Tort Law in America

TORT LAW IN AMERICA

An Intellectual History

G. Edward White

New York   Oxford
OXFORD UNIVERSITY PRESS
1980

Copyright © 1980 by Oxford University Press, Inc.

Library of Congress Cataloging in Publication Data

White, G. Edward.
  Tort law in America.

  Includes index.
  1. Torts—United States—History. I. Title.
KF1249.W48   346′.73′0309   79-1349   ISBN 0-19-502586-5

Printed in the United States of America

for Alexandra Valre White

Preface

There are some books that I suppose one expects to write, but this was not one of them. I have been teaching tort law for several years, but I have not contributed any "orthodox" scholarship to the field and have not regarded Torts as my principal area of scholarly interest. Over time, however, the possibility of applying techniques of intellectual history to a private law subject engaged me, and the subject that naturally came to mind was the one with which I had a passing familiarity.

The experiences of looking at Torts from a different vantage point and reacquainting myself with intellectual history have been sources of considerable stimulation and pleasure to me. This is one instance where an author may well have learned more from a book than his readers. While I am certainly not anxious to deter prospective readers from attempting that comparison, should my intuitions be verified I will not feel unrewarded. The possibilities for continued work on the relationship between private law and ideas in American history now seem varied and exciting to me; it has been gratifying to see them opening up firsthand.

Part of my educational experiences in writing this book have come through the conversations and the aid of others. Tyler Baker, Richard Epstein, Thomas Haskell, James Henderson, Charles McCurdy, Harvey Perlman, Stephen Presser, Calvin Woodard, and Jamil Zainalden have read the entire manuscript and have given probing and helpful commentary. Thomas Bergin, George Fletcher, and Dorothy Ross have read various drafts of individual chapters and have improved upon my language even when they were not always convinced by my arguments. Debra Willen, Nancy Hudgins, and Elizabeth Kemper have given excellent editorial assistance—as has Carol Franz, who also checked sources and prepared the index. Diane Moss and the secretarial staff at the University of Virginia School of Law have provided typing services in several stages. Susan Rabiner of Oxford University Press has done her usual professional job of seeing the manuscript through production. The book was completed sooner than it otherwise would have been because of the generous support of the National Endowment for the Humanities and the University of Virginia Law Foundation.

Alexandra White has seen this book take shape and has been a fine companion to the writer; this book is for her. Elisabeth White and Susan Davis White have also made significant contributions to the writer's well-being. None of the above persons, of course, can be held responsible for any difficulties the book may present (especially Elisabeth White, who is not yet three), but perhaps the critical reader will bear so broad-ranging a list in mind.

G.E.W.

Charlottesville
May, 1979

Contents

Introduction

Tort law * is a field that encompasses material of considerable breadth and diversity and whose existence, as reflected in individual actions seeking civil redress for injuries not arising out of contractual relations, can be traced back to primitive societies. It would therefore be a staggering task to write the history of tort law, and, if some of my subsequent observations about the nature of the subject of Torts in America are accurate, much of that history before 1850 would be difficult to generalize about. My focus in this book is on the intellectual history of tort law in America, and my coverage is limited largely to those years during which Torts has been conceived of as an independent common law subject.

It might be more accurate to say, in fact, that this book is not so much a history of tort law as a history of the way the subject of Torts has been conceived. Although I trace the development of the rules and doctrines that lawyers currently consider staples of tort law, my interest is less in narrating changes in those rules and doctrines than in speculating about why they changed and who did the changing. I see the shifting character of tort law in nineteenth and twentieth century America as deriving from the shifting ideas of legal scholars and judges—especially ideas about the civil responsibilities of a person to his or her neighbors in society and about the manner in which society should respond to injuries and injured people.

* A "tort" is simply the Norman word for a "wrong," but "torts" have typically been distinguished from crimes and from "wrongs" identified with contractual relations. Tort law, then, is concerned with civil wrongs not arising from contracts.

My focus in this study thus differs not only from that of most scholars concerned with the contemporary features of tort law but also from that of historians who have previously approached the subject.[1] This book has sought to combine four perspectives: one from intellectual history, somewhat modified for my own purposes; one from scholarship on the sociology of knowledge; one from scholarship on the phenomenon of professionalization in late nineteenth- and early twentieth-century America; and one from the recurrent concerns of tort law during its history as a discrete field.

My point of view assumes that the ideas of certain elite groups within the legal profession have had an influence disproportionate to the numbers of persons advancing these ideas. I devote considerable attention, for example, to the educational and jurisprudential theories of law professors at elite law schools such as Harvard, Columbia, Yale, and the University of Pennsylvania. Where I have singled out judges for special treatment, the judges have been members of visible and prominent state courts, such as those of New York and California. The different theories of tort law described in this study are those advanced by selected individuals who occupied high-status and high-visibility positions in the legal profession—not those of the great bulk of lawyers. The implicit argument in this study is that, to an important extent, dominant theories of tort law can be identified with the theories of a small but influential group of persons.

I have assumed that proof of the breadth and representativeness of ideas is not necessary if proof of their prominence among influential figures in legal education is available. I have equated influence with institutional affiliation, assuming that by the late nineteenth century law schools had begun to occupy a significant role in the legal profession's training patterns and that a status hierarchy among law schools had emerged, with Harvard occupying a position of prominence. This assumption seems reasonable given the abundant evidence that several aspiring law schools self-consciously modeled themselves after Harvard[2] and since Harvard graduates and former members of the Harvard faculty proliferated in the profession of law teaching in the early twentieth century.

I have postulated that the ideas of certain scholars at prominent law schools have had considerable influence on the legal profession as a whole. I believe the ideas have been "representative" of influential thought among lawyers and legal scholars even though they have reflected the perspectives of a narrow stratum of the American legal profession. I view the influence of these ideas as a sociological phenomenon, linked not to the inherent soundness of the ideas but to the institutional context in which they have appeared. In this sense my approach to intellectual history resembles that of the sociologist of knowledge.

Recent scholarship has revealed the sociological dimensions of the process by which knowledge is acquired and communicated. Thomas Kuhn and others [3] have shown that even in fields such as the physical sciences, where the personal predilections of scholars are not commonly supposed to play a part in shaping the direction of research, scholarship is implicitly directed toward areas about whose relevance and soundness a tacit consensus exists and away from areas tacitly judged to be unpromising. The direction of research is a function of largely unarticulated value choices made by influential scholars.

The emergence of the "case method" of instruction in American law schools illustrates the sociological dimensions of communicating knowledge. Its original advocates, such as Christopher Columbus Langdell, dean of Harvard Law School from 1870 to 1895, supported the case method because they believed that law should be studied through firsthand exposure to original sources, that appellate cases were the "original sources" of the legal profession, that cases were sources of general rules and principles, and that the articulation of rules and principles would make law more "scientific." All of these beliefs ran counter to the prevailing wisdom of legal education before 1870, and none of them was susceptible to proof. The case method triumphed, however, because a relatively small group of persons at influential law schools came to accept these beliefs. These persons encouraged case analysis in teaching, discouraged other forms of communicating knowledge, and produced scholarship which reinforced their beliefs and which conveyed them to a wider audience of persons in the legal profession. These beliefs were also consistent with the broader thrust of late nineteenth-century educated thought in America.[4]

The sociological dimensions of acquiring and conveying knowledge are most readily discernible in the professionalization of educational institutions. The phenomenon of professionalization in late nineteenth-century America was crucial to the emergence of tort law as an independent subject.[5] Professionalization, which affected all fields of knowledge, wrought three major changes in the practice of law. First, it transformed law schools from optional features of a well-rounded "liberal" education into a necessary step for entering the legal profession. Secondly, it created a class of professionals—law professors—who were distinguishable from practicing lawyers and who evolved into lawmakers through their scholarship. And, finally, it changed the character of legal subjects such as Torts by implicitly delegating their composition to professors, who would shape the subjects in accordance with their own prevailing values.

Professionalization is a socialization process: one does not merely learn specialized material, one learns it in a distinctive, "professional" way. There were several educational options available to the Harvard Law School faculty after 1870 when Langdell became its dean. Courses could have been taught through lectures or through "Socratic discussion; either Massachusetts law or the law of numerous jurisdictions could have been taught; individual law cases could have been treated either as discrete entities or as manifestations of broad legal principles; law school could have been considered either ancillary to apprenticeship training or an alternative to it. For each of these alternatives Langdell and his contemporaries eventually chose the latter option, the option ultimately consistent with their conception of law and notions of professional training. The Harvard faculty thus attempted to equate becoming a lawyer with a particular mode of acquiring knowledge.

For professional training to be effective, of course, the "trained" students have to be accepted by the profession as eligible candidates. The phenomenon of professionalization therefore imposes some limits on the educational theories of members of a professoriat. Nonetheless, the autonomy given professors to shape the materials of legal study is considerable, and it is one of the principal themes of this book. While Langdell assumed that the courses he taught at Harvard were relevant preparation for law practice, he did not expose his students in Contracts to situations comparable to ones they were likely to encounter as practitioners. On the contrary, he exposed them to English cases decided well before they were born. Langdell conceived of "contract law" as an aggregate of those rules, principles, and theories about contractual relations that he thought sound. Such rules, principles, and theories did not have to be derived from contemporary experience.

The autonomy of law professors to shape their subject matter has extended well beyond the classroom. Law professors at elite law schools have been expected to be scholars as well as teachers; since their scholarship has been largely directed toward synthesizing and articulating the rules of common law subjects, their unarticulated convictions have affected the staple materials of the legal profession. The appearance of scholarly treatises on legal subjects and the use of treatises as sources of "law" had preceded the late nineteenth-century professionalization of law,[6] but with professionalization treatise writing was delegated largely to law professors and an interface between educational training and treatise writing resulted. A set of cases, examined in the classroom, revealed themselves as manifestations of principles synthesized in a treatise. The case collector and synthesizer were often the same person. Under these circumstances, legal subjects easily became organized around and equated with the views of professors.

While one cannot adequately discuss the history of tort law in America without taking note of the fact that Torts was not taught as a subject in law schools until 1870, my focus in this book is not exclusively on the role of Torts in legal education. The intellectual history of Torts extends beyond the academic community, not only because a significant group of persons who make tort law—the judiciary—is not precisely part of that community, but also because tort cases raise recurring legal issues whose resolution has been affected by trends in American society at large. From the original emergence of Torts as a discrete common law subject, tort law has been regularly concerned with the problem of determining civil responsibility for injury. The attitudes of educated Americans toward injuries have changed dramatically over the past hundred years. A widespread attitude which associated injury with bad luck or deficiencies in character has been gradually replaced by one which presumes that most injured persons are entitled to compensation, through the legal system or some other mechanism. This transformation in what I have called the prevailing ethos of injury in America has been an important determinant of the state of tort law.

This book follows a general thematic structure; its concluding segments leave the realm of history to enter the realm of contemporary theory. The thematic structure juxtaposes the *subject matter* of tort law —which I believe has remained relatively constant, if diffuse, throughout the period under consideration—against changing *conceptions* of tort law. I have found that those conceptions have been self-sufficient and internally coherent, but they have been based on unprovable, though widely shared, philosophical assumptions. Throughout the history of tort law in America creative scholars and judges have sought to shape tort law to approximate their ideal conceptions of the field. But the subject matter of tort law has proved sufficiently amorphous to resist that shaping, so that a fresh supply of material has always existed for new generations of scholars and judges, and the relationship between changing ideas and changing legal doctrines has sometimes been obscured.

Different comprehensive standards of liability in tort (negligence, strict liability) have been formulated at different times. Competing central purposes for tort law (admonishing blameworthy conduct or compensating injured persons) have been articulated. The ambit of tort law's coverage has been expanded theoretically (to include "traditional" areas of the law of sales) and contracted (to exclude areas superseded by constitutional law). Tort law has been thought of as essentially a private law subject or as "public" law in disguise. The image of the subject of Torts has varied from that of a unified collection of comprehensive and interlocking principles of civil liability, embodied in appellate cases, to that of a grab-bag collection of diverse judgments by individual courts. Yet none of these changing intellectual developments has affected the integrity of tort law itself. Tort law's integrity has come from a recurrent need in American society for some legal response to the problem of responsibility for civilly inflicted injuries. In the last hundred-odd years Americans have been injured in all sorts of diverse ways; in that time secular explanations for, and responses to, the problem of injuries have predominated. Tort law has been a major explanatory and responsive device. Its integrity, and its amorphousness as well, can be linked to the place of injury in American life.

My hope is that on completing this book one will have learned something about the changing ethos of injury in America, about the history of a common law subject, and about the ways that legal scholars interact with more orthodox lawmakers—especially judges—and function as lawmakers themselves. Finally, I hope the book contributes to an understanding of the complex relationship between law and ideas in American society.

Tort Law in America

1

The Intellectual Origins
of Torts in America

The emergence of Torts as an independent branch of law came strikingly late in American legal history. Although William Blackstone and his eighteenth-century contemporaries, in their efforts to classify law, identified a residual category of noncriminal wrongs not arising out of contract,[1] Torts was not considered a discrete branch of law until the late nineteenth century. The first American treatise on Torts appeared in 1859;[2] Torts was first taught as a separate law school subject in 1870;[3] the first Torts casebook was published in 1874.[4]

A standard explanation for the emergence of an independent identity for Torts late in the nineteenth century is the affinity of tort doctrines, especially negligence, to the problems produced by industrialization.[5] The process by which Torts emerged as a discrete branch of law was more complex, however, and less dictated by the demands of industrial enterprise than the standard account suggests. Changes associated with industrial enterprise did provide many more cases involving strangers, a phenomenon that played a part in the emergence of Torts as an independent branch of law. But even this new increase in cases in which the litigants had had no prior relationship would not have been sufficient had it not come at a time when legal scholars were prepared to question and discard old bases of legal classification. The emergence of Torts as a distinct branch of law owed as much to changes in jurisprudential thought as to the spread of industrialization.

Historical events as well as ideas played a part in creating the climate of intellectual legal opinion that spawned Torts an an independent category of law. This chapter's emphasis, however, is on events

3

only as they were used by intellectuals in the legal profession to formulate new legal doctrines and theories. My intent is to detail the influential role of certain lawyer-intellectuals in the development of legal doctrine in America. These intellectuals—who were primarily academicians after 1870—fulfilled their professional roles, in important part, through their efforts to derive and articulate theoretical justifications for their working rules of law that had current acceptance. In the process they significantly affected the content of tort rules and doctrines and consequently affected the changing state of tort law in America.

Conceptualism in Late Nineteenth-Century American Thought

Between 1800 and 1850, as Americans became increasingly enamored of such New World privileges as individual freedom, social equality, and occupational mobility, an eighteenth-century European-derived conception of society as an ordered community with designated social roles to each member and relatively limited mobility for all was called into question. Alongside a relatively static hierarchical vision of man's place in society had emerged in America a new dynamic atomistic vision, which emphasized man's potential to alter the conditions under which he might exercise his capacity for achievement.[6] For a time, these visions apparently were not perceived as contradictory. Leading literary figures espoused both the ideal of communal life and individual freedom.[7] National politicians simultaneously portrayed themselves as guardians of a simpler, more orderly republican society and as apostles of democratic progress.[8] The influential Unitarian theologian William Ellery Channing, asserted that the universe was ordered by God's law and then applauded " 'question[ing] [of] the infinite, the unsearchable, with an audacious self reliance.' "[9]

Perhaps the most striking indication that early nineteenth-century legal scholars were similarly affected by these divergent visions was their articulation of both synthetic and atomistic views of law. Blackstone, in his eighteenth-century synthetic view, had seen the "Law of England" as a unified entity, its components distinguishable but nonetheless interdependent.[10] By the early nineteenth century, James Kent's and Joseph Story's treatises primarily conceived of law as the sum of its parts (the "law" of bailments, the "law" of agency, etc.) but still represented law as at least capable of a grander synthesis. Nathan Dane's widely used *Abridgment*,[11] which first appeared in 1823, was an attempt at a broad synthesis, but Dane's organization suggested that American law was a series of diverse interpretations of individual actions that had, one to another, little unity or coherence. By the 1850s, leading treatise writers such as Theophilus Parsons and Emory Washburn stressed encyclopedic coverage more than theoretical synthesis.[12]

Although American law seemed to be dissonant, diverse, and even chaotic, American society was still—to some extent—perceived of as a communal entity, bound together by commonly held values. A major source of these communal values was a common heritage of religious dogma.[13] Parsons's treatise on contracts, for example, distinguished between "the law of God" and "human law." [14] Parsons argued, building on this distinction, that human laws, with which his treatise was concerned, could not entirely sanction "craft and cunning"; but this fact should not be taken to mean that "whatever human law does not prohibit, [one] has a right to do; for that only is right which violates no law, and there is another law beside human law." [15]

The simultaneous espousal, then, of synthetic and atomistic visions of society was a defining characteristic of early nineteenth-century American culture, manifested, on the one hand, by the still binding force of religious dogma and, on the other, by a growing awareness of the value of individual autonomy. After 1850, both visions would be altered. The role of religion as a unifying force among American intellectuals was considerably diminished, and the sense that American civilization offered endless possibilities for individual growth and progress was sharply qualified. These developments signaled a new phase in the history of ideas in America, sometimes signified by the term "Victorian."

"Victorian" describes a cultural and intellectual ethos that originated in England during the middle years of Queen Victoria's reign.[16] The ethos emerged from tensions associated with the perception that material "progress," in an industrializing, urbanizing society, could have disintegrative side effects.[17] American "Victorians" discovered that sudden rises in income levels, massive industrial development, and marked urbanization tended to undermine traditional sources of stability, especially religious dogmas, that complemented a homogeneous, village-oriented, preindustrial society. Since theological explanations of the universe—which were widely shared by early nineteenth-century intellectuals—had assumed an essentially static view of human nature and social organization, such explanations were increasingly hard to reconcile with the apparent "flux" of post–Civil War American civilization.

After the Civil War, scholars repeatedly stressed their interest in deriving secular and scientific theories that would promote order and unity in a modern industrialized setting. Henry Adams explained that his "instinctive belief" in the theory of evolution was based on a need for a "substitute for religion," a "working system for the universe," and a means of "enforc[ing] unity and uniformity." [18] The novelist Hamlin Garland, reading Herbert Spencer in the 1880s, found that "'the universe took on order and harmony.'" [19] The architect Louis Sullivan felt that "Spencer's definition implying a progression . . . to a highly organized complex, seemed to fit" Sullivan's own experience.[20] Some scholars, such as the philosopher John Fiske, even believed that secularly based systematic thinking might be reconciled with a religious faith. Fiske wrote in 1875 that the authority of religious principles was no longer derived "from the arbitrary command of a mythologic quasi-human ruler" but from "the innermost necessities of [the] process of evolution." [21]

In general, post–Civil War "Victorian" intellectuals were interested in restoring the sense of order and unity that had characterized eighteenth-century thought, but they rejected efforts to derive order and unity from "mythologic" religious principles. In the quarter century after the war, these intellectuals were particularly concerned with "conceptualization"—the transformation of data into comprehensive theories of potentially universal applicability. The source of unity was to be methodological: the "scientific" ordering of knowledge.[22] As the sociologist Lester Ward put it: "[T]he origination and distribution of knowledge [could] no longer be left to chance and nature," but were "to be systematized and erected unto true arts." [23]

The two legal scholars most immediately responsive to this conceptualistic impulse were Nicholas St. John Green and Oliver Wendell Holmes, Jr., who, along with Fiske, the philosophers William James and Chauncey Wright, and others, were members of the celebrated Metaphysical Club, a meeting ground of Cambridge intellectuals between 1870 and 1874.[24] Green, a practicing lawyer, taught Torts and Criminal Law at Harvard and Boston University Law Schools in the 1870s and wrote several essays between 1869 and 1876 in the *Ameri-*

can Law Review, of which Holmes was an editor. When he died in 1876, Green had a treatise on Torts in preparation.

Green's approach to legal scholarship, which Holmes called philosophical,[25] was characteristically conceptualistic. Green refused to accept legal dogmas on faith; their effectiveness as working analytical guidelines was the critical test.[26] The classification of legal subjects and the derivation of general principles of law, efforts Green identified with philosophically oriented scholarship,[27] were, in his judgment, pointless undertakings unless a given classification or principle then served some useful purpose. Green also maintained that purposive organization of a legal subject might in certain instances be better accomplished by studying the subject's history, or, as with the law of slander and libel,[28] by examining the practical considerations on which it was founded, as with the doctrine of vicarious liability.[29]

While Green expressed an interest in treating the law as a science and analyzing its developments with something akin to mathematical precision,[30] he conceded that absolute lines could not be drawn because change was constant and "[a]ll things in nature . . . shade into each other by imperceptible degrees." [31] Paradoxically, an acceptance of the inevitability of change provided Green with some solace. If one recognized that "[t]he latest decided cases upon [a] subject *make the law,*" [32] Green believed one could try to "settle more definitely" the analytical rationales for those cases and "to see what, and how many, of such reasons apply, and with what force, to . . . new cases." [33] Through these techniques one derived general principles that had some operative meaning.

Green's conceptualism, like that of other American "Victorian" intellectuals, was thus an effort to derive certainty in the face of continual change. Certainty was achieved not by appeal to received dogma but by a scientific reorientation of techniques of legal analysis. Green was as interested in "perfect[ing] [the law] as a science" [34] as were his conceptualist contemporaries in sociology, economics, or philosophy in perfecting their disciplines.[35] Through these techniques new philosophical classifications of law were made possible.

The strong parallels between Green's approach and that of Holmes in the 1870s suggest a degree of mutual influence.[36] Green's interest in the historical origins of legal doctrines, his conviction that rules and principles derived their primary meaning from the circumstances in which they were used, and his fascination with systems of legal clas-

sification were mirrored in Holmes's early scholarship.[37] Both men saw
themselves as "expounders" of the law, whose interests lay in treating
legal subjects "philosophically," from the perspective of scientific insight.[38] But notwithstanding the increasing acceptance of conceptualistic methodologies in American intellectual life after the Civil War,
Green and especially Holmes might not have been able to apply those
methodologies so readily to the law had not the principal classification
device of nineteenth-century jurisprudence, the system of writ pleading, collapsed, leaving a perceived void that was ultimately to be filled
by the theories of the conceptualists.

The Collapse of the Writ System

As late as the first half of the nineteenth century "Torts" was not an
autonomous branch of law at all but merely, as Holmes noted in 1871,
a collection of unrelated writs.[39] Lawyers knew how to sue in tort, but
they apparently had little interest in a theory of torts. As a classification device, the writ system became increasingly haphazard by the
early nineteenth century, in part because of the growing diversity of
American law and the tendency of courts to create exceptions to the
system's rigorous requirements, and in part because of the absence of
any powerful pressure for interjurisdictional consistency in American
jurisprudence. By the 1850s, this haphazardness had become a source
of irritation to those working with it in the legal procession, and alternatives to writ classifications began to be considered. The conceptualistic tendencies of contemporaneous legal thought influenced the nature of those alternatives.

The conventional explanation for the demise of the writ system, a
system founded on enforced conformity to arcane technicalities, is
that in the early years of the century dissatisfaction arose with writs
as practical and efficient pleading devices.[40] According to this explanation, the dissatisfaction led to the formation of law-revision commis-
sions in states such as New York and Massachusetts. These commis-
sions were charged with making the common law more intelligible to
lay people. At the same time a movement for codification of American
laws emerged, which in its headiest versions advocated total replace-
ment of the common law with an American civil code. Although the
codification movement ultimately failed, its impetus combined with revisionist impulses to produce a reform of the writ system. The first

manifestation of reform came in the New York Code of Procedure, adopted in 1848, which abolished the forms of action on which the writ system was based. Other states quickly followed New York's example, with eleven states abolishing the writ system by 1856 and twenty-three by the 1870s.[41]

Thus related, the story has a nice historical momentum, with the pent-up demands of Jacksonian reformers finding voice in the 1840s through the genius of David Dudley Field, author of the 1848 New York Code.[42] Unfortunately, insufficient scrutiny of the writ system has taken place to justify this conventional explanation. The scrutiny that has taken place, in fact, reveals a more complex series of developments. A study of Massachusetts pleading in the late eighteenth and early nineteenth centuries,[43] for example, has shown that the writ system was not suddenly abandoned in that state, but was gradually and irregularly modified over a seventy-year period. Although fraught with technicalities, the Massachusetts system of pleading was not universally rigid: amended pleas were permitted [44] and multiple actions were common.[45] Thus when Massachusetts eventually abolished writ pleading in 1851, the "reform" was not a major modification of existing practice.

An overestimation of the extent of dissatisfaction with the system, especially among those who were most significantly affected by it, has accompanied this overly dramatic conventional account of the writ system's demise. The writ system served an important jurisprudential function in the early nineteenth century, that of a surrogate for doctrinal classification. The rigor of the writs, as Green pointed out, tended to make procedural requirements the equivalent of doctrinal categories. He wrote in 1871: "Whatever may be said of [the science of special pleading] as a practical method of meting out justice between private litigants, it is certain that the lawyer who was master of it stood upon an eminence which gave him a clearer view of the position of his case, in its relation both to law and the surrounding facts, than there is any other means of obtaining. . . . Indeed, a knowledge of . . . pleading is a knowledge of . . . law." [46] One could master "tort" doctrine by mastering the technicalities of pleading, since, in the writs of trespass and case, the elements of proof that gained one access to a court were often the same elements by which one recovered. Problems of causation were solved by the writ system's requirements, and affirmative defenses, such as justification or contributory fault, usually were not allowed. A plaintiff took pains to show how his injury resulted, either "directly" (trespass), or "indirectly" (case), from a defendant's act. If he was able to establish a chain of direct or indirect causation and used the proper writ, his chance for recovery often were good.[47] Knowing the procedure for suing in trespass or case was the equivalent of knowing the doctrinal elements of those actions.

It is difficult, at least from a twentieth-century perspective, to identify the sources of the widespread dissatisfaction conventionally associated with this system. Few trained lawyers would likely have opposed it, since, once mastered, it proved to be a handy digest of the common law.[48] Neophyte lawyers or nonlawyers might fall victim to its technicalities; however, if customs prevailing in early nineteenth-century Massachusetts were followed elsewhere, rigid adherence to the formalities of pleading was not universally required and leave to amend an ill-considered plea regularly was obtained.[49]

The fact remains, however, that the writ system was abolished in most states in the 1850s with remarkably little opposition. In light of the strong lawyer resistance to the codification efforts that took place in the mid-nineteenth century,[50] the abolition of technical pleading might seem a little surprising, since the common law, so vigorously defended by lawyers, derived its substantive doctrines largely from its pleading requirements. But if one conjectures that the change came from within—that the system was discarded by those who had profited most from it—the collapse of the writ system becomes more understandable. If one recalls that the writ system functioned as a device for classifying substantive doctrine, one might hypothesize that writ pleading lost support when it ceased to function successfully in that capacity. Its failure to perform successfully as a means of doctrinal organization can be traced to the tendencies toward diversity and dissonance that marked early nineteenth-century jurisprudence.

As the ambit of legal concerns in America widened and diversified, different localities adopted different rules of special pleading. In another age, the balkanization of pleading rules might have been intellectually offensive; in early nineteenth-century America, however, jurisprudential order was not universally prized. But with each relaxation of the technicalities of pleading, there was a concomitant loss of certainty and predictability about substantive legal rules. And so it was only a matter of time before the value of the writ system would be undermined as well.

In addition, the writ system's emphasis on arcane particulars ran counter to a growing scholarly interest in deriving universal principles. "Like other sciences," a commentator noted in 1851, the law was "supposed to be pervaded by general rules, . . . [and] to have first or fundamental principles, never modified." [51] Some years later, Holmes linked this search for scientific universals to an admission of the very real failings of the writ system:

> "If those forms had been based upon a comprehensive survey of the field of rights and duties, so that they embodied in a practical shape a classification of the law, with a form of action to correspond to every substantial duty, the question would be other than it is. But [the writs] are in fact so arbitrary in character, and owe their origin to such purely historical causes, that nothing keeps them but our respect for the sources of our jurisprudence." [52]

This same dissatisfaction with the particularistic approach of the writs, and a comparable inclination to seek universal guiding principles in the law, motivated Francis Hilliard to write the first treatise on Torts in America. In commenting on previous treatments of tort actions, Hilliard wrote: "By a singular process of inversion, . . . *remedies* [procedural requirements] have been substituted for *wrongs* [substantive elements of an action]." [53] He found it "difficult to understand,"

> how so obviously unphilosophical a practice became established. . . .
> . . . To consider wrongs as merely incidental to remedies; to inquire for what injuries a particular action may be brought, instead of explaining the injuries themselves, and then asking what actions may be brought for their redress; seems to me to reverse the natural order of things. . . .[54]

For Hilliard emphasis on the writs gave "a false view of the law, as a system of forms rather than principles; [it] elevate[d] the positive and conventional above the absolute and permanent." [55] Hilliard's approach to Torts sought to show that the subject "involve[d] principles of great comprehensiveness, not modified or colored by diverse *forms of action*." [56] In the developing tradition of nineteenth-century scientific methodology, he proceeded from universals to particulars.

In sum, one can associate the demise of the writ system with the rise of conceptualism in intellectual thought. By the 1850s, the haphazardness of the writ system had become a source of irritation to those working with it in the legal profession, and a search had been begun for alternatives to writ classifications.[57] In the effort to replace writs with generalized substantive legal principles and doctrines, the idea of treating Torts as an independent legal subject emerged. The origins of Torts can be traced to the interaction of a conceptualist restructuring of jurisprudence with a deteriorating system of pleading and procedure in post–Civil War America. Because of this interaction, recognition of an independent branch of tort law was possible. Still wanting was the development of theoretical principles by which Torts could identify itself.

The Rise of Modern Negligence

Francis Hilliard conceded in his 1859 preface that although he had "entire confidence in the idea" of treating Torts as a separate subject, he had "much diffidence as to the *execution.*" [58] His treatise, in fact, was not entirely successful in distinguishing Torts from other common law subjects. In his discussion of Torts, he included chapters on crimes and property and, in his treatment of slander, chapters on evidence and damages. Hilliard's effort was representative of early attempts to organize the subject matter of Torts. Classifications like these caused Holmes, reviewing Charles Addison's treatise on Torts in the *American Law Review* in 1871, to assert that "Torts is not a proper subject for a law book." [59] Holmes found an absence of a "cohesion or legal relationship" between the variously treated topics. Trespass, for example, was far closer to "possession enforced by real actions" than to assault, yet the two were paired as "torts." [60] Holmes "long[ed] for the day when we may see these subjects treated by a writer capable of dealing with them philosophically." [61] By philosophically Holmes meant, as Hilliard and Green had, with sufficient consciousness of scientifically derived universal principles.

It was at this point—the 1870s—that an academic search for overriding theoretical principles in Torts seemed to have been commenced in earnest.[62] Two years after Holmes's assertion that Torts was an unfit subject for a treatise, he attempted to formulate a theory of Torts; in passing, he noted that "there is no fault to be found with the contents of text-books on this subject." [63] The study of Torts had become promising for Holmes because he had been able to discover that "an enumeration of the actions which have been successful, and of those which have failed, defines the extent of the primary duties imposed by the law." [64] Examination of the tort writs showed Holmes that in the case of certain civil wrongs, such as allowing dammed water or wild animals to escape, liability attached regardless of the culpability of the actor; that in others, such as assault or fraud, culpability was a prerequisite for liability; and that in still others the culpability of the defendant, although pivotal to recovery, was determined not from an analysis of his intentions but from an assessment of the social utility of his conduct, this assessment based on "motives of policy . . . kept purposely indefinite." [65] The last category of cases constituted "modern negligence." [66] Thus Torts could be subdivided into three categories: absolute liability, intentional torts, and negligence. [67]

Holmes's theory was not remarkable in itself: common law writs had acquired roughly similar classifications through their procedural requirements. Holmes's significant contribution was the isolation of negligence as a comprehensive principle of tort law. This contribution was significant in two respects. First, it systematized an embryonic expansion in American case law of the meaning of negligence from that of neglect of a specific, predetermnied duty to that of violation of a more general duty potentially owed to all the world. Second, Holmes's isolation of "modern negligence" was to provide Torts with a philosophical principle: [68] no liability for tortious conduct absent fault, with fault to be determined by reference to "motives of policy" or "the felt necessities of the times." [69] Within a short space of time, that principle came to dominate tort law. So infatuated was Holmes with his discovery of "the great mass of cases" in which a negligence standard was applied and so convinced was he of the soundness of conditioning tort liability on a policy determination that a general duty of care had been violated, that only eight years after his first theory of Torts he was prepared to argue that absolute liability had never truly existed in tort law and that fault, either in the strict (intentional) or looser (negligent) sense, had always been a prerequisite for liability.[70]

Holmes's belief that liability in tort had always been based on a determination of "fault" was to be challenged by other scholars in the late nineteenth and early twentieth centuries. John Wigmore argued that early tort liability was "indiscriminate," with no distinctions made between intentional or unintentional, careless or careful acts.[71] George Deiser believed that early tort cases merely compelled "the person actively contributing to the injury . . . to pay the sum ascertained as damages." [72] And Nathan Isaacs asserted that tort law had "lapse[d] from the moral fault basis and return[ed] to it," alternating between "fault" and "absolute" standards of liability.[73]

My interpretation of the intellectual origins of Torts in the nineteenth century suggests another view of the state of tort law prior to its conceptualization: that no comprehensive standard of liability then existed for tort actions. It is misleading, in fact, to speak of separate "tort" actions, let alone standards of tort liability, before the nineteenth century. "Tort" originally simply meant "wrong," which S. F. C. Milsom has shown to have been largely synonymous with "trespass" in the early English common law.[74] "Tortious" wrongs were, in their early history, merely wrongs not arising out of contract and giving rise to civil liability; that is all they were. The idea of Torts as a separate category of law was not present in the commentaries of Edward Coke or in those of Blackstone; it was not present, we have seen, until the middle of the nineteenth century.

Nor was a comprehensive standard of liability for "tort" actions present in any developed form prior to the 1870s. When Chief Justice Lemuel Shaw of the Supreme Court of Massachusetts said, in the 1850 case of *Brown v. Kendall,* that a plaintiff suing in trespass "must come prepared . . . to show either that the *intention* was lawful, or that the defendant was *in fault,"* [75] he was merely articulating the common sense of earlier cases: tort liability generally turned on some association of blameworthy conduct with the defendant. If Shaw was attempting a synthesis of the preconditions for tort liability, he was not accurate, for sometimes tort liability had been found where a defendant had neither intentionally nor carelessly injured a plaintiff.[76] The crucial inquiry in tort actions prior to the 1870s was not whether a defendant was "in fault" or had otherwise violated some comprehensive standard of tort liability, but whether something about the circumstances of the plaintiff's injury compelled the defendant to pay the plaintiff damages. Tort liability was no more precise than that. Deiser's observation on early English cases seems apt: "[t]he tests of liability appear sporadically and not as part of any coherent legal consciousness. . . . There is no suggestion in any of the cases as yet, of any approach to a legal standard of conduct." [77]

The historical "debate" between Holmes and his contemporaries about the original basis of tort liability appears, on reflection, to have been a product of the concerns of their own time. Conceptualism had produced an interest in comprehensive theories; the independence of Torts was associated with the formulation of a general standard of tort liability. It was natural that scholars, in an age that used history as a source of present wisdom, would find the "origins" of comprehensive liability standards in earlier tort cases. But the evidence suggests that individual "tort" actions, before the middle of the nineteenth century, tended to be decided with reference to their own features and to current perceptions of equity and justice. Far from assessing individual tort actions with reference to a comprehensive theory of liability, judges and juries prior to the mid-nineteenth century did not even consider tort actions as a discrete substantive category of claims. "Tort" cases were actions in trespass, actions in case, and the like, with their peculiar circumstances and their special considerations. To say there was no encompassing theory of tort liability prior to 1870 should not be startling: there was no conception of Torts as an independent legal subject upon which there should have been an encompassing theory.

Even before Holmes began to marshall arguments in support of negligence as a general standard of tortious conduct, certain nineteenth-century American courts had been groping in that direction. Prior to the 1830s, with the exception of a handful of cases in New York,[78] the term "negligence" generally referred to "neglect" or failure to perform a specific duty imposed by contract, statute, or common law. Examples were the duty of a sheriff to maintain prisoners in custody [79] and the duty of a town to keep bridges in good condition.[80] Suits arising out of the escape of prisoners or damage to bridges or roads alleged that the official responsible had been negligent or neglectful. Commentators used negligence in a similar fashion.[81] There is little to indicate that negligence was equated with "misfeasance": performing an act in a "careless" manner. Suits in neglect rested primarily on "nonfeasance": the omission of a prescribed duty.[82]

During the 1830s certain state courts, among them New York, Massachusetts, and Pennsylvania, increasingly came to associate negligence with acts of misfeasance, which were evaluated with reference to a general standard of care that was not limited to specific persons, offices, or occupations. *Brown v. Kendall* [83] is regularly cited as the first American Torts case that clearly employed a "fault" standard of liability.[84] It was preceded, however, by at least three other cases in New York and Pennsylvania.[85] *Brown v. Kendall*'s significance lay in Shaw's recognition of the capacity of "fault" to serve as a comprehensive standard, which was consistent with his view of the common law as a set of broad and comprehensive principles.[86] Shaw did not originate the association of the term "negligence" with violations of a general "fault" standard, but he suggested in *Brown v. Kendall* [87] that the fault principle had wide application. Negligence, Shaw implied, was more than neglect of specific duties imposed only under certain circumstances; it was the touchstone (and principal limiting factor) of a general theory of civil obligation, under which persons owed other persons a universal but confined duty to take care not to cause injury to another. [88]

Viewed in this fashion, the modern negligence principle in tort law seems to have been an intellectual response to the increased number of accidents involving persons who had no preexisting relationship with one another—"stranger" cases. [89] In this limited sense the conventional identification of the rise of Torts with the advent of industrialism is accurate. Advances in transportation and industry—mills, dams, carriages, ships—made injuries involving strangers more common. As judges and legal scholars sought to establish a theory of liability for stranger accidents, older notions of neglect proved inadequate, for frequently parties involved in accidents had not had any previous relationship with one another and therefore had not been contemplated as owing one another any civil duties. The writ system may have served to distinguish one "tortious" injury from another, but it was not designed to address the principal question raised by stranger accident cases: What duties of care were owed to all by all? [90] Once the import of this question became clear, the ground for a new theory of tort liability in stranger cases was broken. Neglect expanded to encompass malfeasance as well as nonfeasance and thus came to be synonymous with legal carelessness. At the same time a "fault" standard emerged as a limiting principle of tort liability. Modern negligence was born.

Two stranger cases from the 1870s, one of which made use of Holmes's insights, illustrate the increasing dominance of the newer generalized conception of negligence. Both cases, *Brown v. Collins* [91] and *Losee v. Buchanan,* [92] were reactions against the implications of *Rylands v. Fletcher,* [93] the 1868 House of Lords decision holding a defendant liable regardless of fault for allowing water to seep through his land and damage the mines of a neighbor. Both the *Brown* and *Losee* courts concluded that absolute liability for injuries to strangers was not to be retained in modern American tort law. In *Brown* a pair of horses, startled by the engine of a passing train, had shied off the road and damaged a lamp post on an adjoining property owner's lot. The parties stipulated that the driver "was in the use of ordinary care and skill" in managing his horses prior to the time they became frightened. Judge Charles Doe held that, absent a showing of "actual fault" in the driver, no liability would attach.[94] Relying in part on Holmes's observations in "The Theory of Torts," [95] Doe maintained that to extend the *Rylands v. Fletcher* principle of "absolute liability without evidence of negligence" seemed "contrary to the analogies and the general principles of the common law." [96] Holding a defendant liable without showing that he had acted negligently was the equivalent of suggesting that "every one is liable for all damage done by superior force overpowering him, and using him or his property as an instrument of violence." [97] Doe argued that liability in tort, where a defendant had acted unintentionally, should be conditioned on a showing of lack of "ordinary care and skill." [98]

One of the precedents Doe relied upon in *Brown v. Collins* was *Losee v. Buchanan,* a New York case also decided in 1873. In the absence of any New Hampshire precedent for applying negligence in the generalized sense employed in *Brown,* Doe had looked to other courts and to scholars for support for his critique of *Rylands v. Fletcher.* In *Losee,* however, Commissioner Robert Earl had the benefit of a prior New York case [99] that he cited as holding: " '[w]here one builds a mill-dam upon a proper model, and the work is well and substantially done, he is not liable to an action though it break away. . . . Negligence should be shown in order to make him liable.' " [100] Earl's task was to extend that principle to a case in which a steam boiler had exploded, damaging buildings on a neighboring tract of land. He found the extension simple enough. "We must have factories, machinery, dams, canals and railroads," he maintained. "If I have any of these upon my lands, and they are not a nuisance and are not so managed as to become such, I am not responsible for any damage they accidentally and unavoidably do my neighbor. He receives his compensation for such damage by the general good, in which he shares. . . ." [101]

As for *Rylands v. Fletcher,* Judge Earl found it to be "in direct conflict with the law as settled in this country." [102] The "universal" American rule, Earl asserted, was that "no one can be made liable for injuries to the person or property of another without some fault or negligence on his part." [103] Thus negligence was more than a specific duty. It was a general precondition of liability for unintentional torts,

background of Losee might be used.

a "universal rule" that helped define the subjects of Torts itself. As Holmes wrote eight years later in *The Common Law:* "The general principle of our law is that loss from accident must lie where it falls. . . . 'No case or principle can be found . . . subjecting an individual to liability for an act done without fault on his part.' " [104]

The growth of negligence from the omission of a preexisting, specific duty owed to a limited class of persons to the violation of a generalized standard of care owed to all ensured the emergence of Torts as an independent branch of law. Impulses to conceptualize law around a series of universal principles had extracted Torts from a diverse series of writs and transformed it into a discernible academic subject. These same impulses were struggling to find some unity in the various civil wrongs being cataloged. Negligence provided that unity. It also provided a workable standard for the numerous inadvertent injuries involving strangers, which had come to be a characteristic late nineteenth-century tort action. Negligence was simultaneously a universal rule, satisfying conceptualist tendencies in legal thought, an all-purpose cause of action, supplanting both trespass and case, and an evaluative standard for decision making in cases involving unintentional injuries to strangers.

The close identification of Torts with the rise of negligence can be seen in the evolution of Torts casebooks and treatises by legal scholars in the late nineteenth century. As late as the third edition of Hilliard's treatise in 1866, negligence had only a nine-page treatment and most of the cases cited used the term in its earlier sense of failure to perform a specific duty.[105] James Barr Ames's Torts casebook, which appeared in 1874, contained no negligence cases. By 1880, the need for a generalized treatment of negligence had begun to be perceived. Thomas Cooley's treatise [106] still devoted a chapter to "Wrongs from Non-Performance of Conventional and Statutory Duties" and included negligence among them.[107] But Cooley also recognized that "in every relation of life . . . some duty is imposed for the benefit of others" [108] and, in a separate chapter, he discussed "the general principles which must govern them . . . one has been injured by the neglect of another to observe due care." [109] His discussion included references to a great many stranger accident cases.[110] In 1893 Ames's casebook was supplemented by a second volume, authored by Jeremiah Smith, devoting six chapters to negligence, including discussions of standards of care, the concept of a duty, and contributory negligence.[111] Smith retained a chapter on negligence as a duty imposed by contract, but that chapter was omitted in the 1909 edition.[112] By 1911 John H. Wigmore apparently believed that Torts was sufficiently discrete to merit a full-blown conceptualist treatment. He divided the "Science of Law" into "public" and "private" components,[113] and each component into "groups" and their "topic[s]," [114] and proceeded to analyze the legal relations this categorization created.[115] He found Torts to be concerned with universal, "nonrecusable" duties, which created correlative "general rights." [116] He then subdivided "general rights" into three elements—damage, causation, and excuse [117]—and further subdivided these elements [118] in a virtual mania of classification. Wigmore felt that his technique was made possible because Torts, being a branch of law, had *the quality of being uniform and regular.*" [119]

Behind Wigmore's nomenclature was the triumph of an insight of Holmes's in the 1870s: Torts was that part of the law concerned with universal private duties "of all to all."[120] Torts was, in short, virtually synonymous with negligence. Intentional torts were clear violations of duties "of all the world to all the world"; [121] they raised few policy questions and were largely concerned with problems of causation and assessment of damages. Inadvertent, nonnegligent torts were not actionable unless a given duty had been imposed on the nonnegligent actor by statute, custom, or practice. Negligence cases most starkly raised the policy issue that Holmes and his followers found most significant: When does society impose a duty not to harm one's neighbor? Thus by the close of the nineteenth century Torts was no longer a potpourri of leftover civil, noncontractual wrongs. It had become an entity distinct from the other private-law categories of Contracts or Property: it was that branch of private law that dealt with universally imposed duties.

2

The Impact of Legal Science on Tort Law, 1880–1910

The Knowledge Revolution of the Late Nineteenth Century

In the early and middle years of the nineteenth century, the college student, particularly if he received his education at one of the traditional northern centers of higher learning, was exposed to philosophies of learning that increasingly appeared incongruous with the outside world. From 1820 to 1850, an education at one of the leading northern universities or colleges consisted of one's learning basic rules of conduct, being exposed to classical literature and mathematics, developing one's moral character, and preparing oneself to occupy a position of high status in a homogeneous, stable, stratified society.[1] Yet while this process of education was taking place, primarily through formal lectures and recitations, American life seemed to be moving in different directions. Egalitarian political ideologies had begun to clash with extant status and occupational privileges, and those privileges had begun gradually and irregularly to crumble.[2] "Romantic" literature and popular folklore were celebrating the ability of the individual to transcend his social environment.[3] The barriers to entry of professional guilds had become a subject of legislative attack.[4] Advances in the technology of transportation held out the promise that Americans could change their lives simply by changing their locations.[5]

In the face of this awkward relationship between educational philosophies and social experiences, it is not surprising that after 1870 certain Americans educated before the Civil War found their undergraduate years bankrupt of purpose.[6] Nor is it startling that some of their older contemporaries reacted to the seeming irrelevancy of higher education by defining the process of learning as having far more to do with individual self-growth than with institutional training.[7] What is perhaps surprising, however, is the failure of a coherent alternative philosophy of education to emerge at any time from the 1820s through the Civil War. While a variety of "anti-institutional" experiments in living took place during that period,[8] and individual self-expression was highly valued in literature and the arts,[9] no major northern college or university substantially modified the goals of its educational process.[10]

After the Civil War, however, the process through which Americans sought to acquire and convey knowledge was altered so pervasively and so quickly as to constitute a "revolution." [11] The nature of the revolution best illustrated itself in three transformations. The "leading" area of study at American colleges and universities, that area whose methods of research and discourse were adopted by analogy in other areas, gradually shifted from moral and political philosophy to the natural sciences.[12] The specialized professional replaced the "liberal gentleman" as the model of a well-educated American. And, most significantly, a mode of conveying information that stressed the recapitulation and memorization of a finite body of knowledge was replaced with a mode—widely labeled "scientific"— that assumed knowledge to be complex and infinite but capable of orderly classification and analysis through the use of proper methodological techniques.

As in the case of other dramatic convulsions in the history of knowledge, the forces combining to produce this revolution were numerous, complex, and interrelated. From among those forces, however, it is possible to note the emergence of certain suggestive phenomena that appeared during the period shortly after the Civil War, when significant changes were taking place in the process of acquiring knowledge.

Prominent among these phenomena, because of its pervasiveness in shaping the cultural values of educated Americans, was the growing secularization of intellectual life. As the nineteenth century matured, educated Americans became increasingly more receptive to nonreligious explanations for the workings of the universe. Despite sporadic revivals of evangelical religion [13] and a strong interest in the spiritual side of man's nature—which transcendentalism and similar

nineteenth-century ideologies emphasized [14]—theological explanations
for the cosmos began to lose adherents at this time.[15] Codes of morality
persisted, but they tended to be secular: man-centered rather than
God-centered.[16]

The coexistence of secularism and enthusiasm for man's untapped
personal resources produced in the early and mid-nineteenth century
persistent, if random, efforts at self-fulfillment through communal life
or humanitarian reform. But the exuberant sense that accompanied
those ventures began to wane in the 1850s, and the crises and con-
flicts of the next two decades revived older, more pessimistic interpretations of human worth and social stratification.[17] Historians have
advanced various explanations for this cultural change. Some have
stressed that while educated Americans in the antebellum years celebrated the excitement of a growing, boundless civilization, their
counterparts in the generation that came to maturity during the
Civil War identified life in America with perceptions of chaos and
brutality.[18] Others have argued that the Civil War represented an
ironic culmination of impulses designed to liberate man from social
institutions and that the waste and suffering engendered by the war
deadened those impulses.[19] Still others have found that the experience
of war itself brought out in educated Americans, particularly in those
who had fought in the war, a reawakened yearning for the older
values of order, unity, and regularity in American life, a weariness of
romance and reform, a loss of faith in the possibilities of mankind,
and a cynicism toward utopian social arrangements.[20]

A lost faith in the ideal of liberated, transcendental man, combined
with a lost faith in religious dogma, suggested that educated Americans would find life in the late nineteenth century an unsettling experience. Trends toward urbanization and industrialization had not
been checked by the Civil War; the northeastern and midwestern
American landscapes were, if anything, rapidly becoming even more
crowded, more heterogeneous, more outwardly dominated by technology. These new features clearly needed to be understood and
mastered: simply acquiescing in their presence without attempting
to direct their course recalled the mindless carnage of the war. It
was not surprising, in this context, that educated postwar Americans
were attracted to an ideology that imposed upon their universe a sense
of order derived not from religious, metaphysical, or transcendental

dogmas but from an organized control of the new features of the American industrial environment.

"Science," in its late nineteenth-century version, provided that ideology; and a revived interest in specialized training for the professions—professionalization [21]—was viewed as the means by which educated Americans might master the insights of science.[22] The emergence of "scientific" thinking in late nineteenth-century America can best be seen as one component of a revolution in the process of acquiring and conveying knowledge. This revolution would pervasively alter not only the philosophy of learning but with it the practical implementation of American programs of higher education and professional training.

The revolution was premised upon four assumptions.[23] The first was *that knowledge was neither finite nor fixed in content*. This view represented a sharp break with attitudes that had linked education with training in moral philosophy. There was more to "know" in the universe than man could discover; indeed, knowledge itself was continually expanding and changing. One could never truly understand the cosmology of the universe because one could never acquire a truly integrated perspective. There was simply too much, and of too great complexity, for one person to assimilate it all, no matter how rigorous his training in the classics.

One did not despair, however, for related to this altered perception of knowledge itself was a second premise of the nineteenth-century knowledge revolution: *an altered assumption about the proper methods of accumulating knowledge*. Here those who sought to change the philosophy of American higher education were zealous. There was one proper method of study, the "scientific" method. It was most applicable to those areas of knowledge built upon empirical observation, but it was potentially applicable to "subjective," nonempirical areas as well. It allowed one to organize, classify, and ultimately master one's knowledge speciality. As a consequence one developed practical wisdom applicable to contemporary life.

The late nineteenth-century scientific method was organic, inductive, and classificatory in its emphasis. Its adherents posited the inevitability of growth and change ("evolution") and argued that continuity and even permanency were linked to change. By examining the growth of an area of knowledge over time one could extract the core principles that had been retained and refined. This organic mass of data was analyzed by using the technique of inductive reasoning. One examined an isolated piece of information without advancing any preliminary dogmatic propositions about its nature. One then compared that information with another isolated piece. The comparison refined one's initial observations. Ultimately these related independent investigations yielded a hypothesis, which, if proved to illuminate subsequent examinations of data, ripened into part of a system of classifying an area of knowledge.[24] Thus in *The Origin of Species,* Darwin's comparisons of the remains of various mammals led him, through inductive reasoning, to the hypothesis that a later mammal may have "evolved" from an earlier one. With this hypothesis tentatively formulated, he proceeded to classify the features of a variety of organisms, both narrowly (the species level) and more broadly (the genus level) and then to test his hypothesis against this classification. The result was the theory of natural selection and a biological classification scheme organized around that theory.[25]

Ultimately, the scientific method sought classification: a working scheme ordering an area of knowledge in accordance with inductively derived principles based on organic research. Given the changing quality of knowledge, classification systems were not absolutes. But they were orderly, organized working systems that approximated truth and reduced an area of knowledge to manageable proportions. The content of classification systems varied from one field of study to another, but the method by which they were derived could remain uniform so long as knowledge was empirically discernible.

Related to these assumptions about the character of knowledge and the nearly universal applicability of "scientific" methodology was a third axiom of the knowledge revolution: *The process of acquiring higher learning was to consist of an increasingly specialized and intensive exposure to a limited area of knowledge.* Since knowledge was neither fixed nor finite, what one could learn in a lifetime represented only a small part of the whole. Proper application of the scientific method might ultimately result in one's "mastering" at least one field, however, so higher learning was best facilitated by subdividing knowledge into discrete disciplines, each with its own disciplinary boundaries. Intensive concentration on a chosen field was to be encouraged. The late nineteenth century saw the emergence of departments within a university, of professional societies and associations identified with fields of study, of an elective undergraduate curriculum encouraging specialization, and of formal graduate training, emphasizing further specialization.[26] In this expression of the knowledge revolution the interface between science and professionalization clearly revealed itself.

The final component of the knowledge revolution was *the linking of narrowly focused study of a particular area of knowledge with rites of entry into the profession that had evolved around that area.* College and university training became indispensable requirements for admission into a professional discipline. Degree programs were created and professional status began to be linked to the acquisition of degrees. These degree programs, especially at the graduate level, became exercises in socialization. Training a prospective historian or biologist or economist meant socializing an apprentice in the internal mores of his peer community. As areas of knowledge were distinguished and "specialists" emerged, the definition of the boundaries of the area itself was reserved to specialists. For example, "history" became more than merely a field of study; it became a proving ground for a dominant methodological theory. In the 1890s the theory of scientific "objectivity" dominated the thinking of historians who saw themselves as professionals.[27] History as literary art was frowned upon; [28] history as philosophy was "dangerously speculative"; [29] "mere narrative" history was unprofessional.[30]

Ultimately the same intellectual tendencies that spawned a redefinition of knowledge insured that the redefinition would become orthodoxy in centers of higher learning. Science, it was claimed, "taught" that knowledge, although infinite, was capable of being reduced to discernible units; science also taught the proper methods of discernment, the proper goals of those methods, and ultimately the proper persons to be using them. The knowledge revolution of the late nineteenth century eventually resulted in the emergence of an influential class of university-based "scientific" professionals.[31]

The knowledge revolution of the late nineteenth century was, in sum, a response to an inarticulated perception among educated Americans that new features in their environment could not adequately be understood and explained by the systems of thought and belief they had inherited from past generations. Striking features of late nineteenth-century American life—industrialization, urbanization, increased ethnic heterogeneity, markedly increased technological

and social mobility—had helped generate a perception among educated Americans of the sudden complexity and interdependence of
their society. One of the responses to this perception was to revise the
techniques of learning itself.

The Knowledge Revolution at Harvard Law School

Law, like medicine and the ministry, had been regarded, prior to the
knowledge revolution, as a profession requiring specialized practical
training.[32] Yet the same dramatic changes took place in the legal profession after 1870 as did in other more academic disciplines, although
as a result of surfacely different stimuli. Led by Harvard Law School
in the deanship of Christopher Columbus Langdell, university law
schools actively sought to eliminate apprenticeship training as an alternative to academic training for law practice. As in the case of the
new professional academics of the late nineteenth century, the conviction of legal educators that they were the ones best suited to train
persons for the practice of law was based on their participation in the
knowledge revolution, exemplified by their commitment to legal
science.

All the components of the knowledge revolution can be seen in
Harvard Law School after 1870: Langdell declared that "[i]f law be
not a science, a university will best consult its own dignity in declin-
ing to teach it." [33] But the conception of legal science that came to
prevail at Harvard was not synonymous with Langdell's conception.
Langdell was himself a transition figure, a bridge between an older
educational universe of fixed and finite truths and the universe that
emerged after the Civil War.

Langdell's perception of legal science was revolutionary in the methods of acquiring knowledge it espoused, but static in the dogmatic
orthodoxy it adhered to. Langdell believed in an unfiltered exposure
of law students to original source materials, which he defined as appellate judicial opinions. He thus rejected a principal purpose of early
nineteenth-century higher education—conveying a "liberal" grounding
in the general basics of human knowledge through rote learning and
broad exposure to "classical" sources. Langdell suggested that this
focus was unsound as applied to legal study. It was impractical; it ignored the importance of the published judicial opinion (the "case")
as a fundamental source of learning; and it denied the student direct,

intensive exposure to the original sources of his profession.[34] In each of these criticisms Langdell associated himself with a variety of late nineteenth-century educators who came to favor a more "scientific" and less "liberal" and "generalist" approach to higher learning.[35]

Langdell's approach was not, however, intended to free students to "learn" law on their own through original research. On the contrary, it was intended to enable students "[t]o have . . . a mastery of . . . [certain principles and doctrines so] as to be able to apply them with constant facility and certainty to the ever-tangled skein of human affairs. . . ." [36] This "mastery" came from the identification of "fundamental legal doctrines" within cases in which the basic principles of the doctrines had been defined. Samuel Williston, recalling his years as a student under Langdell, said that "the current of thought . . . ran not merely toward the study of original sources," [37] but rather that:

> The impulse that Langdell gave to legal thinking and teaching was primarily toward the discovery from decided cases of the principles that apparently had controlled them, and to apply to every variety of facts these principles, on the assumption that they would continue to be controlling for the immediate future.[38]

Under Langdell's educational system, students were required "to select, classify, and arrange all the cases which had contributed in any important degree to the growth, development, or establishment of . . . essential doctrines. . . ." [39] Langdell recognized that the "number of reported cases in every department of law" was "great and rapidly increasing" by the 1870s.[40] But he was not concerned that this case explosion would complicate his search for the "fundamental legal doctrines" of "[l]aw, considered as a science." [41] His sanguinity stemmed from a belief that "[t]he vast majority [of cases were] useless and worse than useless for any purpose of systematic study" because "the number of fundamental legal doctrines [was] much less than . . . commonly supposed," [42] and most cases did not embody important doctrines. In Langdell's classes "the principle deduced by the first case was followed chronologically through its developments and applications in the later cases, until by constant iteration all doubt or forgetfulness was removed." [43]

Langdell's system was substantively conservative despite the fact that it was methodologically innovative. His "fundamental legal doctrines" were the equivalent of the "rules" and "principles" announced by early nineteenth-century lecturers like Joseph Story at Harvard or Theodore Dwight at Columbia. Both Story and Dwight, in fact, had a far greater sense of the diversity and complexity of American law than did Langdell.[44] Langdell's casebooks were comprised almost exclusively of English cases decided before 1850. His principal criterion for inclusion of a case was the presence of a principle he thought sound; cases disavowing such principles were excluded as "useless." Langdell's analysis of cases ignored their historical context. "[H]is legal thinking," noted Williston, "[did not] sufficiently take account of changes in law as a constant and necessary process, however gradual and slow." [45]

Several of Langdell's fellow scientists differed with him on the question of whether "scientifically" derived principles were capable of change or, once extracted from cases, were static entities. Holmes, for example, remained enthusiastic about law as a science from the 1870s until at least 1899 [46] and praised Langdell's work in 1871; [47] however, in 1881 he called Langdell a representation of "the powers of darkness," whose Contracts casebook was "[a] . . . misspent piece of marvellous ingenuity" containing "explanations and reconciliations of the cases [that] would have astonished the judges who decided them." [48] By 1880 Holmes had explicitly rejected Langdell's search for *"logical* integrity," asserting that while law was "an object of science, [any] effort to reduce . . . concrete details . . . to the merely logical consequence of simple postulates [was] always in danger of becoming unscientific." [49] John Chapman Gray, a longtime colleague of Langdell, thought he saw an arrogant contempt for "the opinions of judges and lawyers as to what the law is" in Langdell's approach.[50] Gray believed that to ignore those opinions was "as unscientific . . . as for a scientific man to decline to take cognizance of oxygen or gravitation." [51]

Even William Keener, a Langdell disciple who taught at Harvard from 1883 to 1890 and subsequently introduced the case method at Columbia, ultimately distinguished his view from that of Langdell. At one point in his career Keener virtually echoed Langdell. He described law as "a science consisting of a body of principles to be found in the adjudged cases," [52] and he asserted that it was possible to study law in its original sources since "while the adjudged cases are numerous the principles controlling them are comparatively few." [53] But Keener also suggested that in studying cases "the student . . . follows the law in its growth and development." [54] Ultimately Keener was to equate "the scientific spirit of investigation" with "independence and self-reliance on the part of the student." [55]

Keener believed that law as a science had fostered a practical method of developing powers of analytical reasoning. This method, traditionally prefaced by the terms "case" or "scientific," was eventually to be identified by Langdell's followers as his greatest contribution. In 1888 Keener listed two "object[s] of legal education: [developing] the power of legal analysis and synthesis, [and] gaining . . . knowledge of what the law actually is." [56] By 1907, however, James Barr Ames, Langdell's successor as Dean at Harvard, maintained that "the object of the three years at the law school" was not "knowledge" but "the power of legal reasoning." [57] Ames's statement, a version of which is still articulated by many contemporary law schools ("our purpose is not to train students to 'learn the law,' but to 'think like lawyers' "), was remarkable in that its celebration of the "power of legal reasoning" stemmed from a basic reassessment of the means of acquiring knowledge in American higher education. "Learning the law" was not synonymous with assimilating a finite body of information but rather with mastering a "scientific" methodology.

Thus the first component of the knowledge revolution emerged at Harvard during Langdell's deanship, although Langdell did not entirely embrace it. Each of the other components, however, was supported by Langdell himself. He distinguished law from the other disciplines of a university,[58] equated the study of law with the study of judicial opinions, and asserted that "all the available materials" of law were "contained in printed books." [59] "Legal" knowledge was in this last respect different from other types of knowledge. Langdell also assumed that a scientific method of learning law could be formulated and applied, that exposure to this method best qualified students to practice law, and that an understanding of law as a science was essential to successful law teaching. He maintained that "what qualifies a person . . . to teach law is not experience in the work of a lawyer's office, not experience in dealing with men, not experience in the trial or argument of causes—not experience, in short, in using law, but experience in learning law . . . the experience of the jurisconsult." [60]

Finally, Harvard Law School under Langdell created patterns of specialization in law study and linked them to professional training. The field of law was divided into discrete "departments" [61] (such as

Contracts, Property, and Torts), which were nascent classifications of types of legal relations.[62] These departments were subdivided into "courses," which initially were required and which were taken in a prescribed sequence. The course of study was lengthened to three years. Elective courses were subsequently introduced, but they were regarded as building on the preliminary first-year courses and were offered only in the second and third years. By the 1890s, only college graduates were eligible for the degree, three years' residency was required, and the successful completion of twenty-eight to thirty hours of work per year was made a degree prerequisite.[63] The addition to the curriculum of courses on Massachusetts and New York law reflected Harvard's increasing popularity and foretold the usurpation of the law office's role as a professional training ground.[64]

By the end of Langdell's deanship in 1895, certain characteristics of Harvard exemplified the ascendancy of the nineteenth-century knowledge revolution in a university law school. One was the presence of a faculty whose members held full-time positions as professors of law. Some faculty members, such as James Barr Ames, who succeeded Langdell as Dean, had no previous experience in practice. Charles Eliot, President of Harvard from 1869 to 1909 and a visible, if somewhat ambivalent, participant in the knowledge revolution,[65] described full-time teachers of law as "expounders, systematizers, and historians," and called their presence at Harvard "one of the most far-reaching changes in the organization of the profession that has ever been made in our country." [66]

Another significant characteristic of Harvard Law School under Langdell was its hierarchical professional structure. Early nineteenth-century law schools, including Harvard, had been notable for the laxness of their requirements and the informal way they interacted with the legal profession. Prospective lawyers attended or left school nearly at will, attended only some classes, often did not take a degree, and generally conceived of law school as only one of a variety of means of training for the bar (which had virtually no formal entry requirements).[67] During Langdell's tenure Harvard developed enforced specialization, a system of formal examinations and grades, and indicia of student distinction (such as the *Harvard Law Review,* which began in 1887 and whose membership was soon reserved for students with high rankings). It had become a well organized filter for the legal profession, winnowing out the stronger candidates from the weaker, fostering relationships that would be useful in law practice, and encouraging its most distinguished students to consider becoming the next generation's expounders, systematizers, and historians.

The Emergence of the "Scientific" Method of Studying Law

No single distinguishing characteristic of Harvard Law School under Langdell had a greater influence on the substantive growth of American law than the triumph of the "case," or "inductive," or "scientific" method of legal study. Among the concerns of those who embraced this method was the abandonment of dogmatic explanations of legal rules and principles. Early proponents of a "scientific" approach to law, such as Holmes and Green, may well have originally acquired their distaste for dogmas from their impatience with theological explanations for the universe.[68] But ultimately they extended their criticism and rejected all untested abstract propositions. Out of this general skepticism evolved their decision to encourage law students to immerse themselves in original sources without prior reliance on any generalizations at all. Keener asked in 1894, "How many students will do independent thinking and critical reading while preparing twenty pages of Parsons on Contracts for a lecture?"[69] Skepticism of dogma manifested itself in a distrust of ancient maxims;[70] in a conviction that legal principles could best be stated in the form of concrete examples;[71] and in an enthusiasm for the appellate case as a training device, since cases, being concrete manifestations of abstract principles, embodied "both the scientific and the practical side of law."[72] The numerous scholarly articles produced by the Harvard law faculty during the period of Langdell's deanship regularly included skeptical dissections of long-standing dogmatic propositions.[73]

Linked to the scientists' skepticism of abstract dogma was their conviction that a legal principle, as Holmes put it, was "better known when you have studied its embryology and the lines of its growth. . . ."[74] A strong interest in "organic" legal history was a second characteristic of those who advocated the scientific method of law study. The legal history practiced by these scientists is best termed "organic" because its principal purpose was to clarify the present state of the law by showing the evolution of various legal principles over time. While each of the early scientists—Langdell, Holmes, Keener, Ames, Green, and William Schofield—and many in the succeeding generation of law professors, each of whom continued to teach law as a science—including John Wigmore, Samuel Williston, Eugene Wambaugh, and Joseph Beale—made forays into history in the course of their scholarship, their use of history was highly particularized. They were certain that judicial opinions embodied principles, that principles "evolved" over time, and that analysis of an historical "line" of cases could give fuller meaning to an extracted principle. The scientists were not interested, for the most part, in the various historical contexts in which principles were first articulated. Even Holmes, who claimed that law was governed by the felt necessities of the times, used history as a means of buttressing contemporary philosophical arguments rather than as a device by which to understand the "felt necessities" of earlier generations.[75] Like his contemporaries, Holmes assumed that history was another means through which the scientific investigator might master his field. Legal history was, by virtue of the inevitability of change in the universe, a prologue to the present; in studying history one studied nothing more than the "origins" and "development" of contemporary phenomena.[76]

The techniques utilized by scientists to study legal history were therefore indistinguishable from those they used to investigate contemporary law sources. One approach, the process of inductive reasoning, sufficed for all "scientific" legal analysis. Writing in 1894, at a time when the concept of legal science was maturing and flourishing, Keener described the inductive method as "the most scientific method" [77] of studying and teaching law. Under the inductive method students were first "referred to the original sources as the basis of instruction," [78] avoiding "deductions that may have been drawn by writers from sources equally accessible to the student." [79] The source material was "the adjudicated cases found in the reports of the decisions of the [Anglo-American] courts. . . ." [80]

A case was regarded as "both a laboratory and a library." [81] It contained facts, analogous to scientific "specimen[s]," and "the opinion of the court announcing the principles of law to be applied to the facts," analogous to "the memoir of the discoverer of a great scientific truth." [82] The study of law consisted of a series of analytical examinations of the relationship between cases and principles. Cases involving like principles "but contradicting each other in many particulars, and perhaps reaching opposite results" [83] were considered. The student or scholar pondered a given principle's extent and its limits; attempted to show "how it . . . emerged as the felt reconciliation of concrete instances, no one of which established it in terms"; and analyzed "its historic relations to other principles." [84] One practicing the inductive method was "forced not only to analyze cases, but to compare them, to discriminate and choose between them." [85] Having "discriminate[d] between the relevant and the irrelevant, between the actual and possible grounds of decision," one became "prepared . . . to deal with [cases in] relation to other cases." [86] In the process one gained "the power of analysis and synthesis" [87] and became "a scientific lawyer capable of applying the principles of law as they exist, and suggesting improvements therein." [88]

The wholesale enthusiasm of the scientists for inductive reasoning did not entirely allay doubts on the part of those who were hostile to or suspicious of emerging late nineteenth-century methods of acquiring knowledge. One of the arguments frequently advanced by critics of the case method was that it consisted of "plung[ing] a beginner into a chaos of undigested and unclassified matter." [89] Keener responded to this argument by making two observations. The first merely echoed Langdell: "While the adjudged cases [were] numerous, the controlling principles [were] comparatively few," and thus analysis of the relationship between case and principle was a comparatively manageable undertaking.[90]

Keener's second observation was more novel and articulated an ultimate goal of proponents of the scientific method of legal study. Keener asserted that "[u]nder the case system . . . the student is not referred to a mass of cases. . . . He is, in fact, referred to a *few classified* cases, selected with a view to developing the cardinal principles of the topic under consideration." [91] For the late nineteenth-century scientists, the primary end of legal scholarship was the extraction and classification of governing principles in an area of law. Scholarship was a "winnowing process," involving the classification of material "by section and sub-section, when necessary." [92] Classification was the principal device through which one sought to achieve one of Keener's "object[s] of legal education," a "knowledge of what the law actually is." [93] While the case method was a training device in analytical reasoning itself, it also was a stimulus for the promulgation of orderly arrangements of substantive legal fields.

The constant consideration of governing principles in diverse factual contexts allegedly produced a refined sense of the relation of the general to the specific. An interplay of general principles and specific fact situations characterized the massize analytical syntheses of the scientist generation of legal scholars: Wigmore's treatise on Evidence,[94] Williston's on Contracts,[95] and Beale's on Conflict of Laws.[96] These efforts at classification were more than compendia of existing rules. They were end products of the knowledge revolution, volumes in which the relationships of principles to cases in a "section" or "subsection" of a field of law were analyzed rather than memorized. A later generation of legal scholars was to denigrate the emphasis on classification in these treatises as being "conceptualist." That comment was fair in the sense that the purpose of the treatises was to provide a working body of legal concepts that purportedly brought order and coherence to an area of law. In making classifications, however, the scientists did not regard themselves as creating meaningless "paper rules." [97] They saw themselves as expounders, systematizers, and historians, clarifying the law and making possible its orderly development. The aim of the great scientific treatises was to produce, out of the chaos of a constantly growing body of case law, syntheses that made fields such as "Contracts" or "Evidence" orderly and manageable.

If the production of massive conceptualist treatises represented one principal goal of the legal scientists, training students in the techniques of the scientific method represented the other. Available sources describing the activities of the scientists do not entirely capture their impact as teachers. Langdell's and Ames's casebooks only hint at what happened in their classrooms. There are histories and reminiscences [98] that suggest that Ames was "unexcelled in the development of coherent legal rules," [99] but that he "aimed not so much to impart information, as to develop the analytical powers of the [students], to make them think as lawyers"; [100] that Langdell in his later years "simply talked, slowly and quietly, stating, explaining, enforcing, and reenforcing the principles which he found in the case under discussion"; [101] and that Keener's "logic was remorseless, and any student who ventured upon a difference of opinion with him found himself engaged in an argument not likely to prove to his advantage." [102] But perhaps the best sense of the manner in which the scientific method functioned as an analytical training device is captured in the short case comments that members of the Harvard faculty wrote in early editions of the *Harvard Law Review*. These comments (then called articles) approxi-

mated, one suspects, the classroom ruminations of the scientist professors, collected and put in the form of logical arguments. Many of
the comments have no particular structure; they introduce the case,
extract various principles, seek to apply them to other cases, become
sidetracked in discussions of technical questions, and end abruptly.[103]
As artifacts of the scientists' conception of inductive reasoning, however, they are highly instructive.

A representative comment is William Schofield's "The Principle of
Lumley v. Gye, and its Application," [104] which appeared in the *Harvard Law Review* in 1888. Schofield began by stating the facts of
Lumley v. Gye,[105] which concerned an action for interference with
contractual relations. Lumley, the lessee of a theater, had contracted
with one Johanna Wagner, a singer, to perform at his theater for a
fixed period of time on condition that she not sing elsewhere during
that time without his written permission. Gye, the defendant, knowing
of Wagner's contract, maliciously induced her to breach it. Lumley
alleged, and the court agreed, that he had suffered damage as a result
of Gye's actions.

Schofield began his analysis by suggesting that two principles could
be extracted from the case: first, "that an action will lie against one
by whose persuasions one party to a contract is induced to break it to
the damage of the other party"; second, "that the action for seducing
a servant from the master, or persuading one who has contracted for
service from entering into the employ, is of so wide application as to
embrace the case of [a professional singer]." [106] The majority opinion
in *Lumley* had affirmed those principles, but had included within the
first principle the element of malice.

Schofield then began an inquiry into the scope and limitations of
the governing principles in *Lumley.* He considered the later case of
Bowen v. Hall,[107] in which the defendant induced a workman who
possessed the knowledge of a secret process for manufacturing glazed
bricks to breach a five-year contract of exclusive service to the plaintiff. The court in *Bowen* held for the plaintiff and cited *Lumley,* but
rejected *Lumley*'s second principle. The *Bowen* court relied on the
rationale that "whenever a man does an act which, in law and in fact,
is a wrongful act, and such an act as may, as a natural and probable
consequence of it, produce injury to another, and which . . . does
produce such an injury, an action on the case will lie." [108]

What, then, was "the principle" of *Lumley* after *Bowen?* Schofield argued that *Lumley* apparently stood for the proposition that "[t]he mere breach of the contract by the obligor supplies to the obligee the element of damage which is necessary to support an action of tort," [109] or, put another way, "the mere existence of the contract imposed upon all third persons who knew of its existence, a duty to forbear from doing any act maliciously, for the purpose of procuring a breach of the contract." [110] The contract "gave to the obligee a right to such limited forbearance as against all the world." [111]

If this general duty existed in third persons, Schofield then went on to ask, what were its limits? Was it confined to cases involving personal service contracts (as *Lumley* would seem to have confined it) or did "consistency requir[e] that it . . . be extended to the breach of any contract?" [112] Was "persuasion" by the defendant necessary to make out the action, or could less calculated forms of violence suffice? [113] Did the duty apply beyond contracts of a fixed term? [114] Did it extend to cases not involving losses suffered from breaches of contract but "merely the failure to make a profit or gain"? [115] For each query Schofield supplied a case where an extension of the *Lumley* principle to these new contexts might be inferred although it had at no time been made explicitly.[116] His purpose was as much to force consideration of the relationship between principles and cases as it was to declare the current state of the *Lumley* principle.

Schofield, however, seemed singularly uninterested in the basic question of policy that *Lumley* had raised: when was "malicious" interference with contractual relations justifiable? He had noted that the "malice" requirement itself seemed to be a question of policy: it was based on a court's sense of "bad motive[s]" rather than any proof of ill will.[117] But although he asserted that "where the act is done by the defendant in the exercise of some right vested in him . . . a malicious purpose will not render the act unlawful," [118] he seemed disinclined to probe that assertion. Why some malicious interferences with contracts were justified and others not was not Schofield's concern. Rather, his concern was to show the potentially broad principle of *Lumley v. Gye*—the imposition of a duty on citizens not to interfere maliciously with the contracts of others—and the limiting factors of context (personal service, fixed term contract, out-of-pocket losses, verbal persuasion) in which the principle had been articulated. While indifferent to questions of policy or philosophy, Schofield's comment on *Lumley* was enthusiastic about the logical interplay between case and principle he had found. If there was excitement in the classrooms of the legal scientists, it may have centered on that interplay. The dialectic of principles and cases was the organizing theme of scientific teaching as well as of scientific scholarship.

⌈A sense of the dynamic interplay of cases and principles dominated legal scholarship and teaching during the late nineteenth and early twentieth centuries, and in that period the effects of this insight on the course of substantive law were profound. Eventually, however, the analytical modes of the scientists led further and further away from the reality of appellate judging, and theoretical insights, applied with uniform rigidity, revealed themselves to be self-contradictory. Predetermined assertions of principles tended to skew what should have been unbiased readings of cases, while the infinite variety of factual settings tended to vitiate the general applicability of the principles to be preserved. Inductive reasoning, conceived as a reaction against dogmatic logic, nonetheless tended to encourage a yearning to return to a reliance on dogmatic propositions. Relentless attempts to reconcile every expression of a general principle, in whatever case found and however applied, often resulted in making increasingly tenuous the very principle the scientists had set out to redeem. ⌋

The scientific method, then, rested on too narrow a definition of science, a definition that became increasingly inadequate in the development of twentieth-century legal scholarship. The rigid reliance on the case method presupposed the exclusivity of judicial opinions as source materials and suggested an indifference to the role of jury determinations as expressions of societally recognized legal principles—an indifference that had caused difficulties for some scientists, notably those studying tort law. Ultimately, the values of legal science came to be perceived as hopelessly in conflict, and the hegemony of the conception of law as a science crumbled. Nevertheless, from 1880 to 1910, the case method as an expression of the law as a science thrived, and its impact on the development of tort law was significant.

The Impact of Legal Science on Tort Doctrines

While commentators who shared a dedication to the late nineteenth-century ideal of law as a science were not unified in their interpretations of that ideal nor consistently successful in implementing their "scientific" theories, their collective impact on late nineteenth- and early twentieth-century tort law was, nonetheless, substantial. Scientists such as Langdell and Holmes, we have seen, had helped develop the original idea of torts as an independent branch of law: Langdell by offering torts as a discrete subject, with its own casebooks and treatises, in the Harvard Law School curriculum; Holmes by developing a "theory of torts" with a heavy emphasis on negligence as a comprehensive principle. And between 1880 and 1910, as legal science flourished, "doctrinal" analysis of specific tort issues such as Schofield's analysis of the "principle" of *Lumley v. Gye* increased. The consequences for tort law were favorable. With each new analysis, Torts was perceived less as a diffuse collection of diverse actions and more as a "field" of legal knowledge with a distinctive theoretical perspective.

In the mature years of legal science, aided by the burst of scholarship that movement had engendered, tort law acquired one dominant theoretical perspective. That perspective represented both a widening and a narrowing of pre-"scientific" viewpoints. It assumed the existence of a universal duty of care owed by persons to their neighbors. The duty, as previously described, was not peculiar to designated statuses or occupations; it was not limited to instances where it had been imposed by statute or custom; it followed from an assumption about the civil obligations of those who lived in society. While early nineteenth-century jurisprudence had not posited such a broad conception of potential liability in the area of civil "wrongs," it also had not developed a device to limit tort liability, which was an equally fundamental component of the late nineteenth-century scientists' theory of torts. The negligence principle, ultimately established as that limiting device, conditioned tort liability on a showing of "fault" in the defendant and the absence of "fault" in the plaintiff. As legal science matured, fault came to be regarded as so fundamental a requirement of tort law that Jermiah Smith, writing in 1917,[119] proposed that those areas of tort law where liability without fault was still permitted, such as defamation, be reclassified so as to eliminate them altogether from the field of "torts."

The contribution of the scientists to tort law, then, was to isolate Torts as a distinct field of study, to supply that field with an overarching theoretical perspective, and to transform its existing rules and maxims into doctrines consistent, where possible, with that perspective. While their efforts were not always successful in terms of their own goals of doctrinal consistency, clarity, and predictability, those efforts placed collective pressure on a whole range of tort rules, ultimately resulting in a redefinition of the approach of the legal profession to questions of noncontractual civil liability. While tort jurisprudence in 1911 had by no means achieved the "scientific" state assumed by Wigmore in his massive casebook-treatise of that year,[120] it had developed a discernible philosophical identity. By the time of Wigmore's casebook, there had emerged a comprehensible ideal of the "science" of torts.

In practice, many of the principles articulated by the scientists first made their way into the body of substantive tort law as arguments and analyses in law review articles and treatises, two forms of legal literature for which a new role was emerging. One of the more enduring offshoots of legal science was the growth of professional literature. Law professors were expected to "expound" upon and "systematize" their fields as well as inculcate their students in the scientific method. Although the casebook, a new form of legal textbook, also made its first appearance with the knowledge revolution, the controlling academic philosophy on legal reasoning was that it was to be learned on one's own. As a result, whereas Langdell's first Contracts casebook had contained a detailed summary of principles to be matched to appropriate cases, Ames's and Smith's casebook on Torts offered very little guidance, simply introducing cases with an accompanying table of contents. But other participants in the legal profession, such as practitioners and judges, began to rely more and more on the scientists for analytical guidance. The treatise and the law review article attempted to meet that need. In the process a relationship was cemented between judicial opinions and legal scholarship that has survived to the present.

As part of the systematizing of their fields, late nineteenth-century legal scholars extracted principles from a variety of judicial opinions. Once extracted, these principles were articulated as working guides to an area of law. Subsequently, courts referred to extant principles in their consideration of new fact situations, sometimes refining or revising them in the process. These judicial refinements were then noted by academicians in scholarly literature, and sometimes new syntheses were articulated. Law professors and the courts, especially the appellate courts, thereby established a symbiotic relationship. Cases became the staple diet for classrooms, treatises, and law review articles; existing scholarship became a point of reference in judicial analysis; judicial innovations stimulated new scholarship.

In its formative years, the late nineteenth-century academic-judicial symbiosis placed a high value on the achievement of order and co-herence in fields of law. A successful law review article or treatise was one that "illuminated" a field by propounding doctrines capable of continuing to organize an increasing number of cases in an intelligible fashion. In their search for systematic principles, however, aca-demicians encountered a difficulty. Despite the rhetorical flourishes of some earlier treatise writers, there had been little use in American jurisprudence of rules and doctrines as "scientific" principles of uni-versal application. Indeed, to the extent that American law had an intellectual organization in the early nineteenth century, that organi-zation had been procedural rather than doctrinal. Jurisprudential rules, we have seen, were linked more to the writ system than to any substantive grouping of "fields" of law. David Hoffman's *A Course of Legal Study* (1817) and Dane's *Abridgement of American Law* (1823–29) derived their "principles" largely from the existing tech-nicalities of the writs.[121] There was no "field" of "Torts" at all prior to 1870; the "tort" writs (trespass and case) had their own separate rules.

In addition to procedural requirements, American jurisprudence had another source of rules, maxims of equity. These maxims, how-ever, had tended to be applied in accordance with the perceived exigencies of a given case. For example, one common law "rule," originally based on considerations of fairness, was that an innkeeper owed a special duty of care toward his guests. He offered himself out as providing a place of shelter; if that place turned out to be unsafe or unfit for habitation, he bore some responsibility. Over time, this sense of obligation in the innkeeper ripened into a status duty, so that innkeepers could be sued for defective conditions in their taverns. A status duty, however, was limited to a particular vocation, just as recovery in equity was limited to the particular circumstances of a case.[122] As the procedural organization of American jurisprudence broke down in the mid-nineteenth century, scientists looked at the newly created fields of law that had emerged from the dissolution of the writs and saw, in each, a legacy of equitable maxims. They identi-fied the systematization of their respective fields with a transformation of these maxims into scientific organizing principles.

In the field of torts, the transformation took the following form. A number of equity maxims had coalesced into status duties. The scientists created a new concept, the idea of a general duty owed to all the world by all the world, but limited this liability to those who were at "fault" via the negligence principle.[123] They then reexamined preexisting status duties from the perspective of modern negligence. Their examination culminated in the extraction of purportedly universal tort "doctrines" from status contexts. Once a doctrine was identified, the status duty to which it corresponded disappeared, since the doctrine was conceived of as applying not only to cases where the defendant's vocation had created special responsibilities, but to all cases. The consequence was a transformation of tort law to conform with the negligence principle. The following discussion illustrates the transformation process by examining the impact of the conception of law as a science on the tort doctrines of assumption of risk, last clear chance, and vicarious liability.

Assumption of risk strikes the twentieth-century observer as the archetypal doctrine of an age entranced with the idea that each man was equally capable of protecting himself against injury. In its most extreme applications the doctrine seems almost a parody of itself, an abstraction, that from current perspectives, lost all touch with reality. In a 1900 Massachusetts case, for example, Holmes, then chief justice of the Supreme Judicial Court of Massachusetts, held that an employee of an axe and tool company could not recover for injuries suffered when a hatchet from a defective rack fell on him.[124] According to Holmes, the employee had complained that hatchets were likely to drop off the rack while he was engaged in painting. "He was answered in substance [by his employer] that he would have to use the racks or leave," Holmes noted.[125] The employee remained at work, and "[t]he accident which he feared happened."[126] Holmes held that the employee was barred from suing his employer in negligence because he "appreciated the danger . . . [and] took the risk."[127] The doctrine of assumption of risk applied even though "fear of losing his place" motivated the employee to remain.[128] Under the doctrine, as Holmes understood it, there was no duty of care on the part of employers to maintain safe working conditions for their employees; or if there was such a duty, it extended only to those employees who did not know about unsafe conditions. Once the employee discovered the unsafe conditions and continued to work, assumption of risk operated as a complete bar.

Such was the state of the assumption of risk doctrine at its high-water mark. It was a principle that, in jurisdictions such as Massachusetts, operated in all phases of employment, regardless of external factors suggesting that exposure to a known risk might not be truly voluntary. It served as a significant limitation on liability. But the doctrine had not always occupied so formidable a place in tort law. It had originated in the "status" context of servants' relations with their masters, had been based on contract analogies, and had been confined to a limited circle of relationships. Gradually, through the efforts of scientists, the doctrine was expanded to become a basic element of early twentieth-century negligence law.

The early Torts treatise writers regarded assumption of risk as essentially confined to master-servant cases. Francis Hilliard, whose treatise first appeared in 1859, did not use the phrase "assumption of risk" at all, but in his discussion of the liability of a master to his servant indicated that if a defective condition "was known to the servant . . . and the servant continued in the service, he assumed the risk himself." [129] Thomas Shearman and Amasa Redfield, in their 1870 treatise on negligence, felt that assumption of risk was "but a branch of the general law of waiver," resting on an implied contract between employer and employee that allocated responsibilities for the risk of service.[130] Seymour Thompson, in his treatise on *The Law of Negligence in Relations Not Resting in Contract* (1880), also regarded assumption of risk as akin to the "[w]aiver of a [r]ight of [a]ction" in contract cases and found it confined to "the relation of master and servant" or "carrier and passenger." [131] Thompson, however, thought the assumption of risk principle "capable of expansion into other relations than those of master and servant." [132]

By the late 1870s, in fact, others had gone well beyond Thompson. Francis Wharton, in the second edition of *A Treatise on the Law of Negligence* (1878), rejected any connection between contract principles and the assumption of risk doctrine. Wharton pointed out that not all servants were competent to contract, and in the majority of American jurisdictions "contracts to relieve a party from the consequences of his negligence" were held to be invalid "as against the policy of the law." [133] Rather than being grounded on the fiction of an implied contract, assumption of risk embodied "the general principle that a party cannot recover for injury he incurs in risks, themselves legitimate, to which he intelligently submits himself." [134] That principle "[had] nothing distinctively to do with the relation of master and servant. It [was] common to all suits for negligence based on duty as distinguished from contract." [135] Assumption of risk applied, for example, against one who stumbled on an obstacle left negligently on a highway, if he previously knew of the obstacle's presence; [136] against one who attempted to rescue property at a fire, once advised of the attendant dangers; [137] and against one who built a greenhouse near an artillery barracks and had his windows shattered, when he knew that the barracks was in his vicinity. [138] "[M]ere volunteer[s]" as well as servants were barred from recovery by the doctrine. [139]

Thus the first stage in the transformation of the assumption of risk doctrine was its liberation from a "waiver" or "contract" context. This had been partially accomplished by the 1880s. [140] The second stage—liberation of the doctrine from "master-servant" cases—was, despite Wharton's efforts, much slower to materialize. It was not until 1895 that Charles Warren's article in the *Harvard Law Review* ushered in the second stage. [141] The principal achievement of Warren's article was its eradication of the "status" aspects of assumption of risk by including the doctrine in a general theory of negligence. Significantly, the basis of Warren's theory was the concept of a universal duty of ordinary care. Warren began by asserting the presence of this duty and the necessary correlation between the terms "duty" and "negligence," [142] and then argued that "[t]he plaintiff in an action of tort for negligence must allege and prove a duty on the part of the defendant towards him. . . ." [143] The defendant could then assert various defenses, such as lack of proximate causation, contributory negligence, or the fact that "the plaintiff himself had voluntarily placed himself in such a position that no duty arose as towards him." [144]

The last of these defenses Warren described as "strictly not a defense, but a rule of law regarding a plaintiff's conduct." The rule was paraphrased thusly: "One who knows of a danger arising from the act or omission of another, and understands the risk therefrom, and voluntarily exposes himself to it, is precluded from recovering for an injury which results from the exposure." [145] It was a rule embodied by the maxim " '[v]olenti non fit injuria.' " [146] It was not confined to master-servant cases or, potentially, even to employment cases. [147] It was not based on any existing or previous contractual relationship. [148] It could be applied in all cases where persons were on a

landowner's property for business purposes.[149] Its only limitation was
its likely confinement to "cases where the plaintiff and defendant
enter into some distinct relation towards each other." [150] Even with
this limitation, the doctrine was a truly universal rule.

By 1906, at the height of mature legal science, one can see the
assumption of risk doctrine full-blown. Francis Bohlen's article that
year in the *Harvard Law Review* began with the statement that the
doctrine was not "isolated or anomalous." [151] It was "not in any way
founded upon anything peculiar to the relation of master and servant
nor [was] it based upon the contractual nature of [that] relation . . .
[I]t applie[d] equally to any relation voluntarily assumed—contractual
or not." [152] Moreover, in a long discussion of relevant cases taken
primarily from the area of employment, Bohlen showed that the
doctrine was a significant limitation on liability. The doctrine was invoked in those cases where an employee was "placed in a position
where he must either encounter some probable . . . danger, or else
give up his employment. . . ." [153] Holmes's hatchet-rack decision
represented the majority view.

Bohlen sought to explain this tendency and to explore the philosophical foundations of the assumption of risk doctrine. One possible
basis for the doctrine was "economic conditions." Bohlen felt that "in
America as yet there is normally no dearth of work for competent
workmen. If one job is dangerous, another can probably be found." [154]
Another basis was sociological. Bohlen referred to "the known
tendency of American workmen to take desperate chances touching
their safety." Risks often were taken "through mere thoughtless reck-
lessness or disinclination to leave a position in other respects satisfactory." [155] But the principal basis of the doctrine was "the in-
dividualistic tendency of the common law, which . . . naturally regards the freedom of individual action as the keystone of the whole
structure." [156] Individuals were protected from "external violence" but
not from "the effects of [their] own personalit[ies] and from the consequences of [their] voluntary actions." Each person was left "free to
work out his own destin[y]." [157]

In successive stages scientists had transformed assumption of risk
from an equitable maxim into a philosophical principle. In transform-
ing the doctrine they had appealed to history, where, for example,
Bohlen found that "[i]n the law of torts . . . the idea of any obligation to protect others was abnormal." [158] They also had relied on their

skills at "inductive" case analysis to correct judicial misstatements, disapprove of misguided doctrinal interpretations, read cases in a strikingly clear doctrinal light, and extract principles.[159] Finally, the scientists had followed their own philosophical predilections towards achieving intellectual order and restricting tort liability. That assumption of risk was functioning well as a liability-limiting principle can be seen from the passage of federal legislation, in 1906, designed to compel jury consideration of work-related suits by employees of railroads operating in interstate commerce.[160] The 1906 legislation did not require that assumption of risk issues be decided in every instance by juries, a qualification that kept Bohlen from total despair. "[O]therwise," he concluded, the legislation "would practically impose on the railroads the payment of a compulsory pension to injured employees." [161]

A striking example of the need to systematize among late nineteenth-century legal scholars can be found in the creation of the doctrine of last clear chance, by which a negligent plaintiff was allowed recovery against a negligent defendant if the defendant had a last opportunity to avoid injuring the plaintiff. The doctrine currently is assumed to have "originated" [162] in 1842 in the case of *Davies v. Mann*.[163] In this English decision a plaintiff who left a donkey tied in a public highway was allowed damages against a defendant whose servant drove a team of horses and a wagon into the donkey. But the doctrine had not in fact originated in *Davies v. Mann,* at least as a principle of negligence law; it was a creation of later treatise writers who extracted it from the *Davies* case and others. No judge in *Davies* had used the phrase "last clear chance" or had given an extended rationale for the result. One judge, Lord Abingor, merely asserted that "as the defendant might, by proper care, have avoided injuring the animal, and did not, he is liable for the consequences of his negligence." [164] Baron Parke, the other judge, suggested that "the mere fact of negligence on the part of the plaintiff in leaving his donkey on the public highway, was no answer to the action, unless the donkey's being there was the immediate cause of the injury." Although "the ass may have been wrongfully there," Parke observed, "the defendant was bound to go along the road at such a pace as would be likely to prevent mischief." [165]

Davies became troublesome for late nineteenth-century treatise

writers because courts generally held plaintiffs' contributory negligence an absolute bar to their actions in negligence. Since the plaintiff in *Davies* was negligent in leaving his donkey on the highway, how
could the case be justified and yet not undermine contributory negligence as a coherent principle? By the 1880s treatise writers had designed two strategies to deal with that question, one attempting to
explain the *Davies* result on causation grounds, the other calling for
the abolition of the *Davies* line of cases. Seymour Thompson's discussion of *Davies* in his 1880 treatise concluded that *Davies* stood
for "the rule that the plaintiff's negligence will not bar a recovery of
damages where it is but a remote cause of the injury. . . ." [166] This
explanation had been offered by Wharton [167] (1878) and was followed by Bishop (1889),[168] Chase (1892),[169] and Bigelow (1896).[170]

Meanwhile, however, Charles Beach was advocating that the "pernicious and mischief-making authority" of *Davies* be "distinctly
repudiated." [171] Beach saw, as had Thompson, that the *Davies* rule
"practically repudiate[d] the entire doctrine of contributory negligence." [172] The result was "uncertainty and confusion in writing and
in thinking upon the subject of contributory negligence," as courts
were "driven . . . into all sorts of vagaries, and . . . endless floun-
dering and confusion." [173] Beach hoped that as the law developed it
would approach "more and more to the fixedness and certitude of the
exact sciences . . . thereby settling and determining point after point
in the law of negligence. . . ." [174] He believed that only when attempts to reconcile *Davies* with the doctrine of contributory negligence
were "abandoned and forgotten" would American negligence law be
"reduce[d] . . . to an orderly and logical system." [175]

In 1886 William Wills reviewed Beach on *Contributory Negligence*
in the *Law Quarterly Review*.[176] Wills was not taken with Beach's
treatise: he maintained that it "cannot be considered to contribute
much to the general theory of the subject" [177] and that it "employ[ed]
on occasion a somewhat 'high faluting' style." [178] Wills recognized,
however, that the *Davies v. Mann* line of cases presented "considerable difficulty." [179] He set out to formulate a workable "rule" for cases
where "there is negligence on both sides." His formulation was thus:
"the party *who last has a clear opportunity of avoiding the accident,
notwithstanding the negligence of his opponent,* is considered solely
responsible for it. . . ." This rule "will be found . . . to be true,"
Wills claimed, "of all such cases, whether the series [of events leading to

injury] be long or short." [180] He was later to say that "the ground" of the rule was proximate causation: "the law . . . holds that person liable who was *in the main* the cause of the injury." [181]

Thus the "last opportunity" or "last clear chance" rule was born. In the 1888 edition of Shearman and Redfield on *Negligence,* Wills's formulation was cited as "the rule in *Davies v. Mann"* and called "just and necessary," although the "actual decision" in the case was regarded as possibly "erroneous." [182] In 1895 a North Carolina court allowed a jury finding for recovery to stand where an inattentive engineer had failed to notice a person sleeping on a railroad track.[183] The court said that the "test rule" it had employed to assess liability was "that he who has the last clear chance, notwithstanding the negligence of the adverse party, is considered solely responsible. . . ." [184] The court derived the rule from a "principle deduced from *Davies v. Mann,* as is said by discriminating law-writers, [that] the party who has the last clear opportunity of avoiding the accident, notwithstanding the negligence of his opponent, is considered solely responsible for it." [185] Shearman and Redfield were cited. That formulation of the doctrine successfully crossed the Atlantic and was adopted, according to the North Carolina court, in "almost all of the Southern and Western States." [186]

In their 1898 edition Shearman and Redfield dropped reference to Wills and restated the doctrine: "the party who has the last opportunity of avoiding accident, is not excused by the negligence of any one else. His negligence, and not that of the one first in fault, is the sole proximate cause of the injury." [187] By 1901, in a new edition of his treatise, Thompson referred to "[a] doctrine which is found in the text of a leading work on the law of negligence [and] has been echoed by the courts in two or three decisions." [188] He "ventured to call it the 'last clear chance' doctrine" and cited Shearman and Redfield and the North Carolina case.[189] Nearly sixty years after *Davies* "last clear chance" entered the common vocabulary of lawyers and judges.

Meanwhile the causation rationale for last clear chance, which Thompson, Wills, and Shearman and Redfield had adopted, was coming under attack. As early as 1889 William Schofield had pointed out that *Davies v. Mann* could be understood as a proximate cause case only if "proximate" was equated with "last." [190] Schofield maintained that the plaintiff in *Davies* "did an act which was likely to result in damage, and which did so result": his having the donkey in

Determining the effectual limits of legal-intellectual history

the highway was a proximate cause of the accident.[191] But even if "proximate cause" were to be equated with "last cause to operate in point of time," *Davies* could not be read as a proximate cause case; no judge in *Davies* inquired "whether the defendant was guilty of the last negligence, but only whether he had an opportunity to avoid the accident by the use of due care." [192]

Hence, Schofield argued, the "great principle" of *Davies* was "the duty of one person to avoid the consequences of another's negligence." [193] The critical question for Schofield was whether an accident, "after the peril was imminent, [could have been] avoided by either party, by the use of due care." If so, "the one who fails to use due care to avoid, cannot recover." [194] Thus the only time plaintiffs should recover in "successive" negligence situations was when "the defendant alone can avoid the accident by the use of due care." If the plaintiff could have avoided it, or if the defendant could not have, the plaintiff could be barred from recovery by the doctrine of contributory negligence.[195]

Although Schofield explicitly rejected the idea that the defendant's failure to act in *Davies* was the "last" cause of the accident, his formulation invited a search for the party who had the last clear chance to avoid injury. Avoiding the consequences of another's negligence assumed an opportunity to perceive the other's acts and respond. If a defendant could show that he did not have that opportunity, or that it was not clear that he alone had it, he could defeat recovery. In practical application, then, plaintiffs sought to show that defendants were solely responsible for the injury not having been avoided. Such a showing invariably became equated with physical proof that the defendant was the last person capable of preventing an accident. The words "last clear chance" nicely described the conduct plaintiffs sought to ascribe to defendants.

But a causation explanation for the last clear chance doctrine still posed analytical difficulties. If the conduct of defendant A, who failed to exercise the last clear chance to avoid an accident, was *the* proximate cause of a collision in which a negligent plaintiff B, was injured, it would seem to follow that an innocent third party C, also injured, would have no recourse against B, since B's negligence was not the cause of the accident. Yet courts repeatedly allowed C to recover from B.[196] Legal sicentists therefore sought still another basis for the doctrine. In 1908 Francis Bohlen argued that the last clear chance doctrine was "an auxiliary rule enforcing, where there are successive acts of misconduct, an arbitrary legal conception of proximity," and that it should be treated "as a separate limitation of legal liability quite distinct from proximity of causation." [197] For reasons of policy, Bohlen maintained, the doctrine sought to retain liability in those instances where a "plaintiff's danger and his inability to help himself was known to the defendant," or in cases where "the defendant, had he been on the alert, as he should have been, could have discovered it." [198] Last clear chance, as another commentator said in 1919, was "an exception to the rule of contributory negligence . . . based as much on [considerations of] sound policy and justice as the rule itself." [199]

With Bohlen's treatment the cycle of last clear chance was complete. The result in *Davies v. Mann* may have been based on no more than unarticulated perceptions of equity and justice: it simply may have seemed unfair to deny a person compensation for the value of his donkey, even though he had left it in a public highway, when, in the end, the accident had been caused by another person's driving too fast to avoid hitting the donkey. Later treatise writers, in seeking to systematize the "principle" of *Davies,* had been baffled by its presence in a system that permitted contributory negligence to be an absolute bar to recovery. Impatient with explanations that rested only on the individual equities of a case, those treatise writers had sought a "doctrinal" explanation for *Davies,* which produced the formulation "last clear chance" and its underlying theory of proximate causation. But the last clear chance doctrine proved inconsistent even with causation theory, and commentators ultimately recognized it as "an arbitrary modification of a harsh rule" [200] or "an exception based . . . on sound policy and justice." [201]

The last clear chance doctrine had never been more than an escape from the inequities of a doctrinal jurisprudence that encouraged the promulgation of universal rules. Universals, such as the doctrine of contributory negligence, sometimes produced harsh results. The sporadic amelioration of harsh results by courts has been commonplace; *Davies* was an example. What was extraordinary about "last clear chance" was the need among commentators to give it doctrinal status. This need resulted in the posing of numerous hypothetical problems involving "inattentive" or "helpless" plaintiffs in which the doctrine did or did not apply and in their straining to link the doctrine to some orderly general principle—even that most unruly principle, proximate causation—of scientific tort law.[202] In the age of legal science, recurrent results admitting of no doctrinal explanation were heretical. If courts could not provide an explanation, academics would invent one.

Although the scientists were highly interested in the development and refinement of all the doctrines of tort law, they were more enthusiastic about some of their doctrinal products than others. In general, doctrines limiting liability were preferred to those expanding it. This preference stemmed from the scientists' sense that although specially conferred tort duties were being replaced by a general duty of care, that general duty needed to be severely limited lest it undermine the premise that one's responsibilities in society were owed largely to oneself. As Holmes had said in *The Common Law,*

> The state might conceivably make itself a mutual insurance company against accidents, and distribute the burden of its citizens' mishaps among all its members. . . . As between individuals it might adopt the mutual insurance principle . . . and divide damages when both were in fault . . . or it might throw all loss upon the actor irrespective of fault. The state does none of these things, however, and the prevailing view is that its cumbrous and expensive machinery ought not to be set in motion unless some clear benefit is to be derived from disturbing the *status quo.*[203]

This "prevailing view" characterized the age of legal science; consequently doctrines that imposed liability on persons who were not at fault were subjected to hostile scrutiny.[204]

Yet one such doctrine, vicarious liability, survived the transition in Torts from status duties to general duties of care with its essential features undisturbed. The principle of vicarious liability held an employer (formerly a master) liable for the negligence of his employee (formerly servant) even though he had neither authorized his employees' torts nor specifically prohibited them. An 1852 U.S. Supreme Court case indicated that vicarious liability did not depend on any contractual relationship or "chain of command" between the employer and the employee, but simply on whether the employee's acts were within the scope of his employment. If so, the employer was absolutely liable for his employee's negligence.[205] John Dillon wrote in 1890, "So far as this rule imposes on the master . . . a liability beyond his authorized acts and defaults . . . it is one of manifest severity, not based on natural justice."[206]

Vicarious liability was itself a holdover from the earlier conception of negligence as a specific duty arising out of a preexisting status or relationship. A master owed a duty to see that his servants did not injure others because his servants were part of his household and he could be regarded as responsible for their conduct, as an innkeeper was responsible to guests for the condition of his premises. But as applied to large industrial enterprises, the doctrine, particularly in its severest forms, seem antithetical to the trend of late nineteenth-century tort law: to condition the existence of a general duty of care to others on a showing of fault. How could management personnel of a giant industrial combine be said to be fairly accountable for all the careless acts of the combine's employees? Yet the doctrine of respondeat superior, which embodied the vicarious liability principle, held the corporation, through its management personnel, responsible regardless of what prior steps management might have taken to forestall or prevent an employee's risky act.

Despite the anomalous status of vicarious liability in a period where the negligence principle was coming to dominate tort law, courts and commentators were slow to attack the doctrine itself. There were, however, significant efforts to limit its impact, the most successful of which was the so-called "fellow servant" rule. That rule, whose first important articulation came in a Massachusetts case in 1842,[207] held that an employee could not successfully sue his employer for injuries sustained from the negligence of a fellow employee. The rule thereby served to relieve employers of vicarious liability for the injuries of a substantial class of potential litigants. It created the anomaly that, if in the course of his employment, an employee negligently injured a bystander, his employer was legally responsible; however, if he injured a co-employee (as was much more likely in most nineteenth-century industrial environments), the employer was relieved from liability. The great success of the fellow servant rule in eviscerating vicarious liability engendered some concern in the courts, which were not uniformly unsympathetic to victims of industrial accidents even in the late nineteenth century. Out of this concern emerged the abortive "vice principal" doctrine, which had a brief and unhappy history in the Supreme Court of the United States.

In the late nineteenth century the Supreme Court was a major source of common law torts decisions. Several factors combined to produce this state of affairs: a significant number of railroad accidents, which regularly resulted in suits in the federal courts under diversity jurisdiction because the injured plaintiffs and corporate defendants were domiciled in different states; the low minimum ($500) required for federal court jurisdiction; the absence of any certiorari power in the Court, which forced it to hear any qualified diversity case appealed from a lower federal court; and the *Swift v. Tyson* [208] rule that the federal courts, including the Supreme Court, were not bound to follow the common law decisions of a state but could declare general common law principles.

The Supreme Court's two primary "vice principal" cases were *Chicago, Milwaukee & St. Paul Ry. Co. v. Ross* [209] and *Baltimore & Ohio R.R. v. Baugh*.[210] Both involved injuries suffered by railroad employees as a consequence of the negligence of their co-workers. In *Ross* an engineer of the Chicago and Milwaukee Railroad was injured when his freight train collided with an unscheduled train carrying gravel. The conductor of the freight train had failed to notify his engineer that their train had been ordered to remain on side tracks while the gravel train was in the vicinity. The conductor also had fallen asleep during the freight train's run. The railroad argued that the conductor was a fellow servant of the engineer, and thus the engineer was barred from recovery. Justice Field, for a five-man majority, held that a conductor of a railroad train was a "vice principal," standing in the shoes of his company, and not a "fellow servant" for the purposes of suits by employees based on the conductor's negligence. Field found significance in the fact that the conductor was responsible to "the general management of [the train], and [had] control over the persons employed upon it." [211]

The *Ross* decision set off some scrambling among commentators. Wharton,[212] Thompson,[213] and Beach [214] had all concluded, before *Ross,* that "the decided weight of authority [was] to the effect that all who serve the same master . . . and are engaged in the same general business, though it may be in different grades or departments of it, are fellow servants, who take the risk of each other's negligence." [215] After *Ross* was decided, Dillon maintained that the decision needed to be confined to its facts and that "the true inquiry" in each fellow servant case was whether "the accident [was] one of the normal and natural risks in the ordinary course of . . . business." If so, the master was not liable; if not, he was. "[G]rades or . . . departments" were largely irrelevant.[216] Beach, on the other hand, called *Ross* "the clearest and ablest production of the law in this behalf, and the fairest and most satisfactory argument upon it to be found." He felt that the *Ross* doctrine was "certainly the rule of humanity" and could "be expected to have a powerful influence." [217]

Unfortunately for Beach, one year after his remarks appeared the Supreme Court rejected the *Ross* doctrine in *Baugh.* The *Baugh* case involved a suit for damages by a fireman of the Baltimore and Ohio Railroad who had been injured in a collision caused by the negligence of his train's engineer. At the time of the accident the engineer and fireman were the sole employees on a train consisting only of a loco-motive and a tender. The engineer had failed to signal the presence of his train, which was proceeding at an unscheduled time and which subsequently collided with a scheduled passenger train. A company regulation provided that whenever a train was being run without a conductor the engineer would "be regarded as conductor and . . . act accordingly." [218]

Justice Brewer, for the majority in *Baugh,* maintained that *Ross* had labeled conductors "vice principals" because they had "the control and management of a distinct department" and argued that the doc-trine could "only be fairly applied when the different branches or departments of service are in and of themselves separate and dis-tinct." [219] Mere control of a department was not enough to merit being called a vice principal. Since the engineer and the firemen were in the "operating" department, they were fellow servants. It was irrele-vant that the engineer's status was superior to that of the fireman, or that he was the only person in authority on the train at the time, or that the railroad's regulations considered him a "conductor" under the circumstances. It was hard to know what was left of the vice principal doctrine after *Baugh.*

A revealing aspect of the *Baugh* decision was an attack launched by Justice Brewer on the broad implications of vicarious liability. Brewer argued that for vicarious liability to attach against a master "there must be . . . some breach of positive duty on his part." If a master had "taken all reasonable precautions to inquire into the competency of one proposing to enter his service . . . [he had] done all that reasonable care requires" and no negligence ought to be imputed to him.[220] Brewer would have confined vicarious liability to those situations where an employer could be shown to have been negligent in his choice of employees or in providing safe working conditions. In short, Brewer sought to convert questions of vicarious liability to ordinary questions of negligence, at least in "fellow-servant" cases.

Justice Field, dissenting in *Baugh,* understood the broad implications of the decision. Not only did the Court's holding "den[y] . . . the correctness of [the vice principal] doctrine," but it demonstrated an impatience with vicarious liability in any form. "There [was] a marked distinction" Field noted, "in the decisions of different courts upon the extent of liability of a corporation for injuries by its servants to persons in their employ." One line of cases "would exempt the corporation from all responsibility for the negligence of its employees, of every grade, whether exercising supervising authority and control over other employees of the company, or otherwise." [221] Another "would hold a corporation responsible for all negligent acts of its agents . . . when exercising authority and supervision over other employees." [222] Field found the latter line of decisions "most in accordance with justice and humanity." [223]

The changing state of the vice principal doctrine unsettled commentators. The 1887 Shearman and Redfield treatise, in the course of discussing the *Ross* case, noted that the doctrine was being followed in sixteen states and the federal courts and would "be adopted . . . probably by others." [224] But in 1898, after *Baugh,* Sherman and Redfield grudgingly conceded that the doctrine did not cover "an engineer running an engine with no train," or "foreman, etc., managing small pieces of work, in which they take part." They argued that the *Ross* decision "has been limited . . . [but] it has never been overruled." [225] By the time of his 1907 edition of Cooley's treatise, John Lewis was prepared to assert as a general proposition that "the mere fact" that one employee had authority over another or served in a different department was not sufficient to create an exception to the fellow-servant rule.[226] Lewis maintained that the vice principal doctrine had come to be "expressly repudiated in many of the states" and was "not generally regarded in determining who are fellow-servants." [227]

The abortive life of the vice principal doctrine illustrates some of the obstacles scientists faced in their efforts to reshape tort law. Where courts had advanced only cryptic explanations for a doctrine or had not attempted to view a line of cases from a doctrinal perspective at all, as in the cases of assumption of risk or last clear chance, opportunities abounded for creative "scientific" analysis by treatise writers. Where courts had been heavily involved in the process of doctrinal creation, however, as in fellow servant and vice principal cases, commentators were reduced to a more passive role. In addition, the abundance of fellow-servant cases, the conflicting approaches of different jurisdictions, and the apparently settled status, in the late nineteenth century, of both the vicarious liability principle and the fellow-servant rule virtually precluded the development of any comprehensive approach to the class of situations that had spawned the vice principal doctrine. The post-Civil War academic-judicial symbiosis acted to limit the creative opportunities of scientists as well as to expand them.

The frustration commentators expressed with the "conflict of judicial decisions" and "diversity of opinion" surrounding the vice principal doctrine, then, may have stemmed in part from a sense of their own powerlessness to abolish the principle of vicarious liability, which they tended to regard as unsound.[228] With the establishment of both vicarious liability and the fellow-servant rule confusion was inevitable, given the differing views of courts on the proper distribution of risks in industrial accidents. The checkered course of the vice principal doctrine not only offended the scientists' desire for order and predictability in tort law, but also underscored for them the anachronistic nature of vicarious liability itself. But while the demise of the vice principal doctrine was generally applauded by commentators, none proposed, even at the height of the influence of universalistic negligence theory, that vicarious liability itself be abandoned.

The doctrinal histories described in this section reveal the ingenuity of late nineteenth-century legal science and also suggest one of its principal weaknesses. When a system of legal analysis, holding as one of its basic tenets the assumption that law is in flux, is employed to establish a set of general principles applicable to all cases, a fundamental tension arises between the goal of the methodology and the methodology itself. Nevertheless, the conception of law as a science substantially affected both the doctrinal state of tort law and the analytical techniques employed in the discussion of tort cases between 1880 and 1910. Legal science was part of a broader theoretical effort to revise the ways in which late nineteenth-century Americans became educated. Other disciplines and professions erected similar frameworks, many of which stressed the importance of "scientific" thinking.

The role of science in late nineteenth-century thought can, from this perspective, be viewed as a metaphorical device through which a new theory of acquiring knowledge was conveyed.

The Legacy of Legal Science

The original formulation of law as a science began to lose its usefulness in the first decades of the twentieth century and while an ideal of legal science persisted, new definitions of "scientific" analysis were created.

The principal tension in late nineteenth-century legal science was between its fluid methodology and the static substantive outcomes this methodology produced. The process of extracting principles from cases assumed a continuing fresh supply of material, for few cases were ever identical. The different ingredients in each fact situation meant a continually fluid application of existing principles to new circumstances.[229] But since a paramount goal of legal science was the achievement of jurisprudential order and coherence, existing principles were supposed to have more than a hypothetical quality: they were formulated as enduring guidelines. How, then, did a scientist maintain doctrinal coherence in the face of a growing and changing body of cases?

Early scientists, such as Langdell, had resolved this dilemma by simply asserting that most cases reflected an imperfect or erroneous statement of a principle and thus could be discarded as "wrong." This approach greatly simplified the scholar's task, but led to a static jurisprudence and was not adopted by many scholars in the mature years of legal science. The Langdellian resolution became a helpful caricature when legal science came under attack,[230] but it was only a primitive response, and Langdell's successors identified their task as integration of the imperfect case rather than simple dismissal. In the work of Schofield, Wigmore, Bohlen, Smith, and Beale one can see efforts to reformulate a principle of liability in light of difficulties with its implementation.[231] None of the authors refrains from a generalization, but each defines his task as refining an existing principle rather than abandoning principles altogether. As Smith put it in a 1912 article on causation:

> . . . [O]ur present purpose is . . . to bring out the most important
> elementary principles underlying . . . decisions. The decisions con-

tain the rough material from which the leading principles are to be evolved; but a detailed statement of each separate decision is not equivalent to a statement of the leading principles. . . . [I]t is not desirable to attempt to add subsidiary rules sufficiently numerous and sufficiently minute to point out unerringly the exact decision in every conceivable specific case.[232]

However much the later scientists may have labored to preserve coherence and predictability in tort law, the subject was vulnerable to atomistic tendencies. This atomism became strikingly apparent as modern negligence concepts evolved. In 1915 Henry Terry wrote that "[t]here is a negative duty of due care of very great generality, resting upon all persons and owed regularly to all persons, not to do negligent acts." [233] This was a restatement of Holmes' "duty of all to all," first formulated in 1873 when negligence was largely limited to existing duties of status or occupation. Terry's assertion of its unquestioned acceptance was itself an event in the history of Torts.[234] But how was a breach of that duty to be established? Terry's tests, intended as statements of "scientific" rules, each involved the creation of a hypothetical "reasonable" or "standard" man and, in most cases, a jury determination as to whether the defendant's conduct in the circumstances of the case had been "reasonable" for that "standard man." Terry pointed out that "[t]he reasonableness or unreasonableness of conduct is an inference from data. The data consist of the conduct in question and the facts of the actor's situation." [235] In other words, in the great majority of cases, a jury asked whether the peculiar factual circumstances gave rise to an inference of negligence.

Where, then, were the "rules" of negligence law? Terry claimed that since some groups of facts tended to recur, "a number of positive rules of considerable generality have been evolved." He gave as one such example the rule "about looking and listening before crossing a railroad track." [236] But was Terry asserting that in every case failure to "stop, look, and listen" constituted conclusive evidence of negligence? If not, then the "rule" was not a rule of substantive law but a rule of procedure. It held that in most railroad crossing cases the judge would take from the jury the question of an actor's negligence where the actor had failed to stop, look, or listen. The "rule" was really a rule of judicial discretion that stated that judges were given the power to depart, in some areas, from the presumption that negligence was a jury-determined question based on discrete circumstances.

It was not difficult for scientists to see the subversive effect of jury determinations on the theoretical integrity of Torts. The more often a principle of tort law, such as negligence, took its operative meaning from individualized decisions by discrete juries, the less meaningful that principle was as a uniform guide to conduct. One might posit the existence of a universal duty not to injure one's neighbor negligently, but if the question of whether one had been negligent invariably turned on a jury's interpretation of a unique set of facts, the universal duty had little meaning as an abstraction. Holmes had seen this in *The Common Law* and had argued in his lectures on Torts for a limiting of the jury's function. "[T]he tendency of the law," he maintained, "must always be to narrow the field of uncertainty," and judicially derived "definite rule[s"] were more "philosophical in spirit" [237] than discrete jury determinations. But Holmes conceded that "[t]he trouble with many cases of negligence is, that they are of a kind not frequently recurring . . . and that the elements are so complex that courts are glad to leave the whole matter in a lump for the jury's determination." [238] As a judge, Holmes enjoyed taking negligence cases away from juries and was one of the architects of the "stop, look, and listen" rule for the federal courts.[239] His fears about the corrosive effects of juries on negligence rules were well founded, for in a later case involving that very rule the Supreme Court decided that "stop, look and listen" needed to be interpreted in terms of the context in which an individual driver found himself and that a jury could best apply the rule to that context.[240]

As complexities in the relationship between principles and cases came to be perceived by legal scholars and the importance of the relationship between judge and jury in tort cases surfaced, an insight emerged in legal scholarship that exposed a major limitation in the existing methodology of the scientists. If "rules" in negligence cases were principally rules of power or procedure rather than rules of substance, then the gist of negligence law was found not in the content of its rules but in the process by which those rules were implemented. In proximate cause cases, for example, the most useful question was not whether a given "rule" of causation (such as the "substantial factor" rule suggested by Smith) [241] was sound as a general explanatory principle. The salient questions were rather whether judges tended to invoke that rule at all; whether, if they did so, they tended to use it as a means of taking proximate cause cases away from juries; and, if they did not, whether juries applied the rule in a meaningful and predictable fashion.[242]

The damaging aspect of these questions for the conception of law advanced by the scientists was that they could easily lead to a belief that "law" was synonymous with the idiosyncratic judgments of officials (including juries) or a complementary belief that two sets of legal "rules" existed: "paper rules" (rules of substance) on which judicial actions purportedly were based and "real rules" (rules of power or procedure), which determined whose individualized judgment would prevail in a given case.[243] This description of law, while not irreconcilable with all "scientific" models, was inconsistent with the model of the late nineteenth- and early twentieth-century scientists, which placed great emphasis on the derivation of meaningful substantive rules.

In positing a gap between substantive and procedural rules and in suggesting a misplaced emphasis in legal science, twentieth-century critics were reviving a tactic of early participants in the nineteenth-century knowledge revolution. Their tactic was to distinguish between dogmatic and inductive reasoning and to suggest that the scientists were guilty of the former. Their argument, as applied to tort law, ran as follows: if substantive rules were largely subject to modification in given cases, then proper scholarly focus should be on the modification process, not on the rules. This was inductive reasoning, since it proceeded from the diverse facts of cases to generalizations about the judicial process or the function of judge and jury. In contrast, the reasoning of the scientists was seen as dogmatic reasoning, emphasizing the formulation of meaningless abstract principles that were asserted to have universal validity. That assertion, critics suggested, ignored the operation of the principles in practice. Thus, in one of the recurrent ironies of intellectual history, critics of the scientists juxtaposed their own "original research" against the "dogma" of their opponents. The scientists had, of course, taken as one of their first premises the importance of legal research in original sources as a counterweight to dogma.

The tension between principles and cases in nineteenth-century legal science was symptomatic of larger tensions in the value orientation of participants in the late nineteenth-century knowledge revolution. The "order" achieved by universal explanatory concepts competed with the "progress" achieved by the common law's perceived capability to respond to the changing context in which legal rules were applied. The "inductive" research techniques of the late nineteenth-century scientific method helped expose the "dogmatic" character of all-encompassing legal principles. And, most significantly, the scientists' perception that the multifaceted character of post-Civil War American society could not be adequately understood through simplistic, derivative educational techniques ultimately threatened their own philosophical assumptions. If life in America was complex and interdependent, how sensible were "scientifically" derived legal rules if their philosophical basis was a vision of society as simply an aggregate of autonomous individuals?

Thus, for twentieth-century critics, a final limitation of legal science was its association with substantive rules that were based on an outmoded view of society. Beliefs such as the free will of the autonomous individual, the undesirability of governmental involvement in human affairs, and the inherent justice of the law of the marketplace were antithetical to a twentieth-century philosophy of affirmative, paternalistic intervention by the state. That philosophy was justified by its advocates as a necessary response to the conditions of life in a society where the activities of persons disadvantaged by the free market affected those advantaged by it. As the ideal of the general welfare state came to have a greater influence in educated American thought, the philosophical positions assumed by the scientists came to be seen as not only dogmatic but reactionary.[44]

The limitations in the late nineteenth-century ideal of legal science were perceived ultimately as outweighing its contributions, and by the third decade of the twentieth century "conceptualism" had become a pejorative term. Before turning to the intellectual activity of that period, however, the state of tort law at the zenith of the scientists' influence should be summarized.

Four features characterized American tort law in the early years of the twentieth century. It was essentially a common law subject, one whose rules and doctrines had been articulated and developed by judges and academicians. Legal problems in Torts were "solved" primarily by the application of common law principles, such as assumption of risk, last clear chance, and the fellow-servant doctrine, rather than through legislation. The apparent capability of tort principles to expand and contract with the dictates of society was viewed by early twentieth-century observers as a testament to the regenerative powers of the common law.

Second, "scientific" tort law was dominated by the negligence principle. Between 1850 and 1910 modern negligence had been created, had developed an interrelated system of doctrines, and had expanded the ambit of its jurisdiction. Strict liability, hitherto a persistent presence in tortious civil actions, had diminished in influence until its existence seemed confined to wild animals, escaping water, and other survivals of what Francis Burdick called "peculiar" liability in tort.[245] Nuisance had virtually disappeared as a common law tort. Tort liability based on intent remained, but was increasingly overshadowed by the dominant policy question of the late nineteenth-century tort law, which was how to treat accidental injury caused by risky, although socially useful, activities. Negligence theory alone addressed that issue.

Third, an observer surveying sources of early twentieth-century tort law, especially those compiled by academics, would find a strong interest in the articulation and application of comprehensive doctrines. Tort law had become systematized: its interlocking rules were allegedly designed to provide guidance in an infinite number of situations. A theory of negligence led to a focus on defenses consistent with that theory, such as contributory negligence and assumption of risk, on refinements on those defenses, such as last clear chance and the fellow-servant rule, and on other related concepts, such as "proximate" causation and the idea of a civil duty "of very great generality" to take care not to injure one's neighbor. The ultimate step in a comprehensive systematization of tort law was to eliminate from the field of Torts all those messy areas not governed by a "fault" standard. As noted, Jeremiah Smith made such a proposal in the early years of the twentieth century.

Finally, the function of tort law as a system for compensating injured persons had been markedly affected by late nineteenth-century developments. If one makes an assumption that increased population, urbanization, and industrialization resulted in more Americans being injured after 1850 (although those injured were not necessarily a higher percentage of the total population), tort law was a potentially significant source of redress for those injuries, especially with the emergence of modern negligence and its widened definition of one's duty to act carefully. But the principal thrust of late nineteenth-century tort doctrines was to restrict, rather than to expand, the compensatory function of the law of torts. Negligence theory, in operation, emphasized limitations on liability as much as it widened the potential scope of civil duties. Of the major doctrinal innovations of the late nineteenth century, only one—the abortive "vice-principal" doctrine—served to expand liability. The creative energies of late nineteenth-century scientists were regularly exercised in the refinement of a principle, such as assumption of risk, that reinforced a disinclination to shift the burden of losses.

In considering this last characteristic of tort law at the height of the scientists' influence, it should be recalled that tort actions, prior to 1900, had not principally been conceived as devices for compensating injured persons. Compensation had been a consequence of a successful tort action, but the primary function of tort liability had been seen as one of punishing or deterring blameworthy civil conduct. A conception of tort law as a "compensation system" is a distinctly twentieth-century phenomenon, brought about by an altered view of the social consequences of injuries. This view is the product of certain changes in intellectual attitudes and assumptions, changes that are the subject of forthcoming chapters.

3

The Impact of Realism on Tort Law, 1910-1945

[handwritten annotation: Sociological jurisprudence]

The emergence of the Realist movement in American jurisprudence appears, in retrospect, to have been tinged with ironies. Leading participants in the movement disclaimed any striking theoretical unity or coherence in Realism and took pains to disassociate their own jurisprudential positions from those of purportedly Realist colleagues. Some self-styled Realists even went so far as to deny that Realism was a jurisprudential theory at all, locating its essence in its methodology. Yet few of the specific methodological innovations associated with Realism gained widespread acceptance in legal education or jurisprudential scholarship, while others were conspicuously ridiculed. At the same time, the theoretical underpinnings of Realism did become staples of American jurisprudential thought, and by 1940 the acceptance of Realism in leading American law schools was so widespread that no competing jurisprudential attitude could have been said to occupy a position of comparable influence.

Realists, for the most part, professed little interest in substantive legal doctrine, claiming that process and procedure constituted the gist of lawmaking. Yet the significant doctrinal changes that occurred in tort law and other private law areas during the years of Realism's hegemony can be seen to reflect the intellectual assumptions of the Realists. Finally, notwithstanding the pervasive and persistent impact of Realism on legal education, notably in a widely shared skepticism about the value of learning substantive "rules" or "principles," the doctrinal analysis of common law subjects pioneered by the scientists survived the emergence of Realism. Scholars and teachers, subjected to persistent criticism for the use of unworkable legal "concepts," continued to employ them and to resent efforts to replace them with more "functional" professional terms. As this chapter illustrates, Realism profoundly altered the intellectual foundations of twentieth-century tort law, but did not fundamentally change its conceptual apparatus.

The Place of Realism in Twentieth-Century American Thought

Legal science had been a product of a generation of creative energies in American higher education. Those energies had stemmed, in important part, from reexaminations of the intellectual bases of educated thought in America. There is evidence that the emergence of Realism can be traced to a comparable, though different, intellectual ferment in the early twentieth century. One can observe, on examining the course of American jurisprudence between 1870 and 1910, the growth, maturity, and nascent ossification of a conceptualist methodology whose principal end was the derivation and application of universal principles of law. One can also observe, especially after 1900, the beginnings of criticism of that methodology. Realism was to emerge as the culmination of a critical appraisal of scientific conceptualism. The creative impulses of those associated with the Realist movement were akin to those of the progenitors of late nineteenth-century legal science in that both groups felt the flush of penetrating new philosophical insights. The insights, though dramatically dissimilar, were comparably perceived as fundamental.

The philosophical presuppositions of the Realists were jurisprudential versions of more generalized intellectual insights developed and refined by educated Americans between approximately 1910 and 1945. The chronology of the Realist movement cannot be made overly distinct: intimations of a critique of scientific conceptualism had surfaced before 1910 and Realist jurisprudential assumptions remained viable among legal scholars after 1945. But the hegemony of Realism lay within those thirty-five years, and the evolution of Realist jurisprudence from a partial criticism of scientism to a thoroughgoing repudiation of its assumptions also took place in that time frame. This section is concerned with the place of the Realist movement in the context of broader developments in American thought in the 1910–1945 period.

The nineteenth-century revolution in higher education had reflected, we have seen, altered assumptions about the character of knowledge in America. The scientists had altered previous beliefs about man's proper areas of intellectual inquiry; they had, in fact, fostered an intellectual revolution by asking what truly might be "learned" and what professional techniques were most efficacious in the learning process. They had made a number of judgments about the utility or inutility of given areas of study ("science" being given a preferred position, theology not); about the relationship between the present and the past (the former "evolved" from the latter, rather than having been in stark juxtaposition to it); about the usefulness of "scientific" methodologies in the derivation of secular "truths" about the universe; and so on.

The Realists held their own set of assumptions about knowledge, which were shared, as had been those of the scientists, by a segment of their contemporaries from other professions. For present purposes I have identified this set of assumptions with a wing of early twentieth-century thought I call reformist. By reformist I do not principally mean committed to reform in politics, although that commitment can be found in several prominent educated thinkers in the segment under discussion. By reformist I principally mean committed to the ostensibly apolitical task of altering the methodological orientations of a profession. And, in particular, I mean committed to making that methodological alteration congruent with certain philosophical assumptions. Reformist thought was methodologically innovative thought resting on shared value premises.

I have designated these premises, or assumptions about knowledge, by the terms presentism, objectivism, empiricism, and anti-universalism. The terms will be defined and discussed in turn. My designation is intended to exclude from the appellation "reformist" those thinkers who did not share *all of the premises simultaneously.* In the early years of the twentieth century numerous educated Americans shared one or more of the premises; it is their combination that I have associated with a reformist perspective.[1]

A basic insight shared by numerous segments of emerging twentieth-century thought was that American civilization in the twentieth-century was radically different from, as well as an improvement upon, the past. Life in America was perceived of as being "new": new in the sense of taking place in a markedly altered environment, new also in the sense

of requiring a revision of political and social values. In the early years
of the twentieth century a vision of society as a constellation of interdependent groups displaced a competing vision, held by the original
proponents of legal science, of society as an aggregate of autonomous
individuals.[2]

A perception of social interdependence was endemic to the presentism of early twentieth-century thought. Presentism can be defined as
a tendency to assess intellectual contributions in terms of their contemporary relevance and applicability. For example, advocates of the
"New Nationalism" and the "New Freedom" identified the "newness"
of their approaches with the soundness of a belief that affirmative
governmental intervention was necessary to redress social and economic disadvantage. The problems of disadvantaged groups came to
be seen by these thinkers as affecting all of society; they were problems
of social living, not of individual character; the recent past had failed
to understand their true nature; the social philosophies of the recent
past were thus irrelevant as a source of wisdom.[3]

Comparable assumptions were made by scholars. Historians were
urged to select for study those aspects of the past relevant to current
conditions.[4] Students of politics were asked to examine the behavior of
contemporary groups in the American governmental "process" rather
than to rely on inherited theoretical wisdom.[5] The "new" contributions
of students of sociology, anthropology, and psychology to an understanding of the current state of American civilization were applauded.[6]
Influential philosophers eschewed metaphysics for "social engineering," which stressed the capability of educated elites to develop philosophically sound solutions to contemporary problems.[7] Within each
discipline thinkers increasingly stressed the novel consequences of
American society's increased interdependence.

Presentism was so widely shared by early twentieth-century scholars,
and has come to be so commonplace a value in modern American
legal thought, that its identification with the Realist movement may
seem insignificant. Yet the nineteenth-century scientists had not assumed that contemporary relevance was the most accurate guide in
assessing the validity of a statement about legal doctrine. Although
Langdell's casebook and others modeled on it were employed throughout the nineteenth century, none of the cases included in his casebook
had been handed down after 1850. The scientists used cases as repositories of principles and attempted to imbue principles with a universal

essence: in their efforts comprehensiveness far outweighed contemporaneousness. The initial twentieth-century critics of the scientists, who came to be called "sociological" jurisprudes,[8] introduced presentist assumptions into modern legal thought. For them nineteenth-century conceptualism was deficient not only because of the overly abstract quality of the "principles" it derived, but because the principles, taken as substantive guidelines, were outmoded. Conceptualists, for these critics, simply did not address the gap between their universal doctrines and the piecemeal character of contemporary American life. In Roscoe Pound's writings, for example, the simple maxims of the nineteenth century were juxtaposed against the "conditions of society today": scholars and judges needed to immerse themselves in their contemporary environment instead of relying, like "monks," on inherited abstractions.[9]

The second and third assumptions of early twentieth-century reformist thought complemented one another. Reformist thinkers assumed that objectivity was a desirable and attainable stance for professional scholars, and they assumed that the preferred mode of scholarly research was empirical. Objectivity had been a goal of late nineteneth-century scientific thought: exposure to "original" sources and the use of "inductive" reasoning were counterweights to dogma for the scientists. In early twentieth-century thought objectivity was revived, but given an altered emphasis. The purportedly neutral and disinterested scientist remained an aspirational model for twentieth-century thinkers, but the ideal of "scientific" scholarship was redefined to remove the emphasis on abstract classification associated with conceptualism and to include, increasingly, direct contemporary observations made by the social sciences.[10]

A shift in the content of a "scientific" scholarly ideal, when merged with the image of a "disinterested" scientist scholar, gave a new meaning to objectivity. Nineteenth-century scholars had been "disinterested" in turning away from the popular nostrums of the outside world to the "truths" found in their laboratories. Twentieth-century scientists were reentering the world around them. How, then, to preserve their objectivity? By suspending judgment about the "facts" they discovered; by altering policies to conform with social "realities" ("letting the facts speak for themselves"); or by demonstrating an enlightened skepticism about the permanency or even the comprehensibility of values themselves. The last technique for achieving objectivity confronted twentieth-century reformist thinkers with the possibility of embracing moral relativism, the belief that the worth of moral values is determined by their context rather than by their nature. Several influential scholars were openly to embrace relativism as twentieth-century thought matured; others were to exhibit considerable uneasiness about it, and some were to openly disassociate themselves from it; none, seemingly, could avoid its close connection with the conception of knowledge they were advancing.[11]

Moral relativism most starkly revealed the antiuniversalist thrust of early twentieth-century reformist thought. The place of universal principles in American educated thought underwent two significant modifications between the 1870s and the First World War. The late nineteenth-century critics who ultimately became associated with conceptualism had attacked dogmatic assertions of organizing principles in the universe, but their attack had been based more on the religious nature of those principles than on a discomfort with the derivation of generalized guides for human conduct. The thrust of their methodology had, in fact, been toward rather than away from generalized intellectual frameworks. Reformist thought in the early twentieth century, by contrast, increasingly exhibited a skepticism about generalizations of any kind. "Institutionalist" economics, "pragmatist" philosophy, and "progressive" history, for example, were linked by an assumption that universal propositions, especially if derived through the use of conceptualist logic, were inadequate guides to knowledge. Advocates of the above "schools of thought" proposed either to eliminate altogether academic quests for universal principles or to ground those quests on a disinterested empirical examination of contemporary social conditions.[12]

Antiuniversalist assumptions seemed to reinforce a conclusion that abstract moral judgments, especially ones that claimed constancy over time, had no place in a properly "scientific" history, economics, philosophy, or jurisprudence. Just as the natural sciences had been the disciplinary model for late nineteenth-century innovations in the acquisition and communication of knowledge, so the social sciences became the disciplinary focus of intellectual excitement after 1910. But if the social sciences were properly "contemporary," "empirical," and "objective" in their orientation, they were also either seemingly indifferent to questions of value judgment or skeptical about the necessity of including conscious value choices in scholarly analysis. Values either followed from the "facts," twentieth-century reformist thinkers seemed to be saying, or could be placed to one side. If the former, one could decide one's moral stance by finding out, through properly detached empirical observation, what was "there"; if the latter, one's moral stance need not intrude on one's scholarly endeavors.

Participants in the Realist movement were to confront each of the assumptions of twentieth-century reformist thought. Realism borrowed so completely the presentist bias of sociological jurisprudence, and made contemporary relevance so important a criterion for effective legal scholarship, that presentism remains a core assumption of American legal thought. And Realism was similarly influenced by the other assumptions: its proponents, at the height of its influence, were openly enthusiastic about empiricist methodologies, especially those of the social sciences, and quick to associate empiricism with objectivity and detachment. Most significantly, they were unabashedly critical of universal guiding principles and, when pressed, dubious about the necessity of infiltrating legal scholarship with appeals to moral values or norms.[13]

The above positions were advanced at a time—the early 1930s—when Realism seemed to its adherents remarkably full of intellectual promise and excitement. The Realist movement had had a lengthy gestation period and was to have a sudden comeuppance, but its brief years of exuberance marked Realism as the jurisprudential posture most representative of influential early twentieth-century thought. To understand more fully how Realism came to achieve its prominence, a brief review of its history is necessary.

The Realist movement evolved in stages. In the first stage, lasting approximately from 1910 to the mid-1920s, jurisprudential ferment centered around the proper function of judges and the utility of existing judicial conceptions of "law." The genesis of this ferment was a tendency in the late nineteenth-century and early twentieth-century judiciary to oppose legislative efforts to alleviate the newly perceived problems of socially and economically disadvantaged persons. The initial strictures of Pound, Arthur Corbin, and other "sociological" jurisprudes were directed at this judicial recalcitrance.[14]

Sociological jurisprudence, as noted, was characteristic of numerous segments of early twentieth-century reformist thought in its "discovery" of new social "problems" and in its confidence in the possibility of their being solved by governmental institutions. Poverty, unemploy-

ment, adverse working conditions, child labor, and industrial injuries
came to be perceived as phenomena for which society bore some
collective responsibility rather than simply as costs of the struggle of
life.[15] None of these phenomena was a new component of twentieth-
century American life, although the presence of each may have been
accentuated or dramatized by the rapid industrialization and urbanization of the late nineteenth century. What was new was the way in
which these phenomena were being perceived.

The perceived failings of the judiciary thus emphasized the need
for better understanding of contemporary social conditions. Sociological jurisprudes, like several other early twentieth-century thinkers,
equated this understanding with an increased sensitivity on the part of
public officials to social problems; a greater emphasis on the "sociology, economics, and politics" of education; [16] the development of a
public consciousness in social and professional elites; the implementation of "scientific" methods in public administration. They defined
their professional goals as many other "progressive" early twentieth-
century professionals defined theirs: alleviating "the backwardness of
law (society) in meeting social ends" and educating the public "on
matters of social reform." [17] Sociological jurisprudence was, in a
phrase, "social engineering." [18]

By the 1920s, when mature statements of sociological jurisprudence
had appeared, its emphasis had centered primarily on efforts to reshape the sensibilities of governmental officials, especially judges, to
be more in tune with the current "body of philosophical, political, and
ethical ideas as to the end of law." [19] The goals of sociological jurisprudes had been expressed in generalities, and their scholarship, although critical of conceptualist methodologies, had given little attention to actual techniques of legal or judicial analysis. At the same time,
however, a group of writings appeared that, while retaining many of
the general perspectives of sociological jurisprudence, focused more
specifically on the areas of legal methodology and pedagogy and
directed substantial critical attention to issues of legal education. With
the appearance of these writings the Realist movement entered its
second and better known stage. Its proponents in that stage, while
attempting to distinguish themselves from sociological jurisprudes,
shared so many of the goals of sociological jurisprudence as to blur
that distinction.

Indeed, when one considers Realism in the context of broad intellectual developments in the early twentieth century, and contrasts those developments with prevailing late nineteenth-century intellectual trends, it is possible to formulate a definition of Realism that incorporates sociological jurisprudence.[20] The Realist movement, in its successive stages, was an extended critique of the conceptualist orientation of late nineteenth-century jurisprudence, with the sociological jurisprudes primarily criticizing the social and political consequences of that orientation, and the self-styled "Realists" [21] primarily criticizing conceptualism's underlying philosophical assumptions.

The difference in emphasis between early and late Realism can be seen in a comparison of Pound's 1908 article, "Mechanical Jurisprudence," [22] with a 1930 essay by Karl Llewellyn of Columbia Law School entitled "A Realistic Jurisprudence—The Next Step." [23] Pound's criticism of the "jurisprudence of conceptions," [24] which he found prevalent in early twentieth-century America was not based on a distrust of legal principles in themselves. He felt, in fact, that "[a] period of legislative activity" could supply "a systematic body of principles as a fresh start for juristic development." [25] Pound's critique of "mechanical jurisprudence" was based on the premise that the existing body of principles had become fixed and sterile, producing "rules . . . that obstruct the way of social progress." [26] In short, Pound was not uncompromisingly anti-universalist. He was not skeptical about the derivation of rules, merely offended by the social implications of certain rules that had been derived. His goal was to have "fresh illustration[s] of the intelligent application of [a] principle to a concrete cause, producing a workable and a just result." [27]

Llewellyn, by contrast, rejected the derivation of principles, whether "sterile" or "fresh," as a central task of lawmaking. The meaningfulness of a rule or principle lay not in the method of its derivation but in whether it was followed in practice. In analyzing "accepted doctrine," for example, Llewellyn proposed that "one lifts an eye canny and skeptical as to whether judicial behavior is in fact what the . . . rule purports (implicitly) to state," that "[o]ne seeks the real practice on the subject, by study of how the cases do in fact eventuate." [28] The focus of study in law schools "should now be consciously shifted to the area of contact, of interaction, between official regulatory behavior and the behavior of those affecting or affected by official regulatory behavior." [29]

At its maturity Realism was to propose a reorientation of legal education nearly comparable in magnitude to that undertaken by the legal scientists after 1870. The three principal innovations marked the reorientation: an expansion of the focus of casebooks, the principal teaching tools of law schools, to include material other than judicial opinions; a greater emphasis on the degree to which decisions by legal institutions, including judges, constituted exercises in social policy-making; and a transformation of the relationship between individual cases and generalized principles in legal analysis.

Realists believed that if Llewellyn was correct in his claim that the significance of legal rules lay in their impact rather than in their derivation or content, the exclusive focus of legal education on cases would have to be abandoned. Most of the "real" rules of law were not reflected in cases but in patterns of behavior: business practices, the activities of criminals, the performance of legislative and administrative officials. Casebooks and the case method needed to be supplemented by empirical studies of the behavior patterns of groups and individuals. The "science of law," one Realist declared, was "the science of the administration of law." [30] In law schools, as in many phases of early twentieth-century American educational life, the techniques of the social sciences were relevant and necessary.

Alongside an expanded definition of "law" and lawmaking went an expanded awareness of the role of the legal system as an instrument of public policy. Early nineteenth-century jurists had been aware of the policy dimensions of law. In the judicial decisions of Lemuel Shaw or the treatises of Joseph Story one can see a conscious interweaving of arguments at the level of technical legal expertise with arguments at the level of "first principles" or "public policy." [31] The late nineteenth-century scientists had elevated arguments from professional "logic" to a stature far surpassing that of arguments on behalf of the "public welfare." An occasional offshoot of conceptualist jurisprudence, in fact, was the explicit disavowal that policy considerations, "morals," or other extraneous phenomena were synonymous with "law." While an elimination of explicit appeals to public policy never occurred even at the zenith of conceptualism's influence, those appeals were not fully congenial with the intellectual assumptions of the scientists. With the advent of Realism arguments based on public policy considerations revived. Their presence in casebook and treatise literature will subsequently be traced.

While a modification of the content of casebooks and an increased emphasis on the policy implications of lawmaking were significant educational innovations, they were overshadowed by the basic revision made by Realism of the relationship between cases and principles in the analysis of common law subjects. The scientists had pioneered the use of individual cases as the paradigmatic units of law study: their casebooks had displaced treatises as the principal vehicle for developing a professional consciousness in law students. The Realists retained this use of cases. They altered, however, the manner in which cases were studied. Since Realists believed that generalized abstractions were suspect, that theory followed from empirical observation, that legal doctrine was constantly changing, and that present-mindedness was imperative, they rejected the scientists' belief that a case could be regarded as representative of a broad legal principle. A case, for Realists, was an autonomous entity whose doctrinal significance might well be confined to its own factual context.

To be sure, argued those influenced by Realism, the opinions that regularly accompanied case decisions contained doctrinal observations that went beyond the confines of the precise controversy individual judges were being asked to consider. But one had to learn to read common law opinions on several levels: first, and most precisely, as an individualized resolution of a discrete controversy; second, as a *potential* general guide to similar controversies; third, as an abstract statement about legal doctrine whose validity was to turn on its future acceptability to other courts deciding other cases. The scientists, they felt, had too easily equated the first level of a case with the third; the Realists sought to train lawyers to distinguish among the levels.

The jurisprudential implications of this revision of the relationship between case and principle were far reaching. The Realists' approach called into question descriptions of common law subjects oriented around broad doctrinal categories. Since the least tangible and least developed aspect of a case was its role as a repository of generalized doctrine, the systematic doctrinal organization of subject matter areas developed by the scientists was highly suspect. The methodological perspective of the Realists required one to ask whether a recent case retained, modified, or abandoned existing doctrine. Doctrine was thus continually in a hypothetical state: once declared, it was always vulnerable to later attack. Some Realists were tempted to see legal doctrine as nothing more than the aggregate of recent individual cases, or, even more skeptically, as the aggregate of the recent opinions of individual judges.[32]

The revisionist character of these Realist educational innovations was not thoroughly grasped by contemporaries, and only the third provoked immediate and heated controversy. In 1938, when Realism had become well established in American legal education, Pound—who had by then disassociated himself from the Realist movement [33]—claimed to have pioneered the movement's interest in "study of the actual social effects of legal institutions," its insistence on a grounding in the social sciences as a precondition of law study, and its examination of the "effects of . . . legal doctrines." [34] There was some truth to Pound's claims: Realism had incorporated many of the insights of sociological jurisprudence. But at the same time the later exponents of Realism had clearly gone further, forcing their predecessors, such as Pound, to ask themselves whether their criticism of late nineteenth-century conceptualism had been partial or total. Was early twentieth-century American jurisprudence prepared to grant the possibility of some enduring principles in social organization, the possibility that legal principles had any permanency? Or was it intending, as Llewellyn said, to see law from a wholly "fresh" perspective?

Dominant phases of American thought, despite their widespread acceptance, seem to create their own special philosophical dilemmas. The central dilemma for the nineteenth-century conceptualists, we have previously seen, focused on the capacity of universal principles to evolve. If universals were static as well as comprehensive, they were truly devices through which order and predictability might be achieved. But if their content changed, which seemed increasingly obvious to late nineteenth-century thinkers, how could they retain their universalistic character? Individual conceptualists tried to resolve this dilemma for themselves, but not without strain.

The principal dilemma of the Realist movement and analogous twentieth-century movements in other disciplines was produced by their apparently relativist thrust. In criticizing an intellectual fetish for universals, in declaring that society was in an endless state of flux, in making contemporary relevance a prime test of the soundness of ideas, and in proclaiming the incomprehensibility or the current irrelevance of traditional moral values the Realists, like their counterparts in history or political science or philosophy, were identifying themselves with moral relativism and with "nominalism"—the denial of the concrete meaningfulness of any sort of intellectual system-building. They thus seemed, to contemporary critics, to be advocating chaos over order, irrationality over rationality, and random data over theory.[35] Few Realists saw themselves as doing any of these things, but the fervor of their protest against conceptualism in any form exposed them to these charges. Thus reformist thinkers of the early twentieth century confronted their special dilemma: how could one erect comprehensible guidelines for social conduct if one denied the "reality" of any generalized abstraction? Was one's guideline merely the observation of current behavior? If so, what standards exsited for distinguishing the humane and inspirational aspects of social living from the inhumane and corrosive?

Individual Realists, under pressure to disassociate themselves from the apparent congeniality of nominalism and moral relativism to the totalitarian regimes of the 1930s, tried to resolve this set of dilemmas.[36] But the vulnerability of Realism to the charges of its critics kept alive in American jurisprudence a point of view that never fully endorsed all the assumptions of the Realists. This point of view retained a partial adherence to conceptulaism, notably in retaining a belief in the viability of doctrinal organization of legal subjects. In tort law the figures whose scholarship most clearly symbolized respectively, the Realist and modified conceptualist perspectives were Leon Green and Frances Bohlen.

The Contributions of Green and Bohlen

For all the diversity and longevity of Leon Green's career, the sources of his development as a torts theorist are not difficult to identify. Green came to law teaching from trial litigation in Texas; he came to torts scholarship from teaching courses whose major focus was civil and criminal procedure; and he came to intellectual maturity at the same time as the Realist movement.[37] He was, by the 1930s, a New Dealer in his politics, a democrat and a humanitarian in his social instincts, and a law professor committed to a belief in the constantly changing nature of the legal system, tirelessly critical of conceptualist abstractions, and convinced of the factual integrity and autonomy of the individual common law case.[38] His experiences in law practice had reinforced his sense that legal doctrines should be workable and practical rather than abstruse and metaphysical. His exposure to subjects that emphasized remedies and procedures had helped develop his sense that the administration and implementation of legal rules was far more significant than their abstract content. And the reformist and iconoclastic strains of his thought found a congenial home in Realism.

In the course of a decade, extending from the mid-1920s to the mid-1930s, Green produced the most original and revisionist torts scholarship of the Realist years. He proposed a major revision in theories about causation in negligence law.[39] He helped redefine the concept of duty in negligence cases.[40] He synthesized and extended emerging insights about the "relational" character of many types of personal injuries.[41] He revived interest in the relationship between judge and jury in tort cases.[42] He suggested that the areas of law that might be illuminated by tort theory were infinitely more numerous than previously thought. And he produced a casebook whose educational goals were avowedly anticonceptualist and whose orientation was markedly presentist and empiricist.[43] By 1948, a year after Green left the deanship of Northwestern Law School to return to teaching at the University of Texas, Charles Gregory, an influential torts scholar in his own right, said that Green's scholarship in Torts had been "sufficiently voluminous to cause wonder, sufficiently authoritative to command deference, sufficiently broad in its scope to excite admiration, and sufficiently original to provoke envy." [44]

If Green was the most influential Realist tort theoretician of the early twentieth century, he was not necessarily the most influential torts scholar in the years of Realism's dominance. Gregory himself wondered "why more of us [in the early 1930s] did not hail Mr. Green as our prophet." [45] A characteristic of Green's career in the Realist years was that he unconsciously revealed the jurisprudential dilemmas of Realism as vividly as he demonstrated the freshness of the Realist movement. Green's reformist assumptions that "government is nothing more than a working adjustment between the activities of men," and that "[e]ach generation demands as its own the privilege of adjusting its own matters," [46] allowed him to detach himself from the tort theories of the scientists. They also led him to adopt approaches to tort law that seemingly sought to replace the entire existing legacy of torts scholarship with his own idiosyncratic perspective.

Green never fully resolved, during the period of Realism's dominance, some basic ambivalences in his thought. He pressed hard his beliefs that "law" was synonymous with "government" and that public policy considerations were therefore decisive in the resolution of any legal issue. But he also seemed to persist in an orthodox characterization of Torts as a "private" law subject with its own unique boundaries. For example, Green sought in his novel casebook, *The Judicial Process in Torts Cases* (1931), to consider tort law "functionally" so as to underscore its implications for public policy. This approach was a major break with the approach of the scientists, and will subsequently be discussed in some detail. But while Green's casebook was intended to correlate with his scholarly writings, those writings reemphasized the importance of certain analytical concepts—notably the notion of the duties of one private party to another—that had been at the core of orthodox scientist tort scholarship.[47]

In addition, Green identified, as no previous torts theorist had, the significance for negligence law of a decision to grant to a jury, rather than to a judge, the power to apply a generalized standard of conduct to a specific case. A determination of "negligent" conduct in a given case, Green argued, could turn on an individual jury's interpretation of what constituted "reasonable" care under the circumstances. Alternatively, the determination could turn on an interpretation of reasonable care by a judge. A judge's decision either to save the interpretation of "reasonableness" for himself (by strict instructions to the jury) or to delegate that interpretive function to the jury was thus, for Green, crucial in the development of negligence law. The more judges took cases away from juries, the more "reasonable conduct" became synonymous with the present and past views of courts on what constituted "reasonableness"; the more they delegated interpretive power to juries, the more "reasonableness" became the aggregate of discrete findings by juries.[48] Other torts scholars, such as Holmes, had seen the importance of judge-jury relations in negligence,[49] but none before Green had shown so powerfully the capacity of generalized tort principles to fragment in their application.

Yet having underscored the significance of the jury in negligence cases, Green seemed ambivalent about its presence. Holmes had identified judge-made tort rules with certainty and predictability and had accordingly attempted to limit jury interpretive powers wherever possible. Green saw that the decision to limit or not to limit a jury was itself an exercise of judicial power and felt that judges should exercise that power. He also felt, however, that judges should exercise their power, in many instances, in favor of jury interpretation. This was because existing rules in Torts were too rigid and outmoded: by delegating interpretation to a jury the judiciary allowed current considerations of equity and common sense to modify anachronistic principles.[50] In an ideal world, it appeared, Green would have preferred judge-made rules, since he had confidence in the wisdom of properly trained government servants.[51] Behind Green's model of judge-jury relations, then, lurked fears about unbridled, uneducated lawmaking by juries comparable to those of Holmes. Yet Green's model appeared to invite those fears to materialize, or, alternatively, simply to allow judges the power to keep tort cases for themselves, outmoded rules or not.

The ambivalences of Green's approach to tort law personified the ambivalences of reformist American thought in the early twentieth century. Green and his reformist contemporaries sought to reconcile a perception that society was inevitably in flux with an ideal of a harmonious government "engineered" by elites. They tried to structure intellectual thought around the proposition that ideas had no structure, since they invariably reflected current social "realities." They attempted to insure that conventional academic theories and moral norms confront contemporary facts and values while also acknowledging some place in civilized society for enduring moral standards. They reconciled these ambivalences for themselves. But they did not always convince others.

Francis Bohlen, a law professor at the University of Pennsylvania and at Harvard, was the leading Torts theorist of the Realist years who remained unconvinced that a Realist theoretical perspective should fully supplant the perspective developed by nineteenth-century conceptualists. Bohlen's approach to tort law, however, was not wholly conceptualist. While a commentator later claimed, with some justice, that Bohlen attempted to "pigeonhole most of [tort law] in compact little categories," [52] Bohlen's conceptualism never approximated the abstract purity of that of scientists such as Joseph Beale, who wrote an occasional essay on Torts in the 1920s.[53] Bohlen, in fact, believed in the primacy of social change, in the necessity of tort doctrines to accommodate themselves to changed conditions, in the futility of static classification systems, and in the value, in an increasingly interdependent universe, of elite policymakers serving as an active force on behalf of progress.[54] For a variety of reasons, however, Bohlen never endorsed Realism nor accommodated his thinking about Torts to that of Green.

Bohlen's disinclination to accept Realism fully stemmed in part from the fortuities of age and personality. Bohlen was born in 1868, twenty years before Green and most of the other principal exponents of Realism, and at least five years before anyone who has been linked to the Realist movement.[55] He began teaching in 1901, before sociological jurisprudence had surfaced. He was recognized as a distinguished torts scholar before the First World War, when Green had not yet begun to teach Torts. He was chosen Reporter of the Restatement of Torts for the American Law Institute in 1922, before Green had entered the field of torts scholarship. Bohlen did not come to maturity along with Realism; he developed his thinking during its embryonic stage. He was in the sixth decade of his life, and the third decade of his career in the legal profession, when Realism came to maturity. Bohlen's approach to mature Realism and its proponents' approach to him took on the dimensions of a dialogue between an elder statesman and young Turks.

The distance between Bohlen and the later Realists was accentuated by certain of Bohlen's personal qualities. Bohlen neither gladly suffered fools nor easily accepted criticism. "He was," a colleague noted, "often impatient and unreasonable. [I]t was typically Bohlen to flare up suddenly and without cause." [56] On his death in 1943 friends unburdened themselves of Bohlenesque vignettes: stalking out of class, subjecting students to "personal and sharp" criticisms, and resigning his position as Reporter for the American Law Institute's Restatement of Torts after criticism of his proposed texts by colleagues.[57] William Draper Lewis, who had been associated with Bohlen at the University of Pennsylvania and at the American Law Institute, spoke of Bohlen's "high strung nerves," his "keen and reckless wit," his "distinct antipathy to intellectual opposition," and his "instinctive determination to see and to express ideas and views without evasion or camouflage." [58]

Some of Bohlen's contemporaries associated his "picturesque personality" with his social background.[59] Bohlen's parents were wealthy and socially prominent descendants of Prussian junkers; his primary education was in local day schools and a New England boarding school; he was, into his forties, an international cricketeer; his "appearance and carriage" struck Lewis as "more nearly that of the high-born European than any American I have known." [60] Colleagues suggested that Bohlen was not snobbish in his relations with students [61] and that Bohlen's approach to tort law, which sought to "bring about equitable adjustments of the financial burdens caused by injuries to persons and property," was "anathema to . . . some of his later cronies at the exclusive and conservative clubs to which he belonged." [62] But in a period in which the sociological character of elite legal education was in transition and class-consciousness was rife, Bohlen's upper-class affect may have had a bearing on some of his professional relationships. [63]

Bohlen's picturesqueness, however, was less jurisprudentially significant than his association with the American Law Institute. That organization had been founded in 1923 by prominent lawyers, judges, and law professors for the purposes of restoring clarity and predictability to American law through the production of a series of massive, annotated "Restatements" of specific legal subjects. [64] The Realists came to regard the Institute, and its various Restatements, as symbols of nineteenth-century conceptualism. In 1948 the Realist Thurman Arnold, reflecting on the Institute's image in the 1920s and 30s, said that the Institute had been seen as preserv[ing] the attitudes and faiths of the nineteenth century" by "confin[ing] itself to the issues of the past as they had been solved by the common law." The Institute's efforts "to restore order and topical unity" to law had failed for Arnold because its Restatements had "nothing to do with the central legal problems of our time." Faith in "nineteenth-century legal conceptions" had made the Restatements, Arnold believed, "further and further [removed] from reality." [65]

Insofar as Arnold's critique had political overtones, identifying the Institute with established nineteenth-century propertied orthodoxy, it was not entirely fair. The Institute's staff contained a spectrum of political views, including persons such as Judge Benjamin Cardozo, Judge Learned Hand, Joseph Beale, and Samuel Williston. But insofar as Arnold's view of the Institute in its early years associated it with a conceptualist perspective, it was accurate. The founders of the Institute believed that "order and logical unity" in legal subjects could be achieved through "agreement among the best minds as to what were the best principles." [66] This assumption was classically conceptualist, and if one believed, as many Realists did, that "law was not and could not be a consensus of the opinion of the best legal thinkers assembled in convention," [67] an issue was fully joined. Those associated with the Institute maintained that abstract legal principles could be derived and articulated by scholars and judges, and that once derived, could be intelligible, if not necessarily fixed, guides to conduct. Realist critics simply denied that set of affirmations. In tort law, Bohlen's impassioned efforts to "restate" doctrines were subject to dismissal by Realists on the grounds of being simply irrelevant. For his part, Bohlen could charge his critics with jurisprudential nihilism, arguing that their ideas were based on a chaos of purported "realities" whose meaning remained unintelligible.

The increasing estrangement of Bohlen and Green in the 1930s personified the debates in that decade between modified conceptualists and Realists. The estrangement was all the more revealing because of the apparent similarity of Bohlen's and Green's starting assumptions. Bohlen agreed with Green that judges, lawyers, and law teachers should "look rather to what the law does than what the courts say; [68] he shared with Green a sense that "much of the legal machinery . . . is archaic, [having been] designed to meet social needs far . . . different from those of the present day"; [69] and his pronouncement in 1926 that there was "no field of law in which rigidity and finality is less probable and less desirable" than the field of Torts [70] could have been written by Green himself. Moreover, Green, for all his professed distaste for conceptualism, was an inveterate classifier, regularly exhibiting a penchant for analytical simplification that Bohlen occasionally applauded. [71]

Nonetheless Bohlen and Green exchanged vigorous and acerbic attacks on each other's scholarship throughout the late twenties and thirties. Green's *Rationale of Proximate Cause* and *Judge and Jury* criticized Bohlen's thinking on causation and his approach to misrepresensentation cases. [72] In response Bohlen cataloged a list of the "grave faults" of *Judge and Jury* and suggested that the book was "dangerous if used by the overimpressionable." [73] Green repeated his quarrels with Bohlen over the proper approach to the area of misrepresentation, and Bohlen forcefully defended his position. [74] A friend and coauthor of Bohlen's delivered a measured but thoroughgoing attack on Green's Torts casebook. [75] Finally in 1934 the Restatement of Torts appeared in print, with Bohlen its principal draftsman. Green responded by subjecting the Restatement to a long and almost entirely critical review. [76] He found fault with the Restatement's classification scheme, its literary style, the clarity and precision of its analysis, and, most pointedly, its authoritativeness. [77] In Green's view the Restatement's treatments of negligence and causation, in particular, were "inaccurate and misleading." [78] Green's general reaction to the Restatement was that "the lawyers and judges who have to do with tort cases . . . will find very little in the Restatement in [a] form that they can use . . . and much that is wholly incomprehensible." [79]

One removed from the passion of the Green-Bohlen interchanges may fairly wonder at their intensity. Much of the splenetic character of the debates was personal: the two men perceived themselves as polar opposites, socially and philosophically, and were prideful, stubborn, and combative personalities. But behind the human dimensions of the Green-Bohlen disputes lay the apparent irreconcilability of two strands of the Realist movement. The more recent and more polemical strand had moved by the 1930s beyond the sociological jurisprudes' original concern for "social justice" in an individual case to a conviction that the processes by which cases were "really" decided be exposed and studied. Instead of "good rules" rather than "bad rules," the mature Realists wanted the mythical nature of all rules revealed. Law for them was a set of governmental judgments about the claims of "interests": the law that was "made" in a given case was a function of the "interests" at stake therein. The legal rules affecting water companies were different from those affecting railroads or coal miners. It was fruitless to generalize beyond the immediacy of the case and the clash of interests that it posed.

Despite the interest of Bohlen and his fellow draftsmen of the Restatements in furthering social justice through law, and despite Bohlen's personal attraction to "interest-analysis," Bohlen and company could not tolerate the apparent abandonment of traditional legal concepts that mature Realism proposed. If the meaning of "negligence" in one case was different from its meaning in another, depending on the context, then, Bohlen and his colleagues felt, order and predictability were undermined and chaos and uncertainty would reign. Bohlen himself simply did not believe that doctrine was meaningless, or that "functional" classifications were the only "reality," or that facts always triumphed over rules. He sensed a recurrent quality in legal disputes; he thought that certainty and predictability were identifiable and legitimate values; he believed that in the main common law subjects could be "restated." He saw the Restatement of Torts not as a reactionary defense of nineteenth-century conceptualism but as a progressive reshaping and clarifying of the staple doctrines of tort law.

The "staple" doctrines of tort law for Bohlen, however, were those that had been created and refined by the scientists. Those doctrines were considerably modified by Green's approach to tort issues. Green reduced the notion of a generalized duty of care—the scientists' "negative duty of very great generality"—to a set of particularized duties owed to individual litigants in given cases. He conceived of proximate causation questions, which the scientists had described in metaphysical terms, as factual inquiries for juries. He described the "reasonable" or "standard" man formula in negligence as merely an articulation of the common sense of jurors. He subsumed doctrinal defenses, such as last clear chance and assumption of risk, in the question of whether a particular defendant owed a duty to a particular plaintiff. He resurrected the importance of damages, an element that did not easily lend itself to doctrinal analysis. And he insisted that political, economic, moral, philosophical, and "administrative" factors were as important in the decision of cases as purely "legal" ones.[80] His perspective, then, was profoundly subversive of the doctrinal mode of analysis on which Bohlen and the Institute had built their Restatements. If a significant thrust of scientism had been the development and refinement of doctrinal analysis, a thrust of Green's version of Realism was to develop an alternative antidoctrinal perspective. With Green's appeaance Torts scholarship had seemingly come full cycle: the discrete "tort" actions of prescientist eras were being resurrected by Green in the guise of a "functional" approach to the subject that stressed its essential fluidity and diversity. A field of Torts had been created, but its lack of cohesiveness had seemingly returned.

The Impact of Realism: Casebook Literature

The Green-Bohlen debates demonstrated that, at least by the 1930s, the jurisprudential perspectives of the mature Realists had not fully supplanted those of nineteenth-century conceptualism. But Bohlen's conceptualism, we have seen, did not retain the enthusiasm for generalized abstractions that had marked mature legal science; nor did Bohlen deny that the field of Torts was in some respects a fluid and amorphous entity; nor was he hostile to widening the range of tort liability to relieve emerging twentieth-century social problems. A self-styled "conservative," [81] Bohlen nonetheless saw himself as an innovator in the field of Torts. And to an important extent he was: his articles and casebooks abandoned the premise that tort law could be a self-contained unit, moving to the measure of its own logical principles. In so doing Bohlen prepared the way for those Realists who sought to embrace within the field of Torts, and within all fields of law, considerations of public policy.

The eventual triumph of a conception of tort law as a conscious instrument of public policy can be seen in the evolution of Torts casebooks in the early twentieth century. The scientists' casebooks, as previously noted, were organized around generalized staple doctrines and principles, such as negligence, contributory negligence, assumption of risk, and causation. Wigmore's casebook (1911) represented the culmination of scientific conceptualism in its relentlessly hierarchical and structured approach. But Wigmore's treatment also anticipated later developments, notably in his identification of tort principles as "general rights" common to all aspects of law. Recalling his early contacts with Wigmore's casebook, Green maintained that Wigmore had "first laid out the boundaries of the vast domain of tort law," since he "thought of torts as general law that ramifies throughout all law." [82] Casebook writers of the twenties and thirties were to build on Wigmore's insight, gradually replacing his notion of "general law" with their notions of public policy. At the same time they were to fight, through methods of casebook organization, the principal jurisprudential battles of the Realist years.

By the 1920s the principal Torts casebooks, including Pound's edition of Ames (1917), Beale's edition of the same (1929), and the 1915 edition of Bohlen's *Cases on Torts,* had all developed a regularized doctrinal form of organization. The subject of Torts was divided into three major parts: intentional harms, negligent harms, and what Bohlen was later to call "unintended and nonnegligent" harms (analogous to the modern area of strict liability). These three parts were usually discussed in sequence, and the orthodox tort concepts of the scientists were introduced in the process. The concept of a privilege was introduced in connection with intentional torts, and the concepts of causation, duty, contributory negligence, assumption of risk, last clear chance, and vicarious liability were introduced in connection with negligence. "Unintended and nonnegligent" harms were then considered, but not given extended treatment. A grab-bag collection of topics—such as misrepresentation, defamation, disparagement, unfair competition, infliction of emotional distress, invasion of privacy, and abuse of process—completed the coverage. The last set of topics involved "civil wrongs not arising out of contract" but were not easily subordinated to the tripartite organizational scheme.

The impression created by these casebooks was that Torts was an area of intelligible principles, capable of being classified and analyzed. Where possible, cases were treated as manifestations of generalized propositions, often explicitly in the editors' footnotes on subject matter headings. But since the casebook writers believed that cases were not only sources of principles but vehicles for developing techniques of analytical reasoning, they regularly grouped together cases with seemingly similar fact situations that reached different results. The original aim of this grouping, for the nineteenth-century scientists, had been to teach students to derive principles by reconciling seemingly opposed viewpoints. But Bohlen, in his 1915 edition, occasionally juxtaposed divergent results to give examples of the common law's capability for growth and change. The implicit message of Bohlen's approach was that principles were continually being considered in new factual contexts.

The casebook writers of the twenties did not, however, regard principles, rules, and doctrines as meaningless. To advocates of doctrinal organization the maddening feature of Green's *The Judicial Process in Tort Cases* (1931) was that he denied the legitimacy of a doctrinal approach. Green's organization, as noted, abandoned the tripartite scheme and arranged concepts "functionally" by reference to the "interests" affected. Green seemed to be saying (to many reviewers) that the participants in a case, the atmosphere it created, and the interests at stake were what determined its outcome, quite independent of rules or principles.[83]

A sense of the differences between Bohlen's perspective in the 1920s and that of the scientific conceptualists, on the one hand, and Green, on the other, emerges from a comparison of casebook treatments of the doctrines of assumptions of risk and last clear chance. The organization of Bohlen's 1925 edition of his casebook represented an intermediate stage between the scientists' tripartite division of tort law and the Realists' ultimate conclusion that tort liability, regardless of the type of "tortious" activity involved, was arrived at through an exercise in interest-balancing. Bohlen's 1925 edition had two major parts, one covering "direct and intentional invasions of interests of personality and property," the other covering "the development of tort liability by the action of trespass on the case."[84] The second part treated both negligent and act-at-peril torts, the latter receiving only sixty pages of coverage in a book of over 1100 pages. Assumption of risk and last clear chance also were treated in the second part of the casebook, under the topic of contributory fault.

Bohlen's treatment of both assumption of risk and last clear chance was doctrinal, as that of the scientists had been. He grouped cases in sections designated "voluntary assumption of risk" and "last clear chance." He added cases in footnotes that were designed to embody doctrinal propositions. He strung citations together that supported the propositions embodied in his selected cases, and he also included citations to cases not agreeing with given propositions. The effect was to make the treatment of assumption of risk and last clear chance in his casebook correspond neatly with a treatise classifying the "rules" of those two doctrinal areas. In subsequent editions of Bohlen's casebook, in fact, regular references were made to Fowler Harper's 1933 treatise on Torts and to the forthcoming Restatement of Torts, which Bohlen was preparing.[85]

Bohlen's approach was not, however, precisely like that of the scientists. By his 1933 edition, for example, Bohlen had adopted an organizational framework that identified tort law exclusively with what he called "invasions of interests." [86] Assumption of risk and last clear chance, in the 1933 edition, were treated under the topic "negligent invasions of interests in personality and property." Seven types of "interests" were identified in Bohlen's table of contents, and various doctrines were distributed among the respective interests. The impression created by such a treatment was that one could read tort cases in a double sense: as manifestations of doctrinal propositions or as examples of an "interest" (in "reputation," in "freedom from fraud and deceit," in "freedom from unjustifiable liitgation," and so on) being "invaded." The conceptual purity of "scientific" Torts was undermined by this latter reading, since the primacy of various social interests rose and fell with the passage of time, and determinations as to whether a given "invasion" gave rise to tort liability could be seen as exercises in "interest-balancing" on a case-by-case basis.

Thus Bohlen's perspective, while retaining the scientists' interest in classifying tort law on a doctrinal basis, did not exclusively endorse the scientists' emphasis on using cases principally as a means of extracting doctrinal propositions. A student exposed to the later editions of Bohlen's casebook could hardly fail to see that tort law might just as well be viewed as a clash between competing social interests.

Even this dimension of Bohlen's perspective, however, diverged from Green's approach. Green began by noting that his emphasis was "not [on] doctrinal integrity," but on the "processes which the courts employ" in deciding tort cases. Green's working "hypothesis" in his 1931 casebook was that "persons have interests which are subjected to harms against which the judicial process gives protection." [87] While this hypothesis was not dramatically different from one of the levels of Bohlen's presentation, the manner in which Green chose to present it entirely subordinated doctrinal analysis to "functional" considerations.

A student using Green's casebook, for example, would not have found "assumption of risk" or "last clear chance" in the table of contents, nor as separate categories in the index. Nor would the student have found "negligence" or "contributory negligence" in the table of contents. Upon searching for those latter two terms in the index, the student would have been referred to "automobile traffic"; "counties, towns, cities, boards"; "manufacturers and dealers"; "passenger transportation"; and other "functional" categories. Moreover, even if the student discovered "assumption of risk" or "last clear chance" under one of those categories, he would be referred to a case where the doctrine, although employed by the court, was often neither identified by the court nor by the casebook editor.

Nothing about Green's casebook, in short, encouraged students or teachers to think of tort law as a collection of doctrines. On the contrary, the entire organization and presentation of the casebook encouraged students and teachers to emphasize the interests at stake in a discrete litigation. Green's notes, which were relatively sparse in comparison to Bohlen's, focused on whether the defendant in a case was a power company or a railroad or a landowner or a surgeon; or on whether the plaintiff was a tenant or a passenger or a woman; or on whether the relationship between the parties was a commercial one or a social one or a professional one; or on whether the transaction spawning the litigation involved a sale of personal services or a sale of timber. The unmistakable inference from Green's treatment was that a doctrinal organization of tort law failed to grasp its essential features.

Between the early 1930s and the opening of the Second World War, mature Realism emerged and scientific conceptualism declined in influence in elite American law schools.[88] But the prototypically Realist Torts casebook, Green's, was slow to gain acceptance. By the late

1930s and 1940s, however, signs of change had appeared. In the preface to the fourth edition of Bohlen's casebook (1941), Fowler
Harper, who had assisted and then succeeded Bohlen as editor, regularly cited Green, even though he retained Bohlen's organization.[89]
The second edition of Green's casebook (1939), provoked milder
reviews than the first. An increasing number of reviewers, while not
necessarily applauding Green's organization, conceded that they were
enamored of his "functional" perspective. One reviewer applauded
Green for suggesting that inquiries as to "whether or not the given
facts . . . can be found to fall within or without some one or another of the familiarly available legal precepts" reversed proper logic:
facts should lead to principles, not the reverse.[90]

Under pressure from Realism the process of "scientific" reconciliation of inapposite cases had been subtly altered. Rather than searching for a reconciling principle that, once articulated, was regarded as a
guidepost for future cases, scholars began to suspend the application of
a principle to a new fact situation until they were convinced that it
produced a sound result. This subtle shift suggested that even comprehensive general principles might become useless if they had been
derived in factual contexts that could no longer be duplicated. The
degree to which legal doctrines bore an inescapably factual component became more apparent.

In 1942 two new Torts casebooks appeared, and both reflected this
new sense of the significance of a factual context in the derivation of
tort doctrines. The casebooks were seemingly distant from one another
in their methodology, yet they shared certain common intellectual assumptions. Edward Thurston's and Warren Seavey's *Cases on Torts*
retained Bohlen's tripartite classification scheme, and their table of
contents suggested that their approach was doctrinal. But the casebook contained virtually nothing but cases, most of which were reduced to their bare essentials, and many of which, when grouped
together, reached contradictory results. Almost no guidelines were
provided for the student. The clear impact of Thurston's and Seavey's
organization was to force students to consider doctrines in a factual
context. The editors believed that "the subject of Torts can best be
taught by putting before the student . . . a summary statement of the
facts, with the court's decision thereon, of a very large number of . . .
cases." [91] A reviewer noted that Thurston's and Seavey's approach left
"the student to seek out his own interpretation of the legal materials

from which he must select controlling precedent . . . for application to novel situations." [92] The implicit message of Thurston and Seavey was that the efficacy of doctrines was dependent on their ability to be applied to new factual contexts.

If Thurston and Seavey had implicitly incorporated one of the principal tenets of Realism—that legal doctrine was in large measure dependent on its factual setting—Harry Shulman and Fleming James, in their 1942 casebook, were more explicitly Realist. Their approach, however, was reminiscent of an earlier focus of the Realist movement. Shulman and James spoke, in their preface, of the "effects" of law "upon the social good"; of the concern of law "not so much with rule or doctrine as with problems in human relations"; of "the potentialities of tort liability as a means of distributing losses"; and of "social engineering." [93] There were echoes, as well, of Green: Shulman and James expressed an interest in "the way in which the judicial process actually operates," and organized three chapters "functionally," devoting one to "occupiers and owners of land," one to "motor vehicles," and one to "suppliers of goods and remote contractors." [94] But the principal distinguishing characteristic of Shulman's and James's approach was their integration of materials from legal scholarship and the social sciences with conventional law cases. Their casebook was entitled *Cases and Materials on Torts:* they included excerpts from law review articles, the Restatement of Torts, law treatises, medical journals and treatises, studies of law administration, statistical reports on motor vehicle injuries, and articles on insurance. This emphasis was stressed by reviewers, one of whom claimed that "the editors [were] not concerned primarily with the training of the student as a practitioner of law," but rather with "inculcat[ing] in the student the point of view of the social scientist trained in law." [95]

Integration of law with the social sciences, the development in judges of a "sociological" perspective, an interest in the manner in which law was administered, a "functional" approach to cases, and a general interest in the "policy" implications of legal doctrines were each concerns of the Realists, and each was manifested in Shulman and James. But for all the novelty of Shulman's and James's approach (theirs was perhaps the first of what has now become a long line of "Cases and Materials" volumes), their analytical framework was closer to that of Bohlen than to that of Green. Shulman and James retained, for example, the intentional tort-negligence-strict liability demarcations of the 1920s casebooks. In addition, while Shulman and James created an impression that the significance of doctrines, principles, and rules was to be gauged by their current social utility, they did not suggest that traditional tort doctrines were meaningless or not worth mastering by students.

The relationship between Shulman's and James's approach and Green's version of Realism was revealed in a 1940 review James wrote of Green's *The Judicial Process in Torts Cases*. James claimed that Green's approach had gone "too far in abandoning the conventional framework and in relying upon types of fact situations for its categories." James believed that "legal concepts, principles and rules play [an] . . . important part in determining the operation of the judicial process." Moreover, James felt that Green's effort to derive new "functional" categories for tort law had simply not succeeded as well as the conventional clasisfication.[96] At the same time James (and Shulman, as indicated in an earlier review of Green) [97] had been stimulated, through their exposure to Green's work, to explore the policy implications of tort law. As Shulman put it, "[i]ndividual cases should be studied not merely as particular private disputes, but as instances of larger social problems." An interest in policy issues led Shulman to the inclusion in casebooks of nonlegal materials. He argued that "materials for study should present . . . not only decided cases but also, if possible, the factors which create the social problems." [98] Thus Shulman's and James's "cases and materials" approach may have emerged from exposure to Green's scholarship and their reflections on it.

The primary difficulty scholars had in adopting a thoroughgoing "functional" perspective in Torts was the apparent failure of "functionalism" to create an analytical framework that gave students and teachers a sense of solidity. Fowler Harper advanced this argument in a 1939 review of the second edition of Green's casebook. "The gist of the argument against the funcitonal arrangement in Torts," Harper wrote, "is that a mastery of doctrine must logically precede a knowledge of its use. How can a student understand the variations and shadings in the application of a legal principle to varying fact-patterns unless he has first commanded a thorough mastery of the principle in question?" [99] A Realist-inspired rejoinder to Harper, of course, would be that legal principles could not be understood apart from their application to varying fact situations. But that rejoinder left an empty feeling that there was nothing concrete in the subject of Torts except countless fact situations. One simply took the grade-crossing accident cases in a batch, the child trespasser case in another batch, and so on. While this may have been "realistic" to Green, it was profoundly unsettling to his contemporaries, since it seemingly stripped Torts of its common modes of analysis and even its conventional vocabulary.

Tort scholars inspired by Realism never produced a wholesale transformation of treatise and casebook literature, as had those inspired by the late nineteenth-century ideal of legal science. Nonetheless the organization of Torts casebooks was significantly altered between the 1920s and the 1940s. Each of the major alterations—a greater emphasis on the policy dimensions of tort law, a growing inclusion of social science literature in casebooks, and a revised treatment of the relationship between legal principles and their factual context—reflected the jurisprudential insights of Realism. But the "triumph" of Realist perspectives was incomplete. The most striking insight of mature Realists, that rules and norms and even values were meaningless as abstract general guides to social conduct, seemed to lead to anarchistic methodologies or nihilistic philosophies. A striving for order and coherence in law, so marked in the thought of the scientists, did not entirely vanish with Realism's unveiling of the unsubstantiated assumptions of late nineteenth-century scientific jurisprudence.

The Impact of Realism: Doctrine

Just as each dominant phase of American thought can be seen to contain its own set of influential insights and to create its own set of philosophical dilemmas, each phase can be shown to give certain professional issues concentrated attention. Realism, the legal professional's variant of early twentieth-century reformist thought, exhibited a special concern with particular issues in legal education and jurisprudence, several of which have been previously discussed. At the same time the Realist movement had a professional impact at another level, that of substantive legal doctrine. The impact of Realism on tort doctrine can be demonstrated through a consideration of doctrinal areas that tort scholars, in the years of Realism's influence, identified as especially novel or significant. Three such areas are addressed here: causation, infliction of emotional distress, and the theory of "strict" liability for personal injuries.

No area of late nineteenth-century tort law had been more confusingly and inadequately treated, Realists felt, than that of causation. Causation analysis, which was principally employed in negligence law, was dominated by doctrinal formulas, each of which sought to provide workable definitions of "proximate" or "legal" cause, and each of which seemed to be used in highly ambiguous and misleading ways. After laboring in frustration with received tests and formulas, jurists influenced by Realism eventually abandoned much of orthodox causation analysis. In its place they offered an analysis that made a sharp separation, in negligence, between questions pertaining to causation and questions pertaining to the violation of legal duties. The refinements made possible by this separation were the isolation of causation from other issues in negligence law, the conversion of causation to a "factual" rather than a "legal" issue, the expansion of duty analysis, which explicitly dealt with interest-balancing, and the consequent reduction of the significance of causation issues in Torts. The principal scholarly contributor to this altered treatment of causation was Leon Green, whose voice on this occasion was heard and heeded.

The origins of scholarly interest in causation were closely tied to the emergence of negligence as a major principle of tort law. Early treatises and casebooks devoted no space to causation issues: Jeremiah Smith's 1893 casebook represented the first significant treatment.[100] The significance of causation for negligence law can be linked to the character of negligence itself. In other areas of tort law civil liability followed from the presence of a document binding the parties in advance (a contract or a lease) or from strong public policy concerns (as in defamation, intentional torts, or torts following from the nonnegligent use of "dangerous" substances). Where, as in those areas, tort liability had been apportioned in advance or was linked to moral blame, causation issues were easily resolved once an injured party could trace his injury to an accountable defendant. Negligence law governed a different set of civil wrongs, those inflicted on strangers by strangers who had been "careless." The "careless" parties had often been performing some socially useful function, and since they could not be shown to have "intentionally" injured anyone, their liability, from perspectives of utility or fairness, was not as clear-cut as the liability of intentional tortfeasors or tortfeasors whose civil responsibilities had been apportioned in a written document.

Thus courts came to conclude that some injuries traceable to the negligent conduct of a party were nonetheless too marginal to give rise to liability, lest the negligent party be unfairly burdened with extensive financial outlays. The language of causation provided helpful ways of describing injuries that as a matter of policy were deemed too marginal or "remote." "Cause," then, came to be used in two senses: a factual link between a defendant's act or omission and a plaintiff's injury, and an implicit policy judgment that the defendant was legally responsible for the injury. The term "proximate" or "legal" was regularly attached to "cause" as employed in the second sense, although the policy judgment was not made explicit.

The emergence of causation doctrines in tort law paralleled the coming to maturity of legal science. An interest of orthodox Torts scholarship in the early twentieth century, consistent with the jurisprudential goals of legal science, was in developing orderly and workable formulas for causation. Thus Smith, in a three-part article in the *Harvard Law Review* in 1911 and 1912, exhaustively reviewed the various "tests" for causation in order to determine which possessed the clearest set of practical guidelines for courts, and, in the event that none adequately performed that function, to derive a test of his own.[101] Having found the tests of "proximate cause," "last (or nearest) wrongdoer," and "probable (and natural) consequence" each deficient, Smith substituted his own formula: causation sufficient for liability was to be found if a "defendant's tort [was] a substantial factor in producing the damage complained of."[102] Smith conceived his task as the conventional one of the scientist: "bring[ing] out the most important elementary principles underlying . . . decisions."[103]

Smith's "substantial factor" test, although adopted by Bohlen in his drafting of the *Restatement of Torts,* was not sufficiently "definite" for Joseph Beale. In an article in 1920 Beale sought to provide a "definite principle of law" to govern causation, so that "the court [could] determine the general limits of proximity, and not leave it at large to the jury."[104] The principle that Beale ultimately derived, while "scientific" in its imagery, was something of a caricature of conceptualist jurisprudence. "[P]roximity of result" was achieved, Beale maintained, when a defendant had violated a duty, thereby setting a force in motion, and the force thus created had "a) remained active itself or created another *force* which remained active until it directly caused the result; or b) . . . created a new active *risk* of being acted upon by the active force that caused the result."[105] One might have been able to diagram Beale's formula, but as a guide to courts it was close to gibberish. Green, when he came to consider causation in the late 1920s, argued that "in attempting to apply . . . quantitative determinants to a problem calling for good judgment," Beale had "misconceived the nature of the problem."[106]

Beale was not the only scholar who, in Green's view, had approached causation from a faulty perspective. Green's *Rationale of Proximate Cause,* which appeared in 1927, represented a sharp break from the doctrinal approach to causation of earlier scholars. Green's perspective was not entirely unprecedented. As early as 1909 John Bingham, a law professor at Stanford, had suggested that existing generalizations about causation were largely meaningless,[107] and in 1924 Henry Edgerton, a law professor at Cornell who was to become a distinguished judge, had responded to Beale by calling for a theory of causation that produced results "not merely fair as between the parties, but socially advantageous."[108]

Green built on those contributions, but his theory was typically idiosyncratic. He began by asserting that the "bearings" of the courts in the field of causation had been "incorrect." He then suggested an approach to causation that would "clean up" the area by considerably narrowing the range of issues to which the term "cause" was applicable.[109] In brief, Green's theory removed from the area of causation all questions that did not pertain to a determination of the "causal relation" between the defendant's conduct and the plaintiff's injury. He suggested that such questions—previously termed "proximate" or "legal" cause issues—were in fact related to a determination of the scope of a given defendant's duty to a given plaintiff.

Green's theory was more than a new treatment of causation. It signified an abandonment of the idea, originated by Holmes and later popularized by the scientists, of a "negative duty of very great generality" owed by all the world to all the world. For Green duties could only be owed to particular persons. The "duty" issue in every negligence case was whether the defendant owed a duty to protect the plaintiff from the injury that the plaintiff had suffered. That issue was to be resolved by the judge; if answered negatively, no liability could ensue. The judge's resolution of the "duty" issue was, invariably, a question of policy, involving "the weighing of interests." [110] Many judges used the language of causation to justify their resolution of the "duty" issue, but Green believed that the issue had nothing to do with causation; rather, it focused on the relationship between the plaintiff and defendant and the social utility of protecting the plaintiff from the hazard to which he had been exposed.

If, under Green's analysis, a judge decided that a given defendant owed a given plaintiff a duty to protect the plaintiff from the hazard to which the plaintiff had been exposed, the judge asked the jury to determine whether the defendant had violated his duty. It was at this stage of negligence analysis that familiar concepts such as "reasonable man" and "foreseeability" could be invoked. But those concepts, as well, had nothing to do with causation, according to Green. Asking whether a reasonable man in the position of the defendant should have foreseen that his act or omission would expose a given plaintiff to a foreseeable risk was not the same as asking whether the defendant's act or omission or carelessness had caused the plaintiff's injury.

Green believed that causation should be reduced to a factual inquiry about the connection between the defendant's act and the plaintiff's injury. The inquiry, which should usually be made by the jury, was necessary, but not sufficient, for a finding of negligence. All juries were required to do with respect to causation was to determine whether a causal connection existed between the defendant's act or omission and the plaintiff's injury. If such a connection existed, issues pertaining to the defendant's duty to the plaintiff were raised. If no factual connection existed, the defendant could never be found negligent. Thus if a judge concluded that no reasonable person could have found a causal link between the defendant's act and the plaintiff's injury, he could dismiss the plaintiff's suit; otherwise the issue of causal relation was determined by the jury.

Green's "chief point of pride" in his approach was "the simplicity of [its] process." [111] His effort was to avoid the complexities caused by orthodox treatment of causation, which confused factual with "legal" or "proximate" cause. Under Green's approach causation became a relatively simple problem in negligence. The complexities of negligence analysis were shifted to another area, the relationship between the defendant and the plaintiff.

Negligence for Green became a term of relation. Persons did not owe duties in the abstract, but rather to particular injured persons with respect to specific risks. Whether a given defendant owed a duty not to expose a given plaintiff to a particular risk and whether he had violated that duty were not simple questions. Their analysis involved, among other things, an assessment of the risk-bearing capacities of the respective parties and the degree to which society had an interest in placing the risk on the one or the other. This assessment, which the judge was to make under Green's analysis, required an implicit judgment about the worth of the defendant's activity that had exposed the plaintiff to a risk of injury, and the value of protecting the plaintiff from that exposure. The judgment was not made any easier for Green by the use of doctrinal formulas. In particular, it was not alleviated by the use of a formula—proximate causation—that in Green's view only obfuscated the judgmental process.

Green's *Rationale of Proximate Cause* was widely reviewed. The reviewers' enthusiasm for Green's approach varied considerably (one called *Rationale of Proximate Cause* "one of the great law books of this generation"; [112] another said that "[u]pon . . . the greater part of the field of legal cause as commonly understood Mr. Green's formula . . . throw[s] no light whatever" [113]), but most commentators agreed that Green had demonstrated that judging involved "policy, or the balancing of interests . . . and that solution by formula [was] impossible." [114] The widespread scholarly convergence on this point of view was significant. If interest-balancing and policymaking had replaced rule making as jurisprudential goals, orthodox doctrinal analysis was suspect, because it stressed the extraction and promulgation of definitive rules, and the definitiveness of those rules was now regarded as fictional. Moreover, if the social policies of tort law were more important than its doctrines, searching for comprehensive doctrines of causation or negligence was a misguided effort. The way was opened for a reorientation of negligence law around concepts such as interest-balancing and risk distribution, concepts that stressed the relationships between litigating parties and the implications of those relationships for the rest of society.

The new perspective on negligence issues suggested by Green and seemingly approved by others received a classic test in the late 1920s. That test was the case of *Palsgraf v. Long Island Railroad*,[115] perhaps the most famous case in the history of tort law. *Palsgraf*'s fame, which has puzzled some commentators, does not rest solely on its combination of delightfully bizarre facts, forceful judicial rhetoric, and ample room for disagreement about the result; [116] the *Palsgraf* case was also one of those moments in the intellectual history of a legal subject when two theoretical approaches stood in solid opposition. The fundamental obscurities and ambiguities in the *Palsgraf* opinions, to which countless students of the case have alluded, can be traced to the interaction of the opposing theories of negligence used to analyze the case.[117] *Palsgraf* represents an episode in American legal history where a clash of ideas resulted in an intellectual communication of genuine ambivalence.

The theoretical approaches employed in *Palsgraf* were those of "universal" and "relational" negligence, and the facts of the case were perfectly suited to show the role of causation in those separate approaches. As almost everyone who has studied law in the last forty years knows, in *Palsgraf* two men attempted to board a Long Island Railroad train as it was departing from a station. Guards on the train helped boost the men onto it while it was moving. In the process one of the guards jostled one of the men, dislodging a nondescript package from his arm and causing it to fall onto the rails. The package, which contained fireworks, exploded. A prospective passenger of the railroad, Helen Palsgraf, was standing on the platform some distance from where the package fell. She heard an explosion and was then injured when some scales, apparently toppled by the explosion, fell on her. She sued the railroad, claiming negligence on the part of its guard in dislodging the package. The case ultimately reached the New York Court of Appeals.

Between the time the *Palsgraf* case was decided by an intermediate New York court and the time it was appealed to the New York Court of Appeals the American Law Institute's advisors on Torts discussed it at a meeting. Judge Benjamin Cardozo, who was to write the majority opinion in *Palsgraf,* attended the meeting in his capacity as an adviser, but did not participate in the discussion and did not vote.[118] The simple issue in the *Palsgraf* case, which was to evolve into an issue of considerable complexity in its articulation, was whether the railroad was liable in negligence to Mrs. Palsgraf.

If liability were not to attach to the railroad, two explanations for that outcome presented themselves. The orthodox doctrinal explanation was to label the railroad's guard hypothetically "negligent" in causing the package to be dropped, but to find that the negligence was

not a "proximate" or "legal" cause of Mrs. Palsgraf's injuries, since
she was sufficiently remote from the explosion that injury to her could
not have been expected to have been foreseen by the guard. This
rationale assumed the existence of a duty on the part of the guard to
take care not to injure prospective passengers such as Mrs. Palsgraf,
but mitigated that duty through the rubric of causation.

The alternative rationale was reminiscent of Green's approach to
causation issues in negligence. The railroad owed no liability to Mrs.
Palsgraf because the guard owed no duty to protect her from the risk
of injury from exploding fireworks. She was not close enough to him—
injury to her was "unforeseeable"—and therefore she was not "within
the range of apprehension." Since the guard owed Mrs. Palsgraf no
duty, it was irrelevant whether a "causal relation" existed between his
dislodging of the package and her injury. The case was not one of
"causation" at all.

This rationale, which was adopted by both the A.L.I. advisors
and Cardozo for a majority of the Court of Appeals, forced its
adherents to contemplate the reorientation of negligence theory inherent in Green's approach. If duties were only owed to specific
persons with respect to particular risks, then negligence as an abstract
duty of very great generality did not exist. Negligence, Cardozo said
in *Palsgraf,* was "a term of relation": "the risk reasonably to be perceived defines the duty to be obeyed, and risk imports relation; it is
risk to another or to others within the range of apprehension." [119]
Negligence in the abstract, Cardozo maintained, was "surely not a
tort, if indeed it is understandable at all." [120]

In dissent, Judge William Andrews voiced the traditional view:
"[d]ue care is a duty imposed on each one of us to protect society from
unnecessary danger, not to protect A, B or C alone." [121] "Every one,"
Andrews felt, owed "to the world at large the duty of refraining from
those acts that may unreasonably threaten the safety of others." [122]
The limits on this general duty were achieved by mitigating concepts
such as "legal" or "proximate" causation. Legal causation demonstrated that "the law arbitrarily declines to trace a series of events
beyond a certain point." "Proximate" for Andrews was a term "of
convenience, of public policy, of a rough sense of justice." [123]

A juxtaposition of Cardozo's majority opinion in *Palsgraf* with
Andrews' dissent reveals some ironies of the case. Cardozo's approach,
while less orthodox, was at the same time more "doctrinal" than that

of Andrews. Cardozo defined negligence as a term of relation and conditioned liability for negligence on a showing by plaintiffs that defendants had exposed them to specific foreseeable risks. Through the elevation of "risk" and "relation" to fundamental concepts in negligence law, Cardozo's approach apparently eliminated both "unforeseeable" plaintiffs and "unforeseeable" risks from the scope of an action in negligence. No "duties" were owed to such persons; no obligations of protection existed with respect to such hazards. Cardozo also proceeded as if his recasting of negligence theory had been received from on high. Nowhere in the *Palsgraf* majority opinion was there any concession that the question of whether a defendant owed a duty to protect a particular plaintiff from specific risks was a question of "interest-balancing" or "practical politics." In contrast, Cardozo suggested that the existence of "duties" in negligence turned on foreseeability, as determined by physical proximity. "[T]he orbit of the danger as disclosed to the eye of reasonable vigilance," he said, "would be the orbit of the duty." [124]

Andrews's opinion, on the other hand, while retaining the orthodox concepts of an abstract, universal duty of care and of "proximate" causation, was explicitly an exercise in interest-balancing. And the *Palsgraf* case was a peculiarly attractive one for that sort of exercise. Mrs. Palsgraf was a passenger of the Long Island Railroad, and her presence on the platform was linked to her passenger status; she had not herself contributed to her injury. The railroad had liability insurance and the opportunity to absorb the costs of its liability to Mrs. Palsgraf either through a claim against its insurance carrier or by incremental raises in its rates. On the other hand, Mrs. Palsgraf could not be distinguished, in terms of her exposure to the risk of injury from falling scales, from any other passenger on a railroad platform. Perhaps she could not even be distinguished from a bystander, since no effort was made to segregate bystanders from passengers on railroad platforms. Thus if the railroad was liable in negligence to Mrs. Palsgraf, it was potentially liable to anyone else injured on a railroad platform whose injuries could be traced to some careless act of a railroad employee. In short, the *Palsgraf* case balanced the "justice" of Mrs. Palsgraf's position as an innocent passenger injured by the carelessness of a solvent enterprise against the threats to the future financial solvency of that enterprise posed by too extensive an ambit of tort liability.

The ambivalence of the *Palsgraf* case came from the failure of either Cardozo's or Andrews's opinions openly to concede that in cases involving liability in negligence for remote consequences, or to remote persons, the process of resolution was explicitly one of interest-balancing. Both opinions retreated to formulas—Cardozo to his "duty-relation-risk" formula, Andrews to a more familiar one of "proximate" causation, in which he distinguished between "direct" and "indirect" injuries. The use of the formulas made the message of *Palsgraf* highly ambivalent. Was the concept of negligence now a "relational" one, so that if a given plaintiff could not show that he was in a class of persons to whom a given defendant owed a duty of protection against a specific risk, he could not recover? And if so, was this a more *restrictive* meaning of negligence, since it abandoned the concept of an abstract general duty owed to all the world by all the world, or a potentially more *expansive* meaning, since it allowed judges to decide, through interest-balancing, whether a given plaintiff was deserving of protection in a given case, regardless of the "remoteness" of his injury?

Green, whose insights contributed to the perspectives of both Cardozo's and Andrews's opinions in *Palsgraf*,[125] was nonetheless not enthusiastic about either of them. While applauding Andrews's dissent as "the high water mark of judicial expression explanatory of the proximate cause concept," [126] Green felt that the proximate causation rubric only concealed difficulties in negligence cases. Nor had Cardozo "clearly articulate[d]" the grounds for his decision; he had retreated to " 'pat' phrases and formulas," notably "risk" and "foreseeability." The issue in the *Palsgraf* case for Green was "far deeper than any matter of foreseeability or experience." *Palsgraf* involved the "adjustment by government of risks which . . . cannot be eliminated from the hurly-burly of modern traffic and transportation." Rather than facing risk allocation openly, Cardozo and Andrews had "transport[ed]" their inquiries "into the realm of metaphysics," where effective legal reasoning was "lost in a flood of words." [127]

Thus the final irony of *Palsgraf* was that while it seemed to usher in a new approach to negligence theory, in which causation would play a much less significant role, it also seemed to be an unsatisfactory statement of that approach. Bohlen, through the *Restatement of Torts,* endorsed the majority result in *Palsgraf* and incorporated both Cardozo's and Andrews's opinions within the doctrinal organization of the 1930 edition of his casebook.[128] Nevertheless commentators, from Green on, have not been able collectively to decide what the *Palsgraf* case means. Some have suggested, with Green, that the opinions avoided the true issues;[129] others have regarded the case to be so bizarre as to resist generalized classification;[130] others have implied that *Palsgraf* was merely an academic excursion of the American Law Institute;[131] still others have taken judges and commentators to task for ignoring the human dimensions of Mrs. Palsgraf's injury.[132] While *Palsgraf* continues to fascinate, its fascination has regularly taken the form of exasperation and bewilderment.

Yet *Palsgraf* represents one of the clearest instances in the history of tort law of a theoretical confrontation that could be described as a minor intellectual crisis. Both opinions in *Palsgraf* conceded, implicitly, that orthodox doctrinal concepts developed by late nineteenth-century tort theorists could not satisfactorily resolve the liability issue in the case. Cardozo found causation inapposite as an analytic framework, and Andrews, while employing causation analysis, admitted that "proximate cause" was not doctrine, merely "practical politics." Cardozo's "duty-risk-relation" rationale, while suggesting that the use of doctrines in negligence was still a viable enterprise, abandoned the scientists' formulation of a universal civil duty that had been at the very core of orthodox negligence theory. Andrews's "universal duty" rationale appeared to be meaningless without consideration of the limits on "duties," which seemed, at least in the area of causation, to reduce themselves to the equitable claims of the parties in discrete fact situations.

Palsgraf thus marked the end of conceptions of causation as a generalized legal doctrine and the emergence of conceptions of causation as an issue of public policy. After *Palsgraf* questions of "proximate cause" were increasingly seen as questions involving "considerations of fairness, justice and social policy which are often difficult to explain and frequently have their basis in vague feelings or intentions of what is proper and desirable."[133] In his 1941 treatise on Torts, William Prosser summarized the state of affairs. " 'Proximate cause,' " Prosser maintained, "cannot be reduced to absolute rules. . . . 'It is always to be determined on the facts of each case upon mixed considerations of logic, common sense, justice, policy and precedent.' " The "fruitless quest for a universal formula" of causation ought to be abandoned.[134]

Causation had perhaps been the weakest link in the doctrinal super-structure created by the late nineteenth- and early twentieth-century legal scientists. As the jurisprudential insights of Realism became more widely publicized, "proximate cause" cases increasingly ap-peared as instances where courts resorted to formulas to conceal the bases of their decisions. Treatments of causation seemed to confirm the Realists' belief that rules of law were meaningless apart from their administration, since different courts cut off liability at different points through the use of causation doctrines. Moreover, orthodox causation analysis was especially vulnerable to attack because doc-trinally oriented scholars could not themselves unite on any universal causation formula. Hence a shift of emphasis in the analysis of causa-tion questions from doctrinal to policy considerations was not markedly difficult to achieve, and perhaps not even striking in itself. But the demise of orthodox treatments of causation in the 1930s was highly significant in another respect. The vulnerability of causa-tion revealed the more general vulnerability of orthodox negligence theory.

Doctrinal change in the Realist years was not limited to modifica-tions of the staple concepts of the scientists. Early twentieth-century reformist legal thought also "discovered" new tort doctrines. In 1939 William Prosser announced that "the courts" had "created a new tort," [135] the intentional infliction of emotional distress. Given the fact that as late as the 1920s many courts continued to hold that mental pain and anguish were too vague for legal redress [136] but that by the 1930s mental distress without accompanying physical injury was being compensated in several courts,[137] Prosser's statement had an element of accuracy. But it was also unnecessarily modest. A major contribu-tion to the "creation" of the "new tort" had been made by Prosser himself. He organized the diverse cases where recovery for emotional distress had been granted, criticized the existing rationales employed to avoid liability for emotional distress, and generally sought to treat emotional injuries in terms of the emergent theoretical framework of tort law in the 1930s, which suggested that tort liability be assessed through a "common sense" balancing of social interests.[138]

Prosser's "discovery" of a "new tort" redressing purely emotional injuries was, despite his language, the culmination of a series of doctrinal developments. The recognition that emotional injury could be compensated through tort litigation can be traced to altered attitudes about mental discomfort that emerged in early twentieth-century America and can be linked to the general intellectual trends that were reflected in Realism.

The historic rationale for limiting tort claims to those resting on discernible physical injuries was the "speculative" nature of mental or emotional distress. The term "speculative" subsumed two distinguishable characterizations of emotional discomfort: a sense that emotional illness was hard to diagnose and a sense that, given the diagnostic difficulties, emotional illness was comparatively easy to feign. Taken together, these characterizations suggested that society was not confident of its capacity to evaluate emotional distress apart from its physical manifestations, and perhaps even that on some occasions emotional injuries were taken less seriously than physical ones.

Realism, we have seen, reflected an enhanced early twentieth-century awareness of the psychological dimensions of human behavior, an awareness that was linked to a growing interest in the explanatory powers of the behavioral sciences. As psychology came to be regarded as a "science," its diagnostic techniques, which sought to identify and to explain mental disorders, came to be regarded as capable of distinguishing bona fide emotional distress from the feigned variety. At the same time psychological explanations of human character exposed educated Americans to the widespread presence of emotional stress and its debilitative effects. Thus emotional illness became less "speculative": through the aid of expert testimony it was easier to diagnose and consequently more difficult to feign.

In addition, emotional distress was increasingly regarded as a legitimate illness that was neither a consequence of character weakness nor an unfathomable individual idiosyncrasy. Like poverty, alcoholism, and illegitimacy, emotional discomfort was increasingly perceived in the 1920s and 1930s as a problem for which society bore some collective responsibility. The enhanced seriousness with which emotional disorders were taken was paralleled by an enhanced confidence that affirmative action by governmental institutions could help relieve emotional discomfort, just as it could relieve other newly perceived social problems.

An altered awareness of the "seriousness" of emotional distress led to increased efforts in the courts to seek redress against its infliction. As claims based wholly or in part on emotional distress mounted, commentators discovered that compensation for emotional injury had been, despite dogmatic language to the contrary, a fairly common-place feature of late nineteenth- and early twentieth-century tort law. If emotional distress could be closely linked to physical injury, even though it was not solely related to that injury, courts allowed re-covery.[139] If the distress was the result of an intentional tort, many courts allowed recovery, even if no physical symptoms surfaced.[140] Technical batteries [141] or trespasses,[142] regardless of how slight, were made the basis of recovery where the substance of the claim was for emotional injury. Emotional distress without accompanying physical injury had been regarded as worthy of compensation where contrac-tual relations existed between the parties,[143] where workman's com-pensation legislation governed the claim,[144] or where the defendant had allegedly committed a nuisance.[145]

By 1936 a survey revealed that twenty-one states had allowed re-covery for emotional distress alone and that of the thirteen states that denied recovery, only three had adopted that problem in the twentieth century.[146] Thus the torts of negligent and intentional infliction of emotional distress were not "new," in the 1930s, at least in the sense of their appearance in the courts. While a trend in the direction of ex-panded liability for emotional injuries alone had gained momentum in the 1920s and 1930s, recovery for emotional distress had been granted, if sporadically, from the late nineteenth century onward.

The contribution of Prosser and other tort scholars in the 1920s and 1930s was therefore not to invent the principle of compensation for emotional distress, but to expand the locus of that principle from isolated "exceptional" cases to an established doctrine of tort law. In this effort the scholars relied on three familiar tenets of Realism: a heightened interest in the insights of the behavioral sciences; an im-patience with judicial "fictions," whose purpose was to preserve the apparent integrity of established doctrines that were in actuality being subverted; and a developing conception of tort law as an exercise in social policymaking. Herbert Goodrich, later to become the director of the American Law Institute, showed in 1922 that "mental" suffer-ing was no less real, or susceptible of "scientific" understanding, than physical suffering.[147] Green demolished the rationale of "fright" cases that had attempted to limit recovery to physical injuries.[148] Calvert Magruder, a professor at Harvard Law School who subsequently served as a judge on the U.S. Court of Appeals for the First Circuit, exposed some fictions employed by courts in emotional distress cases, such as allowing recovery where defendants had committed trivial "impacts" or "trespasses," but denying recovery where none existed.[149] Harper cataloged the various "interests" (bodily security, privacy, courteous treatment, memories of loved ones) that claims based on emotional distress sought to protect.[150] Even the Restatement of Torts gave qualified support to recovery in both intentional and negligent infliction of emotional distress cases.[151]

By the late 1930s the material for Prosser's synthesis was present: he could demonstrate, in his 1939 article and in the 1941 edition of his Torts treatise, that a "new" area of tort liability had emerged. While conceding that "objections" against allowing recovery for the intentional or negligent infliction of emotional distress still existed, Prosser gave them short shrift. "[I]t is said," he wrote in 1941, "that mental disturbance cannot be measured in terms of money, and so cannot serve in itself as a basis for the action; that its physical consequences are too remote, and so not 'proximately caused'; that there is a lack of precedent, and that a vast increase in litigation would follow. All these objections have been demolished many times [here Prosser cited the contributions of Goodrich, Green, Bohlen, and several other scholars], and it is threshing old straw to deal with them." [152] Mental suffering, Prosser observed, was "no less a real injury than 'physical' pain," and it was "the business of the courts to make precedent where a wrong calls for redress, even if lawsuits must be multiplied." [153]

Several features common to the climate of educated opinion in which Realism came to prominence had interacted in the "discovery" that tort law could compensate persons for emotional discomfort inflicted by others. The "speculative" nature of emotional injuries had been purportedly eliminated by the insights of the behavioral sciences. The seriousness of the "interests" at stake in emotional distress cases had gradually been recognized, and the possibilities for using tort law as a means of protecting various social interests had emerged as a source of intellectual excitement. Finally, scholars of the 1920s and 1930s had shown a willingness, uncommon in their earlier scientist counterparts, to concede that the doctrinal state of an area of tort law was indeterminate and capable of dramatic change.

Nineteenth-century conceptualists achieved doctrinal consistency and uniformity in the emotional distress area by making a sharp distinction between "physical" and "mental" injuries and invariably denying that the latter, by themselves, were compensable through tort law. When twentieth-century scholars helped extend tort liability to the area of emotional distress they implicitly demanded a further set of inquiries: what criteria were to govern recovery in marginal cases; what were the limits in potential recovery for emotional damage; was negligently inflicted emotional distress to receive protection comparable to that afforded to intentionally inflicted emotional harm; was emotional distress to be limited to fear for oneself and, if not, what third-party relationships were to be recognized. The essence of Realism was an appreciation that doctrinal uniformity was never completely achieved; that an area of law was never made fully predictable. Interest-balancing, case-by-case adjudication, and a sense of doctrinal indeterminacy were compatible with the insights of the Realist movement. Legal scholars influenced by early twentieth-century reformist thought believed that if emerging problems in human relations generated pressure for a set of legal remedies to emerge, those remedies would emerge even if they seemed novel or doctrinally impure or even anomalous. Emotional distress was the stuff of "real" life in twentieth-century America, and hence the stuff of tort law.

The extension of tort law into the emotional distress area implicitly signified the presence of a new perception about the boundaries of the field of Torts. Bohlen, Green, and the other scholars who had been influenced, in varying degrees, by reformist thought shared a confidence in the capacity of private law subjects to respond to the perceived imperatives of public policy. Torts, especially, seemed promising in this regard, since a significant percentage of its litigated issues involved parties that had had no prior business or personal relationships with one another. Reformist legal scholars had regularly argued that the problems of one set of "interests," in an interdependent society, inevitably affected the lives of other sets. They had called for an enhanced role for agencies of government, including courts, as social engineers who balanced the claims of competing interests on behalf of the public good. The resolution of tort issues, in his view, might be perceived as an exercise in social engineering.

But the theoretical framework of nineteenth-century tort law, with its emphasis on the primacy of the negligence principle, had been developed in an age in which perceptions of social interdependence and the mechanisms of affirmative government were not highly developed. Negligence theory, we have seen, had been conceived of by nineteenth-century conceptualists essentially as a device for promoting order and predictability in private relationships. As an analytical superstructure for tort law began to be refined by the scientists, and as the potential ambit of the negligence principle widened, the field of Torts came to be seen as governed by a fairly predictable set of rules. Once requirements of factual causation had been satisfied, one then asked if a defendant had been "at fault," invoking the "reasonable man" test. If so, one considered defenses and other barriers to liability—contributory negligence, assumption of risk, legal causation. Each defense had its own analytical formula: had a plaintiff "voluntarily" exposed himself to a risk; was the defendant's act a "substantial factor" in bringing about the plaintiff's injury; and so on. The nineteenth-century version of negligence theory, in short, functioned to narrow the range of tort liability to a set of predictable instances.

With the transformation of negligence theory in the 1920s the purposes and consequences of the negligence principle shifted. To recapitulate, the notion of an abstract universal duty was gradually abandoned and a "relational" concept of duty was substituted. Relational negligence theory introduced questions of "interest-balancing," inviting judges to compare the magnitude of the risks to which a plaintiff was exposed, and the social worth of the class of persons a plaintiff represented, with the social utility of a defendant's conduct. In the process the uniformity of the negligence principle was lost, since different judges might balance interests differently in given cases and thus give different meanings to "negligence." In addition, the capacity of the negligence principle to be predictably applied was lost, because a general hierarchy of social "interests" could not invariably be agreed upon by judges, and thus even a routinized judicial balancing of interests would not produce predictable results.

Relational negligence theory was to prepare the way for a more sweeping attack on negligence as the gist of tort law. This attack, which only originated in the Realist years, sounded two themes. First, if determinations of "negligent" conduct were essentially exercises in interest-balancing in discrete cases, the concept of "fault," a basic element of orthodox negligence analysis, confused rather than clarified matters. One was not "careless" in the abstract; one could be deemed legally careless or not legally careless for the same conduct depending on the circumstances surrounding that conduct. To say that the Long Island Railroad's guard in *Palsgraf* would surely have been at "fault" if the package he dislodged had injured the person carrying it, but that he was not at "fault" in dislodging the same package and thereby setting off a chain of events that injured Mrs. Palsgraf, was to strip the term fault of its significance as a generalized proposition. The usefulness of a traditional element of negligence analysis was thus called into question.

Second, if negligence analysis was to consist of the balancing of social interests, why should that balancing not be done openly, through a candid weighing of the social costs and benefits of various injury-producing conduct, rather than through use of traditional negligence formulas such as "duty" or "proximate" causation? If a decision to extend tort liability in a given case actually represented a judgment about the compensability of the plaintiff's social interest, why not make that decision explicit by announcing that this class of plaintiffs deserved compensation from this class of defendants for being exposed to this kind of risk and ultimately being injured by the exposure?

Here relational negligence anticipated an approach to tort libability that bypasesd negligence theory altogether. The approach—"strict" liability theory—revived an older notion of acting at one's peril: defendants would be held liable for injuries caused by their risk-creating conduct whether they were "at fault" or not. Even if a given defendant had taken reasonable precautions to avoid creating a risk that a given plaintiff would suffer a particular injury, the defendant was required to compensate the plaintiff because the plaintiff's injury was of a kind worth compensating and because the defendant was in a better position than the plaintiff to pay for it.

Despite the primacy of the negligence principle and despite scholarly efforts to make torts virtually synonymous with negligence,[154] bastions of "strict" liability had persisted in the late nineteenth and early twentieth centuries. These included liability for damage incurred by wild animals and liability for the use of "extrahazardous" substances, such as explosives. Even these areas, however, were regarded as highly exceptional. In the fourth edition of Francis Burdick's treatise on Torts (1926), as indicated, such instances of "strict" liability were grouped under the heading "peculiar liability." [155] Burdick argued, in fact, that injuries suffered from wild animals or explosives were compensable without a showing of fault "only when the defendant's conduct amount[ed] to the maintenance of a nuisance." [156] Otherwise he believed such cases were to be governed by negligence principles.

By the 1930s, however, scholars had begun to treat cases imposing strict liability as a separate category of Torts rather than as a "peculiar" set of exceptions. The principal change in the analysis of strict liability in treatises was not so much in expanded coverage as in recognition that strict liability theory was founded on a conception of tort law as an instrument of social policymaking. Harper, in his 1933 treatise, called strict liability analysis a process of "allocating a probable or inevitable loss in such a manner as to entail the least hardship upon any individual and thus to preserve the social and economic resources of the community." Strict liability was dictated "from considerations of social expediency"; it was "a pure matter of social engineering." [157] Prosser expressed similar views in his 1941 treatise. Strict liability theory, he maintained, consisted of "allocating a more or less inevitable loss to be charged against a complex and dangerous civilization, and [placing] liability upon the party best able to shoulder it." The conduct of a defendant held liable under strict liability theory was "regarded as tortious not because it [was] morally or socially wrong, but because as a matter of social engineering the responsibility must be his." [158]

As thus articulated, the connection between strict liability theory and relational negligence became apparent. Relational negligence, while retaining the concept of fault, had made the determination of where fault lay in a given case a process of interest-balancing. Strict liability theory proposed to conduct the interest-balancing altogether unburdened by notions of fault. In 1917 Jeremiah Smith had found those isolated instances of "strict" liability in tort law exceptional in their repudiation of the general fault standard.[159] By 1941 Prosser was prepared to "question whether 'fault,' with its popular connotation of personal guilt and moral blame, and its more or less arbitrary legal meaning, which [would] vary with the requirements of social conduct imposed by the law, [was] of any real assistance in dealing with . . . questions of [risk allocation], except perhaps as a descriptive term." Once the legal concept of fault was divorced from current standards of moral wrongdoing, Prosser argued, "there [was] a sense in which liability with or without 'fault' must beg its own conclusion." [160]

This renewed interest in strict liability theory among scholars in the 1930s was not paralleled by a significant renaissance of strict liability cases in the courts. Prosser's 1941 treatise, to be sure, showed that in many familiar "tort" areas statutes, such as workman's compensation, had replaced common law negligence standards with strict liability. He also demonstrated that in some other areas, such as cases involving warranties of the quality of food, "the common law . . . has shown some tendency to extend strict liability into new fields." [161] The great explosion of strict liability theory in the area of defective products was, however, a post-World War II phenomenon. But the significant modifications of negligence theory made in *Palsgraf* and contemporary articles and treatises, and the attacks on "fault" as a meaningful concept that accompanied those modifications, had paved the way for an alternative comprehensive principle of tort law to emerge. While that theory was not to emerge full-blown until well after Realism had lost its preeminence in American jurisprudence, and while the strict liability principle has never achieved the exalted status negligence once held, the emergence of modern strict liability theory in the Realist years has significantly affected the course of mid-twentieth century tort law.

The Legacy of Realism

The interaction of the "scientist" phase of the intellectual history of Torts with its "Realist" phase gives rise to a generalization about the intellectual foundations of law in the late nineteenth and twentieth centuries. A recurrent problem for commentators and judges in common law subjects has been the relationship of general principles to particular cases. Since the staple units of the common law have been individual cases, those charged with the task of deciding cases or assessing those decisions have necessarily had to direct their attention toward particularized results. But the intellectual origins of Torts has also demonstrated that part of the identity of a common law subject is derived from general guiding principles or doctrines through which that subject seeks to define and systematize its boundaries. The interplay of the particular case with the generalized principle has thus been a continuing theme of common law adjudication and scholarship.

Different jurisprudential theories have, however, defined the interplay of case and principle in strikingly different ways. The late nineteenth-century scientists emphasized the extent to which particular results could be seen as emblematic of general principles. While they sought to extract principles "inductively" from cases, they also sought to apply extracted principles as broadly and fully as possible. The result was a doctrinal emphasis in Torts: the promulgation of doctrines that served to identify and organize the subject. While individual commentators differed on how rigidly existing doctrines ought to be followed in new case contexts, they continually referred issues in tort law to a doctrinal framework. Those jurists influenced by Realism, on the other hand, were far less confident that cases embodied general principles, far more inclined to question the meaning of established doctrine, and far more willing to allow an area of Torts, or even the subject itself, to rest in a disorganized or fluid state.

Realism, we have seen, emphasized an approach to the interplay of cases and principles that differed significantly from that of the scientists. For Realists a case was not so much an embodiment of a principle as a testing of that principle anew. Doctrines, from a Realist perspective, were merely working hypothetical guidelines in the solution of cases that might well prove inapposite to the facts at hand. Some Realists, such as Green, seemed to suggest, further, that doctrines were nothing more than vague embodiments, employed for convenience, of a particularized result. Tort "law," in Green's scholarship, appeared as the aggregate of tort cases as currently administered. Its "doctrines," he suggested, were nothing more than efforts to achieve some (quixotic) theoretical unity in an extraordinarily diverse subject.

A tort case, then, for Realists, overwhelmed any principle that it allegedly stood for; a tort case for conceptualists was overwhelmed by the principle that it embodied. Tort law was seen by the conceptualists as a unified entity, integrated by the overarching negligence principle. For the Realists it was seen as a collection of individual claims, linked, if at all, by the interests they affected, or the social policies they tested, or, perhaps, the analytical inquiries they regularly posed.

This last Realist assumption—that there could be, despite the diversity of tort issues, a common methodological approach to tort questions—indicates that the Realists cannot be characterized as antithetical to systematized thinking or unsympathetic to the notion that law could be a "science." The Realist simply made a different definition of science and argued for a different locus for systematic thought.

For them "science" was not the hierarchical classifications of nineteenth-century naturalists but the empirical observations of contemporary social scientists. Law for the Realists was not a set of disembodied universal principles, but it was nonetheless capable of systematic analysis. One observed the social, psychological, and economic conditions of American life as they "really" were, identified meaningful phenomena, such as "interests," or "relations," and sought to reorient the analysis of tort issues so as to make use of those phenomena.

Green dismissed the doctrine of "proximate cause" as a vague metaphysical phantom, but then proceeded to substitute his own formula for deciding causation questions. Cardozo found that the conception of an abstract universal duty in negligence was barely comprehensible, but then derived his own formula for analyzing negligence cases. Differences between the scientists and the Realists centered not so much on questions of the worth of tests and formulas used in legal analysis, but on the issue of whether those tests and formulas could have a substantive content. "Principles," for the scientists, were more than methodological devices: they were rules with substantive implications. The various formulas of the Realists were seemingly intended to be methodological only.[162]

Tort law was not the same after the impact of Realism. It was not the same in that it was no longer conceived of as the autonomous, orderly subject that had been the ideal of the scientists. Its integrating principle, negligence, had been reduced to an exercise in balancing the interests of plaintiff and defendant in a given case. Tort law was also not the same in that its boundaries were less well defined. A consequence of the growth of the negligence principle had been an attempt to narrow the range of tort law virtually to those instances where legal fault, either in its "intentional" or "negligent" forms, was at issue. Although this effort had not been entirely successful, it had lent a sense of boundaries to the subject.

With the advent of Realism and its characterization of Torts as a field that was congenial to "social engineering" and other styles of policymaking, the ambit of tort law was potentially expanded. As new social problems emerged, and cognizable "interests" were affected, tort law could be called upon as a potential solution. The fact that problems had not been traditionally addressed by tort law (emotional distress) or had not been adequately treated by the negligence principle ("extrahazardous" substances) did not mean that tort law was precluded from including them in its concerns. Thus by the publication of Prosser's treatise in 1941, Torts was an unwieldy, diverse, fluid subject. The great success of Prosser's approach to Torts, which will be subsequently discussed, was his ability seemingly to reduce tort law to manageable proportions while not underemphasizing its diversity and capacity for change.

With Prosser's treatise a new phase in the intellectual history of Torts was to begin, although that development was by no means clear at the time, even to Prosser himself. While some of the jurisprudential assumptions of Realism persisted in the adjudication and scholarly articulation of tort issues, subtle shifts were taking place. Most striking among those shifts was a renewed search for unity in the field of Torts. But the perceived source of the unity was not principles as understood by the legal scientists. It was the institutional processes through which private and public law was made. Just as "principle" was a watchword for one generation of legal scholars, "process" came to be one for another. The jurisprudential concept of "process" preserved some of the assumptions of Realism while subtly modifying its central thrust. A consideration of the relationship between process jurisprudence, the "consensus thought" of the years after 1945, and tort law, however, must await a fuller explication of the role of appellate judges as participants in the intellectual history of tort law.

4

The Twentieth Century Judge As Torts Theorist: Cardozo

Thus far the attention of this study has focused primarily on the contributions of academics. Preceding chapters have argued that legal scholars, influenced by intellectual assumptions comparable to those made by scholars in other disciplines, created a "subject" of Torts, attempted to shape its doctrinal superstructure to conform to a conception of law as a science, and then, having abandoned that conception, attempted to reshape tort doctrines to reflect the insights of early twentieth-century reformist thought. In each of the chapters judges and courts have been discussed, but not given central treatment, and where interactions between academic thought and judicial decisions have been examined, emphasis has been placed primarily on academic sources.

The preceding chapters have indicated, however, that nineteenth- and early twentieth-century tort law was not exclusively the product of academic thought. The corpus of tort law between 1850 and 1930, of course, primarily consisted of judicial decisions. The significance of academic thought in those years lay in its subtle, sometimes almost imperceptible, modification of judicial decisions through intellectual analysis and synthesis. In one phase of the intellectual history of Torts the preconceptions influencing this modification were those of late nineteenth-century conceptualism; in another, those of early twentieth-century reformist thought. In each instance widely shared philosophical assumptions stimulated scholars to emphasize one dimension or another of a judicial decision. Scholarly emphasis was to affect the content of future decisions. But the scholars were not the principal decision-makers.

In the history of American tort law the relationship between judicial decisions and academic thought has been, as noted, symbiotic. Judges, particularly those on the highest courts of the states, have articulated generalized tort doctrines in the course of their decisions. The decisions have been analyzed by academicians and their doctrinal emphases commented upon. From the perspective of this study, the decisions of appellate courts, upon being issued, are just beginning their history as "acceptable" responses to emergent issues in tort law. The implicit philosophical assumptions on which these decisions rest are subsequently reinforced, or questioned, by academic commentators, primarily through a process of selecting certain "doctrinal" features of a decision as significant or troublesome. This selection process, we have seen, may affect the influence of a judicial decision not only among commentators, but among courts, ultimately determining the extent of its viability. The life and death of theories and doctrines in tort law can be closely linked to the interaction of the philosophical assumptions of judges with those of commentators.

One can single out those nineteenth-century judges who contributed in one way or another to the intellectual history of Torts, and several have surfaced in early portions of the narrative. Lemuel Shaw's impressive, if ambiguous, statement of the test for tort liability where an injury had been unintentionally inflicted may have hastened the triumph of modern negligence. Charles Doe's broad repudiation, in 1873, of "strict" standards of liability in American tort law likewise contributed to the increased identification of Torts with the negligence principle. Thomas Cooley wrote a widely cited treatise on Torts and sought, during his term on the Supreme Court of Michigan, to preserve a consistency between his perspective as a commentator and his decisions as a judge.[1] Holmes tried, not always successfully, to put his theoretical insights into practice in his Torts decisions on the Supreme Judicial Court of Massachusetts. None of those judges, however, made a greater impact on the state of American tort law than Benjamin Cardozo, who served as associate justice and then chief justice of the New York Court of Appeals during the period 1914 to 1932. Cardozo's impact was not exclusively a function of his skills as a judge. It was also a product of an altered role for judges that emerged with the triumph of reformist thought in the early twentieth century.

The Early Twentieth-Century Judicial Role

Numerous scholars have documented the rise of a conviction among early twentieth-century educated Americans that judges "made law," and the consequent emergence of a belief that judges should not equate exercises in lawmaking with the imposition of their own views on social policy. Although evidence of these changed attitudes towards the nature of judging and the role of the judiciary is abundantly evident, the character of the changes was more complex than most works of modern scholarship have suggested.[2]

Late nineteenth-century conceptions of judging were affected by the presence of two potentially contradictory theories of judicial interpretation. One theory, regularly articulated by prominent judges since the early years of the century, described the role of judge as an oracle, a passive "finder" or "declarer" of laws that had been "made" by some other branch of government. From John Marshall's assertion in 1824 that "courts are mere instruments of the law and can will nothing"[3] to David Brewer's claim in 1893 that "[t]he courts . . . make no laws, they establish no policy, they never enter into the domain of public action,"[4] a theory of the judge as oracle commanded considerable influence, especially among judges. Other theories, however, coexisted with the oracular theory, and by the late years of the nineteenth century a view of the judge as articulator and implementor of comprehensive legal principles had come into prominence.

On first impression the judge as an oracle and judicial interpretation as the declaration of universal principles seems to be a consistent and self-reinforcing arrangement. But complexities appear when one emphasizes the creative aspects of "declaring" principles in a conceptualistic mode of legal analysis. A general rule of law had to come from somewhere, and regularly in the nineteenth century it came from a judge's intuitions, reinforced by a skillful marshalling of academic and judicial sources.[5] Creative judging was rife throughout the century, but it was not commonly conceived of, or presented as, an exercise in policymaking. Open concessions that judges "made law" offended against an oracular interpretation of the judge's role.

Thus the creative dimensions of nineteenth-century judging were largely covert in expression, especially in the latter stages of the century when conceptualist modes of analysis, with their emphasis on technical professional techniques of reasoning, became prominent. The interest of conceptualists in using law as a means to achieve and preserve intellectual order tacitly encouraged emphasis on the predictability and regularity of legal doctrines. The model late nineteenth-century judge found, articulated, and applied a governing principle. Where his "finding" was creative, his opinions tended to minimize that creativity; where his articulation or application of principles constituted substantial innovations in the state of legal doctrine, his opinions did not often emphasize those innovations. Innovative judges, in fact, regularly suggested that their decisions preserved intact the corpus of an area of law.[6]

The substantial alteration of attitudes about judging that emerged in the early twentieth century developed from a central perception about this nineteenth-century model. The perception was that judges did not act as they and orthodox commentators said they did. Judges had been portrayed as passive beings who did not infuse their wills into their decision-making, but in fact, it was argued, they subtly, or at times crudely, equated their personal beliefs with "law." Additionally, law as interpreted by judges had been portrayed as a stable body of enduring principles, but in fact it was a constantly changing entity, and judges contributed to its changing state.

This altered perception of law and judging was yet another expression of the insights of early twentieth-century reformist thought previously described. Not only did the claimed existence of a mystical yet finite body of law inspire skepticism among reformist thinkers, a stark separation of that body of law from the values of the officials who applied it contradicted their common sense observations of the world. It was hard to imagine, let alone to verify, law as anything other than the act of human officials, including judges.

Moreover, the behavioral sciences had shown the ease with which rhetorical statements could be made to serve as rationalizations for official conduct.[7] Early twentieth-century critics looked at the results reached in judicial opinions and explored the possibility that the reasoning of judges was serving to "rationalize" those results: that is, conceal their true basis. The economic or political consequences of an opinion became more interesting than its rhetorical dimensions; the policymaking aspects of judging were revealed; commentators functioned as social and political scientists.

From this critique of the nineteenth-century model of judging evolved a competing model, one more compatible with the thrust of reformist thought. In this model the judge, revealed as a lawmaker, was conceived of as an architect of social policy, responsive to contemporary problems and conditions. An acceptable test for the effectiveness of a judicial opinion was its sensitivity to the "new" imperatives of twentieth-century American life. Reformist critics found some judges' decisions reactionary and their conceptualist modes of analysis isolated from contemporary social and economic conditions. They applauded other judges who openly attempted to change legal doctrine to reflect its altered context. They especially approved of judges whose understanding of their new role was expressed by two concessions: a concession of the need for affirmative governmental action to solve social problems in an interdependent universe, and a concession that the judiciary should use its own powers to support such action only in those instances where it was merely implementing the power of some other lawmaking institution or redressing its own previous lack of responsiveness.

Early twentieth-century judges, however, might acknowledge their function as lawmakers and seek to be responsive to "new" social conditions, but they could not ignore pressures within the legal profession toward uniformity, predictability, and orderliness in common law subjects. These pressures, manifestations of the continued existence of conceptualism among lawyers and legal scholars in the twentieth century, interfused with the insights of reformist thought to shape a unique role for the twentieth-century common law judge. He was to appear as both contemporary-minded and orthodox. He was to emphasize the ability of common law doctrines to change and yet remain continuous over time; he was to respond to emerging social needs yet to preserve traditional values; he was not to base his decisions on abstract metaphysics, but he was to emphasize the common law's capacity to serve as a guide to human conduct. The model early twentieth-century common law judge was a creative theorist whose theoretical contributions were designed to preserve as well as to reform.

The approved role for judges that emerged during the early years of the twentieth century had its own balance between creativity and constraints. But creativity had become overt, and constraints had come to be derived from the professional obligations of a judge rather than from the metaphysical nature of law. Meanwhile perceptions of the work of judges and of their relationship to law had radically changed. Judges were not primarily oracles, they were primarily human beings. They could not, like priests, dissolve their humaneness in the mystical trappings of their role. Judicially interpreted law was no longer conceived of as a "brooding omnipresence." [8] The central insight of reformist critics of the judiciary—that orthodox descriptions of judging inadequately represented its creative, human dimensions—was eventually to mean that judging in twentieth-century America could no longer be conducted in the modes of the late nineteenth century.

Cardozo's Conception of Judging

Cardozo's skill at performing the role of a model twentieth-century common law judge was a primary source of his stature and of his impact on common law subjects such as Torts. The approved early twentieth-century role for judges seemed almost perfectly designed to accommodate Cardozo's intellectual strengths without exposing his weaknesses.

"I was much troubled in spirit in my first years on the bench," Cardozo wrote in 1920, "to find how trackless was the ocean on which I had embarked. I sought for certainty . . . I was trying to reach land, the solid land of fixed and settled rules." Eventually Cardozo was "reconciled to the uncertainty" by seeing judging as "not discovery, but creation," and understanding that when "principles that have served their day expire," new principles could be "born" at the hands of judges.[9] The above passage links three of the insights on which Cardozo's conception of judging was based. Certainty, despite its elusiveness, was a value worth aspiring toward; the exercise of judicial creativity, though inimical to the achievement of certainty, was nonetheless an inevitable consequence of judging; and a search for certainty interacted with creativity in the judicial formulation of generalized but fluid principles of law.

Deriving and articulating general principles on which his results could be based was a recurrent interest of Cardozo as a common law judge. One can take nearly any Cardozo majority opinion in Torts, or another private law subject, and find, sometimes in very explicit language, a principle through which he intended to generalize the narrow holding in the case. Cardozo was fascinated with the capacity of common law opinions to serve as tentative guidelines for a vast number of similar present and future legal controversies. In this fascination he resembled the mature legal scientists, perhaps even sharing some scientists' conviction that properly articulated principles could have long life histories.

To derive meaningful and enduring principles, a judge needed to be creative; to be allowed to be creative he had to make his exercises of power palatable. A strong interest of Cardozo as a judge was the preservation of his creative opportunities. He sought to further this interest surreptitiously, by making his exercises of power inconspicuous and by giving his innovations in common law subjects the appearance of doctrinal continuity. This aspect of Cardozo's judging has been widely commented upon [10] and shall not be belabored here. The best known example in Torts is probably *MacPherson v. Buick Motor Co.*,[11] where Cardozo extended the negligence liability of an automobile manufacturer beyond car dealers to consumers.

The *MacPherson* case involved an injury to a car driver when a defective wheel broke. The decision, allowing recovery by the driver, contravened an established precedent that had been recently reaffirmed in New York.[12] The result was reached by Cardozo's lifting an exception to existing rules governing liability,—an exception carved out for poisons—to the status of a majority rule governing non-poisonous substances as well. One commentator has written that Cardozo's *MacPherson* opinion "imposed liability on [a defendant] who would almost certainly . . . not have been liable if anyone but Cardozo had been stating and analyzing the prior case law." [13] Cardozo claimed, in *MacPherson,* that the "principle" of earlier cases had been that manufacturers of "imminently dangerous" products were liable to all persons who could trace injuries from those products to negligent conduct on a manufacturer's part. He also claimed that "the principle that the danger must be imminent does not change . . ." [14] In both of those claims he was indulging in something of a gloss on the sources, innovating in the guise of following precedent.

In *The Nature of the Judicial Process,* his most famous work, Cardozo attempted to describe how he made decisions by cataloging four judicial "methods" for responding to legal issues. He implied that the decision of every common law case could be seen as involving a tacit choice by a judge of one or more of the methods. But in practice Cardozo's methodology was more fluid. He used the four methods— "logic," "custom," "tradition," or "sociology"—essentially as types of justifications, and he chose the justification that best suited him at the moment. A tort case decided shortly after Cardozo wrote *The Nature of the Judicial Process—Hynes v. New York Central Railroad Co.—*[15] will illustrate.

In the *Hynes* case a sixteen-year-old boy was killed when a cross-arm from a high-tension pole fell and struck him, knocking him off an improvised diving board into the Hudson River. The point in space occupied by the boy when struck had considerable legal significance. The base of the diving board was on land owned by the New York Central Railroad, which had erected and maintained the pole. The end of the board, however, jutted out into airspace that was directly over the Hudson River, a public waterway. Thus the boy, at the moment he was struck, was in a "public" space, although standing on a fixture attached to "private" land. This technical distinction made a great difference. In climbing onto the board the boy had trespassed on the railroad's property. Landowners in New York at the time of the *Hynes* case owed no duty of care to trespassers. But in standing on the end of the board the boy had moved into a "public" space, although his feet were still attached to a board whose base was on private property. Was he still a trespasser, or had he become, by virtue of his position, a bather using the public waterways? If so, the railroad owed him a duty of reasonable protection from injuries caused by the cross-arms of its poles.

Cardozo's opinion in *Hynes* extended the duty of a landowner to cover the boy's injury. The opinion blurred, in the context of the case, the "private space"–"public space" distinction, but it did not obliterate the distinction so completely as to recast the extant categories for determining the liability of landowners. Cardozo achieved this compromise by describing the boy as something other than a "trespasser," despite the fact that in mounting the board the boy had trespassed on the railroad's land.

In the *Nature of the Judicial Process* Cardozo had suggested that the exercise of judicial discretion was to be "informed by tradition, methodized by analogy [and] disciplined by system." [16] In *Hynes* he sought to demonstrate that those constraints were not incompatible with equitable results. The equities in *Hynes* nearly all pointed to recovery against the railroad. The railroad had tolerated the practice of boys diving off a homespun board erected on its land. It had the resources to keep the cross-arms of its utility poles from falling into disrepair. Unsecured cross-arms were extremely dangerous objects, capable of electrocuting bystanders as well as maiming them. The boy was engaging in an activity that, although not without hazards, was one that American culture has regularly condoned, especially among adolescents. The only troublesome equitable feature of the case, from the boy's point of view, was his status as a trespasser. Although a particularly attractive sort of trespasser, especially since he and his companions had been tolerated by the railroad, the boy threatened, through his potential recovery, the shield of protection for land-owners against liability to unknown persons who might intrude on their land. American society has been as indulgent of the autonomy of landowners as it has been of the swimming habits of teenagers.

Thus Cardozo's opinion in *Hynes* was constructed so as to allow recovery without disturbing the status categories that affected the tort liability of landowners. In developing his argument Cardozo did not choose one judicial method over another. Instead he used several methods as techniques for buttressing his reasoning. He used "logic" or "philosophy" through analogy:

> "[t]wo boys . . . stop to rest for a moment along the side of a road or the margin of [a] stream. One of them throws himself beneath the overhanging branches of a tree. The other perches himself on a bough a foot or so above the ground . . . Both are killed by falling wires. The defendant would have us say that there is a remedy for the repre-sentatives of one, and none for the representatives of the other. We may be permitted to distrust the logic that leads to such conclusions." [17]

Logic was thus one justification device of Cardozo's *Hynes* argu-ment; "custom" and "tradition" constituted another. Hynes was essen-tially "a bather," Cardozo maintained; his primary purpose in being on the board was "the enjoyment of the public waters." [18] A tradition of regarding navigable waterways as public property in America united with a custom of allowing persons enjoyment of such water-ways to endow a privileged status on persons who could be designated public bathers. "The rights of bathers," Cardozo argued, "[did] not depend upon . . . nice distinctions" [19] between "public" and "pri-vate" space.

Finally, considerations of "convenience, of fitness, and of justice," associated with Cardozo's method of "sociology," [20] were introduced into the *Hynes* opinion. The expectations of landowners with respect to trespassers and to public travelers were necessarily different. Landowners did not "regulate their conduct in contemplation of the presence of trespassers," but they were required to consider the presence of public travelers. Bright distinctions between trespassers and public travelers did not help in the *Hynes* case, since although the "diver at the end of the springboard [was] an intruder on the adjoining lands . . . he [was] still on public waters in the exercise of public rights." The "law," Cardozo claimed, "must say whether it will subject him to the rule of the one field or of the other." A pragmatic reading of the equities "place[d] him in the field of liability and duty": [21] a duty was owed him, and his representatives could recover against the railroad.

The most striking aspect of *Hynes,* a 4–3 decision, was Cardozo's apparent conviction that the distinctions between categories of persons injured by the negligence of landowners were meaningful and worth preserving, even though nearly useless in the *Hynes* case. While Cardozo linked the categories to " 'a jurisprudence of conceptions,' " [22] and called them "quicksands" [23] as applied to the boy's accident, he never suggested that they be abandoned. In fact he claimed that "there are times when there is little trouble in marking off the field of exemption and immunity [in landowner cases] from that of liability and duty." [24] The categories were "appropriate to spheres which are conceived of as separable and distinct," Cardozo said in *Hynes,* even though they could not "be enforced when the spheres become concentric." [25]

Cardozo's technique of judging, then, was not, as he implied, a picking and choosing among "methods," but rather a use of various justification devices in combination. His "methods" more accurately reflected his conception of how types of legal transactions could be grouped. His use of the methods illustrated his instincts for subtlety and artistry and his recurrent concern with preserving a power in common law judges to be creative. Cardozo's conception of judging was activist, innovative, and as his career progressed, increasingly self-confident. But it was articulated in modes of analysis that deemphasized activism, miminized innovativeness, and suggested that judicial wisdom lay in tentative, measured, incremental decisionmaking. In its self-conscious melding of creativity with contraint Cardozo's view of judging was admirably suited to impress his early twentieth-century contemporaries. He helped make palatable a lawmaking judiciary by suggesting that judicial power necessarily had its boundaries.

Cardozo as Torts Theorist

It remains to consider Cardozo's impact on the doctrinal state of twentieth-century tort law. Cardozo was fortuitously situated to make an impact on common law subjects, being a judge on a visible and prominent state court of last resort at a time when doctrinal uniformity in common law subjects was still regarded as a viable jurisprudential goal. In addition, Cardozo was a common law judge at a time when freedom to be creative was implicitly delegated to the judiciary in common law areas; when judges were regarded as important sources of doctrinal change; and when a symbiotic relationship between the appellate judiciary and a community of legal scholars had developed, personified by such institutions as the American Law Institute. Cardozo thus had opportunities to perform the role of the judge as common law theorist; he was, in addition, personally comfortable in that role.

Previous chapters have traced the gradual maturing of Torts as a discrete common law field, and have discussed the special importance for late nineteenth- and early twentieth-century tort law of the modern negligence principle. By 1914, when Cardozo joined the New York Court of Appeals, the primacy of negligence was well-established and doctrines affiliated with negligence, such as assumption of risk and last clear chance, were firmly in place. At least three aspects of modern negligence law, however, remained troublesome for both judges and scholars. First, the function of causation in negligence law was obscure, and where discernible, ambivalent. Second, a conception of negligence as "a negative duty of very great generality" raised persistent difficulties about the limitations of liability in negligence. Third, the ambit of the negligence principle remained undefined. While judges and commentators seemingly accepted the primacy of negligence, other standards of tort liability existed, and the potential of the negligence principle to intercede into other areas of tort law had not fully been tested. Cardozo was to clarify each of these puzzling aspects of modern negligence.

The *Palsgraf* case, Cardozo's fullest articulation of the role of causation in negligence, has been previously discussed. It is worth repeating at this juncture, however, that the approach adopted by Cardozo in *Palsgraf* tended to reduce causation questions in negligence to inquiries, made by the jury, about the factual connection between a defendant's "careless" act or omission and a plaintiff's injury. Inquiries about the "legal" components of causation were deemphasized: in their place inquiries were made by the judge about whether a given defendant owed a duty to protect a given plaintiff from the risk of the particular injury that had occurred. In Cardozo's analysis judge-controlled standards such as "reasonable foreseeability" and "ambit of risk" replaced ambiguous standards such as "proximity" of causation.

The *Palsgraf* case, as noted, reflected Cardozo's interest in avoiding metaphysical speculations about such matters as "proximity," an interest shared by many of his early twentieth-century contemporaries. It also helped usher in a new approach to negligence issues and a new way of articulating limitations on liability in negligence. This latter dimension of *Palsgraf* invites a comparison between that case and *MacPherson v. Buick.* The Buick Motor Company had argued in *MacPherson* that its duty not to make wheels carelessly was limited by its contractual relations; it did not owe such a duty to "all the world." Cardozo flatly rejected that argument: "we have put aside the notion that duty to safeguard life and limb, when the consequences of negligence may be foreseen, grows out of contract and nothing else." [26] *MacPherson,* at one level, was a "universal duty" case, a case where Cardozo suggested that the negligence principle, at least in the area of supplied goods, was not tied to status or vocation or contract, but was a reflection of generalized civil obligations. "[T]he presence of a known [or foreseeable] danger, attendant upon a known [or foreseeable] use, he said in *MacPherson,* "makes vigilance a duty." [27] Read in this light, *MacPherson* appears as a classic modern negligence case, where a broad universal duty of care is substituted for particularized obligations owed only by certain persons.

In its role as a universal duty case *MacPherson* raised squarely the problem of determining the limits of liability in negligence. The plaintiff in *MacPherson* had not been contributorily negligent, nor had he voluntarily assumed any risks that the car's wheels might be defective. The manufacturer, being a private corporation, could claim no immunities. What prevented countless suits by similarly situated consumers injured by negligently manufactured products? The Buick

Motor Company had alluded to that possibility in *MacPherson,* arguing that extending a duty to supply safe products beyond persons having direct contractual relations with the manufacturer would lead to unlimited liability to remote persons.

Cardozo's opinion in *MacPherson* attempted to meet the unlimited liability argument by articulating three limiting criteria: the "dangerousness" of the product, the "probability" that defective manufacture of a given product would make it dangerous, and the "proximity or remoteness of the relation"[28] between the manufacturer and the person injured. The first two criteria, however, were soon miminized in practice. A "dangerous" product became nearly anything capable of inflicting serious injury, and the "probability" of a defectively made product being dangerous was regularly assumed.[29] Cardozo's third criterion, however, resurfaced in *Palsgraf.* The "relation" between Mrs. Palsgraf and the railroad's employees was arguably "remote." Although Mrs. Palsgraf was a prospective passenger on one of the railroad's trains, she had not boarded the particular train where the fireworks had been dislodged; she was not even in the immediate vicinity. But Cardozo's *Palsgraf* opinion substituted for the language of causation of duty and risk, arguing that the railroad owed no duty to Mrs. Palsgraf, one of its passengers, to protect her from the risk of falling scales on its platforms. Cardozo made this argument despite the fact that the Buick Motor Company owed a duty to Mr. MacPherson, one of its customers, to protect him from the risk of broken wheels.

There are several ways to distinguish *MacPherson* and *Palsgraf* on their facts, but that is not my present concern. My point is rather that the cases, taken together, suggest that by 1928 Cardozo had abandoned all of the criteria for limiting liability in negligence that he had formulated in 1916 in *MacPherson* and substituted another, the "relational" character of negligence itself. Mr. MacPherson bore a relationship to the Buick company such that he was a "foreseeable" victim of a defective wheel. Mrs. Palsgraf's relationship to the Long Island Railroad suggested that she was an "unforeseeable" receipient of an injury from scales felled by an explosion set off by fireworks dislodged from the possession of a person boarding a train. Duties in negligence, Cardozo seemed to be saying in *Palsgraf,* were not universal, but were derived from an evaluation of the relationship between the protagonists. Alternatively, if the duties of motor companies to manufacture their products carefully were "universal," the duties of railroads to protect their prospective passengers from injury were "relational."

The theory of negligence charted by Cardozo from *MacPherson* to *Palsgraf,* then, doubled back on itself. In *MacPherson* Cardozo extracted negligence from a relational context (contract) and identified it with a universal duty of care, subject to vague limitations. In *Palsgraf* he recast negligence in a relational context. The chief limitation on the negligence principle became, once again, its context. A civil obligation to take care not to injure one's neighbor was not limited to certain statuses or occupations, but its existence was nonetheless dependent on the relationship between the prospective obligor and the person he or she had injured. Within a span of twelve years the negligence principle had, theoretically, been dramatically expanded and potentially dramatically limited by the same judge.

While Cardozo was considering limitations on the negligence principle, he was also considering the ambit of its influence. The thrust of late nineteenth-century scholarship in Torts, we have seen, was to favor general standards of liability in tort law and to suggest that of the available generalized standards—one based on intent, one based on modern negligence, and one based on acting at one's peril—the negligence standard was the most central and significant for the field of Torts. Other standards were recognized, however, and on occasion judges were given a choice of treating a given tort claim by one standard or another.

Such a choice was presented to Cardozo in *McFarlane v. City of Niagara Falls.*[30] Employees of the city of Niagara Falls, in constructing a sidewalk, had melted cement irregularly, so that a fanlike projection jutted out about sixteen inches at the junction of the sidewalk and a private driveway. Two or three years after the construction of the sidewalk a woman, who lived in the area and had previously noticed the projection, stumbled against it and injured herself. She sued the city of Niagara Falls, alleging that it had created a public nuisance in constructing the sidewalk and that her injuries were the result of the nuisance.

The alleged public nuisance in *McFarlane* was not the unauthorized construction of the sidewalk—the city itself performed the construction—but the manner in which the sidewalk was constructed. The city in *McFarlane* had arguably committed a nuisance only because of the projection in the sidewalk. And the projection amounted to a "nuisance" only because it created foreseeable risks to prospective users: the nuisance was based on negligence.

Calling the city's act in *McFarlane* a "nuisance" rather than "negligence," however, arguably made a difference. Traditionally in New York the commission of a nuisance, whether public or private, had been treated as an "act-at-peril" tort: the person committing the nuisance was liable to others even if he had taken all available precautions [31] and even if the injured person should have foreseen the risks of injury.[32] While the injured woman in *McFarlane* perhaps should have noticed the projection in the sidewalk (it was dark at the time of her accident) she clearly had not seen it; she was at most contributorily negligent. Earlier cases had intimated that contributory negligence might not be a defense to an action based on nuisance.[33]

Cardozo, however, read those cases and others to yield the following proposition: "Where the substance of the wrong is negligence, a plaintiff, though pleading nuisance, is under a duty to show care proportioned to the danger." [34] The proper inquiry in *McFarlane* was whether the injured woman had used reasonable care in seeking to avoid catching her heel over the sidewalk projection. If she had not, taking into account "the conditions of light and shadow prevailing when she fell," [35] she was contributorily negligent and barred from recovery.

The *McFarlane* opinion was one of Cardozo's best. He combined a skillful reading of relevant precedents, which produced considerable logical momentum for his argument, with a series of careful distinctions intended to shelter the broad proposition he extracted from his limited holding in *McFarlane,* which was to grant a new trial in which the consequences of tripping over a visible but dangerous sidewalk would be clarified. Cardozo made the result in *McFarlane* seem so inexorable and sensible that one might overlook the fact that his opinion sought virtually to eliminate nuisance as a separate category of tort actions.

After *McFarlane* not only were nuisances whose "basis" was negligence to be governed by the ordinary rules of negligence—with its battery of defenses—but other nuisances were not exempted from like treatment. "We are not to be understood," Cardozo said, "as holding by implication that where the nuisance is absolute, the negligence of the traveler is a fact of no account." [36] He then proceeded to examine some additional cases that blurred the line between the defenses of contributory negligence and assumption of risk, and concluded by "leav[ing] the question open whether, in cases of absolute nuisance . . . the test is greatly different." [37]

Nuisance had been an important cause of action in tort law prior to the growth of the negligence principle; [38] it has had something of a renaissance recently in environmentally-based tort suits. [39] But in the golden age of negligence, whose latter years encompassed Cardozo's tenure, nuisance and other pockets of "act at peril" liability were subjected to severe analytical pressure. The ambit of the negligence principle widened and broadened under the guidance of scholars and judges. At the same time the liability-restricting tendencies of negligence were kept firmly in mind.

Like many of Cardozo's innovative decisions, *McFarlane* was a decision restricting potential liability. It was also a decision that preserved uniformity and predictability in tort law even though it apparently changed some rules. The more comprehensive the ambit of the negligence principle in tort law, the less likely would it be that anomalous or contradictory standards of tort liability would coexist. The more often litigants in a tort case could anticipate the set of rules that would be governing their conduct, the more skillfully might they plan their affairs. Thus in calling Cardozo an innovative judge one should recall that his innovations were not inconsistent with the jurisprudential goals of late nineteenth-century scholars. Cardozo did not think of himself as a "scientist" but rather as an artist. He joined early twentieth-century reformist contemporaries in criticizing "mechanical" conceptualism. But an important thrust of his Torts decisions was the formulation of general principles designed to promote intellectual order and coherence.

The maturity of Cardozo as a judge paralleled the maturity of Torts as a common law subject, resulting, in the late stages of Cardozo's tenure, in opinions that drew upon the theoretical insights of scholars and at times improved upon them. But if Cardozo's career was one of gradually increasing success and influence, there were flashes of frustration. One source of such episodes was Cardozo's abiding interest in preserving the moral values he saw as foundations for tort law and other common law subjects. Felicitously situated in so many respects, Cardozo found himself somewhat out of phase with his contemporaries where moral issues were concerned. He firmly believed in the sanctity of moral codes of conduct, but his judicial tenure took place at a time when that belief was being seriously called into question.[40] He was convinced that material progress and morality could be self-reinforcing, and that American society need not become less honorable as it became more affluent,[41] but he witnessed among his contemporaries disenchantment with unregulated capitalism and skepticism about the validity of time-honored moral values.[42]

As the modern negligence principle came to be applied in early twentieth-century tort law, its sources in morality were increasingly ambiguous. Fault was a cornerstone of modern negligence, but scholars and judges quickly made a distinction between "legal" and "moral" fault, a paradigmatic example being the absence of any affirmative duty to help one's neighbor, however morally heinous failure to help seemed. A drowning person could be let drown with impunity; only a botched rescue attempt precipitated a potential negligence claim.

Despite presumptions among early twentieth-century scholars that fault was to be treated as a legal rather than a moral concept and that the standard for liability in negligence was to be "objective" rather than "subjective," the capacity for tort law also to serve as an instrument for the preservation of morality was implicitly recognized.[43] Nowhere was this recognition clearer than in the theory of common law judging articulated by Cardozo. Judges, in Cardozo's theory, were interest-balancers, exercising their limited creative powers for the benefit of others in an interdependent society. Interest balancing allowed the judge's own perceptions of fairness and justice to surface; while those perceptions could not be his only guide to decision, they could be a factor in the decision-making process. It might have been illegitimate for a judge to decide a case on the basis of *his* standards of morality, but it was not illegitimate for him to decide on the basis of *community* standards of morality as *he* interpreted them. Thus armed, Cardozo set forth to do battle for the moral principles in which he believed.

Negligence, with its slippery standards of "fault" and "reasonableness," was not to constitute Cardozo's moral battleground in the law of torts. He reserved that place for the law of misrepresentation, or "deceit," whose very name suggested a more morally charged context. The law of misrepresentation, during Cardozo's tenure, was affected, as were other areas of tort law, by the expansion of the negligence principle. Nineteenth-century common law rules governing misrepresentations had reflected the conceptions of commerce then prevailing. Implicit distinctions between the ethics of "business practices" and the ethics of other spheres of life had been made, so that in commercial relations one was given a greater leeway to make misrepresentations without suffering legal consequences. Moreover, the prevailing nineteenth-century model of a commercial transaction was a two-party exchange, so that, despite the increasingly multiplex character of commerce in the late nineteenth century, the effect on third parties of misrepresentations made by one person to another was not reflected in common law doctrines. Finally, misrepresentation was treated as a category of torts distinct from negligence: its rules were thought to govern intentional efforts to deceive as well as careless misstatements.[44]

The growth of modern negligence had an effect on each of these features of the law of misrepresentation. Through negligence decisions such as *MacPherson,* liability for careless acts that resulted in physical injury had been extended for the benefit of third persons. In addition, the liability in negligence of commercial enterprises was not treated differently from the liability of private persons. The capacity of unintentional acts or omissions to give rise to tort liability was, of course, a cornerstone of the modern negligence principle. If "careless" acts that led to physical injury were compensated through actions in negligence, why should not careless acts that led to economic loss be similarly compensated? Twentieth-century developments in negligence, in short, offered powerful analogies for the law of misrepresentation. In the course of investigating those analogies, scholars "discovered" that many misrepresentations were "negligent" rather than intentional; that on numerous occasions misrepresentations made to one party affected others; and that bright lines between "commerce" and other aspects of life—or between the jurisdictional boundaries of "contract" and "tort" law—were breaking down.[45]

Cardozo approached misrepresentation cases with two apparent goals in mind. One was to revise common law rules that he perceived as having been rendered inadequate by the insights of modern negligence law; the second was to insure that misrepresentation doctrines reflected commendable standards of morality. The goals did not always complement one another, and their coexistence in Cardozo's thought produced some of his most strained opinions.

Glanzer v. Shepard,[46] a 1922 opinion, was reminiscent of *MacPherson.* Cardozo's opinion potentially signalled a dramatic extension of liability; his argument was principally based on a selective reading of prior authorities; a broad statement of principle was accompanied by careful qualifications; the opinion's effect was to broaden and deepen the ambit of the negligence principle. *Glanzer* involved an erroneous certification by public weighers of the weight of a shipment of beans. Both the seller of the beans and the buyer were in the business of buying and selling vegetables. As part of the ordinary course of their business, shipments of beans were weighed at the request of the seller, who then paid for the shipments in accordance with their weight. Public weighers hired by the buyers provided the sellers with a copy of a document certifying the weight of the beans. On one occasion the weighers erroneously certified the weight of the beans to be 11,854 pounds more than it actually was. The buyers consequently overpaid the sellers and ultimately sued the weighers for a refund of the amount of the money they had overpaid.

Glanzer was thus analogous to *MacPherson,* the contractual relationship between the weighers and the seller resembling that between the Buick Motor Company and its dealer. As in *MacPherson,* Cardozo maintained that "[w]e do not need to state the [weighers'] duty in terms of contract or of privity. Growing out of a contract, it has nonetheless an origin not exclusively contractual. Given the contract and the relation, the duty is imposed by law." [47] He then cited the *MacPherson* case. But *Glanzer,* of course, differed from *MacPherson* in a significant respect: the injury complained of was economic loss, not physical injury. Moreover, no previous case in New York had allowed recovery for negligent misrepresentations relied on by third persons. Cardozo, by stressing the "independent calling" of the weighers,[48] by analogy to third-party contracts,[49] and with a citation to one of Bohlen's early articles,[50] simply brushed aside contrary precedent. A duty of "diligence" on the part of the weighers, he asserted, was owed "not only to him who ordered, but to him also who relied." [51]

Glanzer suggested that the negligence principle had made significant inroads into the law of misrepresentation. In cases where members of an "independent calling" owed a duty to represent things accurately to those who could show reliance on their representations, *Glanzer* intimated that recovery in negligence would result even if the injury suffered was merely economic losses. Or so it seemed until Cardozo's opinion in *Ultramares v. Touche,*[52] decided nine years after *Glanzer.*

Between Glanzer and *Ultramares* the Court of Appeals had followed a curious course in three-party negligent misrepresentation cases, extending liability only sporadically, confining its results to specific facts, and, on one occasion, maintaining that *Glanzer* itself should be so confined.[53] Cardozo had written none of those opinions; in *Ultramares* he assigned the case to himself.

Ultramares seemed a mere variation of *Glanzer*. A firm of public accountants had been hired by Fred Stern & Co., a corporation, to prepare a report on its financial condition. The accountants produced a certified statement of audit, representing the condition of Stern & Co. and attaching a balance sheet. Thirty-two copies of the statement, signed by the accountants, were made for potential distribution to interested parties. One such party, the Ultramares Corporation, loaned money to Stern & Co. on the basis of the accountant's statement. The statement was erroneous in that it listed about $900,000 of assets, including one item of $706,000 for "accounts receivable," that Stern & Co. did not possess. Without those assets Stern & Co. was insolvent. Stern & Co. subsequently went into bankruptcy; Ultramares Corporation sued the accountants in both fraud and negligence for its losses.

Cardozo held that if the accountants' actions amounted merely to a negligent misrepresentation, they were not liable to Ultramares Corporation. If, however, their actions could be found by a jury to constitute a fraudulent misrepresentation, liability would ensue. His holding was highly ambivalent and his accompanying opinion was opaque. The case can be seen as an illustration of Cardozo's sense of the inadequacy of the negligence principle as a moral force. *perhaps*

Cardozo's principal reason for denying recovery for a negligent misrepresentation in *Ultramares* was his fear of unlimited liability. "If liability for negligence exists," he claimed, "a thoughtless slip or blunder . . . may expose accountants to a liability in an indeterminate amount for an indeterminate time to an indeterminate class."[54] Moreover, if liability in negligence were upheld in *Ultramares,* it would "extend to many callings other than an auditor's." The most frightening possibility was that "[l]awyers who certify their opinion as to the validity of municipal or corporate bonds" would become "liable to the investors if they have overlooked a statute or a decision."[55]

But was the "indeterminacy" of the accountant's potential liability so clear? The accountants, after all, had made thirty-two copies of their statement: they expected it would be distributed to others. Further, they knew that the primary purpose of the statement was to induce third parties to rely on the solvency of Stern & Co. Finally, the statement spoke only to the financial condition of Stern & Co.; it was not a comprehensive description of that company's business activities. Limited classes of persons—investors, Stern & Co. stockholders, creditors and prospective traders—would find meaning in the statement. If "the risk reasonably to be perceived" defined "the duty to be obeyed" and "risk import[ed] relation," then the relation between the accountants and the Ultramares Corporation would seem sufficiently close and foreseeable as to create a duty in the accountants to avoid errors of $900,000 on the statement on which the Ultramares Corporation and others interested in Stern & Co.'s solvency could be expected to rely. That class of persons might be numerous, but not indeterminate.

In addition, Cardozo's effort to distinguish *Ultramares* from *Glanzer* was subtle to the point of being obscure. He argued that "the service rendered by the defendant in *Glanzer v. Shepard* was primarily for the information of a third person . . . and only incidentally for that of [the sellers of the beans]." In *Ultramares,* by contrast, "the service was primarily for the benefit of the Stern Company." [56] That distinction was specious. The weighing of the beans in *Glanzer* was an essential part of the transaction for *both* parties: the seller needed to know how much to charge, the buyer how much to pay. And, as noted, the financial statement prepared in *Ultramares* was not primarily for the use of Stern & Co. but for others. Cardozo attempted to use the word "benefit" in a slippery fashion: Stern & Co. may have "benefited" from the preparation of the statement, but only if others had the benefit of seeing it.

One may wonder why Cardozo, who was zealous to uphold morality in business practices, apparently tolerated such an egregious misrepresentation in *Ultramares.* The answer is that he did not. He merely argued that such misrepresentations were not successfully punished through the negligence principle, the extent of whose liability needed to be limited. The accountants in *Ultramares,* he suggested, might nonetheless be found to have made a "reckless" misrepresentation which amounted to fraud. And if so, liability to the Ultramares Corporation would ensue. This suggestion was as puzzling as his earlier efforts to distinguish the *Glanzer* case.

The accountants, Cardozo conceded, had not deliberately represented that Stern & Co. possessed approximately $900,000 more in assets than it in fact did. But they perhaps had had such an easy opportunity to discover the fictitious nature of the item for $706,000 for "accounts receivable"—merely by checking Stern & Co.'s "books of original entry" against its "general ledger"—that their failure to discover the fictitious item amounted to gross negligence.[57] It was possible, therefore, that the accountants' audit had been "so negligent as to justify a finding that they had no genuine belief in its accuracy." Gross negligence, "even when not equivalent to fraud," was "nonetheless evidence to sustain an inference of fraud." A jury might therefore find, Cardozo concluded, that "in certifying to the correspondence between balance sheet and accounts" the accountants had "made a statement as true to their own knowledge when they had . . . no knowledge on the subject." [58] Such a jury finding would constitute fraud and give rise to liability.

But why should the fraud principle allow recovery to third persons in the *Ultramares* context when the negligence principle did not? And why should a negligent misrepresentation that was held insufficient for liability to a third person be allowed to form the basis for a fraud action at all? Cardozo's *Ultramares* opinion gave no answers. The *Ultramares* case thus stood for one highly questionable proposition and one unsupported pronouncement. The proposition was that while the negligent misrepresentations of professional weighers subjected them to liability to third persons, the negligent misrepresentations of accountants did not. The pronouncement was that while the negligent misrepresentations of accountants did not subject them to liability to third persons in negligence, those misrepresentations, if "gross" enough, could subject them to liability to third persons in fraud. This last pronouncement was not only unsupported but represented a departure from prior case law, which had limited liability for unintentional or reckless misrepresentations to persons who were parties to the original transaction. The extension of liability that Cardozo had refused to make in negligence he willingly made in fraud.

The tensions in Cardozo's *Ultramares* opinion stemmed from the ambivalence with which he approached its facts. Cardozo was anxious to deter and even to punish civil conduct he regarded as immoral, tort law serving as his principal weapon. Nevertheless, he was concerned about the expansive potential of negligence, the leading principle of early twentieth-century tort law. Consequently in *Ultramares* he avoided using negligence to chastize conduct that he viewed as possibly reprehensible, thereby preserving limits on the negligence principle, and chose instead to allow a jury to chastize the conduct through fraud.

Ultramares was, from this perspective, part of a sequence of Cardozo decisions that tightened the liability rules for fraudulent conduct. An agent could not profit at the expense of his principal by taking advantage of confidential information imparted to him during his agency.[59] A person undertaking a "joint enterprise" with another was to be considered, with respect to jointly acquired property, a "constructive trustee" for the other's benefit, even though a small amount of the property was purchased in the enterprise.[60] And a case for fraudulent misrepresentation was made out when a seller of land revealed the existence of two minor encumbrances on the land and failed to mention a third major one.[61] Once fraud was established, the stigma of moral blame could attach; once it attached, defenses developed in connection with the negligence principle were inconsequential. The moral ambiguity of negligence was replaced by the moral righteousness of fraud.

Yet the law of misrepresentation contained elements of both fraud and negligence, just as the law of nuisance was a hybrid of negligence and strict liability. Cardozo dissected the hybrid qualities of nuisance, but failed to perform a comparable dissection of misrepresentation. At one time Cardozo had sought a "certainty" in tort law that he eventually abandoned; similarly, a uniform, unchanging code of moral conduct did not seem capable of being reflected in the law of torts. Tort law, as dominated by the negligence principle, revealed itself to Cardozo and his contemporaries as an amorphous, evolving mass, its status as a moral force ambiguous and ephemeral.[62] The *Glanzer-Ultramares* sequence reveals Cardozo struggling with that insight.

Cardozo's impact on tort law was, I have suggested, primarily that of the theoretician. He was, to be sure, a judge as well as a jurist: he did not confine his thinking about Torts to law review articles, treatises, or Restatements. As a judge he had more opportunity to apply theory to actual disputes than did, say, Bohlen or Green or Harper. But he made his major impact on the course of twentieth-century tort law not so much in the mass of his decisions but in the theoretical perspective his opinions revealed. That perspective treated Torts as a bundle of creatively derived general principles, capable of continued creative development. The leading such principle was negligence, whose influence Cardozo regarded as established but whose nature he viewed as capable of reinterpretation. In *MacPherson, Palsgraf,* and his numerous other important negligence opinions Cardozo demonstrated that the negligence principle and its attendant concepts and doctrines—duty, causation, contributory negligence, last clear chance, and so on—could change to reflect altered attitudes and values.

Yet the intellectual motivation for change in tort law was linked, in Cardozo's thought, to a search for continuity, uniformity, and predictability in common law subjects. One reexamined and reformulated causation theory because one wanted to make the concept of "legal" or "proximate" cause more comprehensible and useful in application, and one wanted judges, where possible, to be the appliers as well as the formulators. One developed a "relational" view of negligence because the terms "relation" and "risk" seemed to capture common elements of most negligence cases and seemed therefore more conducive to the achievement of conceptual uniformity. One searched for the extent and limits of the negligence principle because understanding its ambit facilitated the orderly classification and categorization of law. And one accepted the amorphous and fluid character of the subject of Torts because that acceptance supposedly helped distinguish Torts from other more regularized common law areas.

Cardozo's theoretical perspective on Torts reflected his conceptions of judging and his personal values, which often fused but sometimes stood side by side in an awkward coexistence. Cardozo's sense that tort law was a repository of general principles harmonized with his strong interest, as a judge, in the creative derivation of rules intended to have broad application. The task of deriving generalizations required, given the jurisprudential climate of Cardozo's tenure, subtle distinctions, a skillful marshalling of precedents, and a tone of expression that was neither too assertive nor too candid. The strengths of Cardozo's mind were often exhibited in his efforts to meet those requirements. Moreover, the theoretical perspective Cardozo applied to tort issues reflected a balance between tradition and innovation that suited his temperament. Tort law for Cardozo was neither a collection of static rules to be mechanically applied nor the aggregate of idiosyncratic decisions by individual judges. Torts was a field peculiarly susceptible to interest-balancing, the juxtaposition of antinomies, the attempted fusion of continuity and change, and the interspersion of general doctrines with particularized fact situations.[63] As such Torts was an admirable testing ground for Cardozo's conception of the proper role of the early twentieth-century common law judge.

But Cardozo's considerable talents as a judge did not entirely shield him from the inherent contradictions embedded in his characterization of tort law. Difficulties posed by the relationship of broad generalizations to their particularized application, which troubled advocates of "realism" in tort theory, also troubled Cardozo. The promise of the negligence principle was clouded by fears about its unsettling effect on other areas of tort law with different standards of liability. Cardozo's opinions did not entirely alleviate such fears. The apparently fluid nature of Torts sometimes permitted creativity and innovation, but other times offended Cardozo's interest in preserving some traditional values he believed in. On occasion, in the course of facing one or more of these contradictions, his opinions lost their remarkable fusion of methodology, style, and outcome and became obscure or strained or dogmatic.

On balance, however, Cardozo not only successfully applied the theoretical insights of his contemporaries to tort cases, he developed and refined those insights. None of his most influential opinions— *MacPherson, Hynes, McFarlane, Palsgraf*—has endured in the sense of representing the current wisdom on their subjects. But their diminished influence can be traced to the emergence of alternative theoretical frameworks for allocating liability in torts that have reduced the primacy of the negligence principle. In the period of his tenure Cardozo's best efforts were classics, reorienting early twentieth-century tort theory without fundamentally disturbing its startling assumptions.

The narrative now turns to issues in twentieth-century tort law that Cardozo's theoretical perspective did not contemplate. By 1932 Cardozo had been a judge for sixteen years, had fully developed his thinking, and had disassociated himself from the more distinctive and controversial aspects of Realism.[64] He was, in short, beginning to "place himself" in time. By 1945 the theoretical perspectives of the most reformist-minded Realists in the 1930s were seen as possessing their own limitations; yet another phase in the intellectual history of tort law was surfacing. As Realism itself diminished in influence Cardozo, who had died in 1938, assumed the sanctification and the remoteness of a historical personage.

5

William Prosser, Consensus Thought, and the Nature of Tort Law, 1945–1970

The Emergence of Consensus Thought

One has the sense, on surveying the writings of legal scholars and judges in the 1930s and 1940s, that in those decades American legal thought quickened its pace, increased its intensity, and lost its sense of direction. The doctrinal perspective on legal issues developed and refined by the scientists had been severely challenged by Realism: in the most powerful critiques launched by Realists doctrine appeared as an artificial smoke screen. Yet no competitive perspective on thinking and writing about legal subjects had fully emerged. Realists talked, some eloquently, of the "functional approach," but "functionalism," as numerous scholars pointed out, seemed incapable of formulating a comprehensive analytical framework that trained professionals could use in thinking about legal problems.

Militant Realists conceded the absence of any analytical comprehensiveness in a "functional approach"; argued that maturity and wisdom came with the recognition that legal issues were endlessly diverse, complex, and fluid; scorned certainty and predictability as ends of the legal system; and seemingly denied that there was any recurrent set of analytical problems that could be called peculiarly "legal" and thereby be made part of a "taught tradition" [1] of professional training. In holding these positions Realists invited polemical exchange, and in the 1940s, especially, polemics emerged, with scholars accusing advocates of Realism of being nihilists, atheists, and totalitarian sympathizers. From the early 1930s, when Pound and Cardozo mildly chastised some philosophical positions associated

139

with Realism,[2] to the middle 1940s, when polemical attacks on Realists claimed to be exercises in patriotism,[3] American legal thought
seemed, as Lon Fuller said in 1940, to be "in quest of itself." [4]

But when academicians returned to full-time teaching and research
after the Second World War, certain subtle shifts in legal thought
appeared to have taken place. Legal scholars seemed to have implicitly agreed upon an altered set of starting philosophical assumptions from which to conduct their teaching and research. Unlike the
intellectual shifts that had taken place during the knowledge revolution of the late nineteenth century, those taking place at the close of
the Second World War did not constitute dramatic breaks with the
recent past. Nor did the new startling assumptions of postwar professional scholars represent a break with the past comparable to that
represented by the emergence of Realism. The dominant thrust of
postwar legal thought was derivative and incorporative; previous assumptions were modified rather than rejected; the insights of Realism,
although sometimes caricatured, were not widely abandoned. Nonetheless legal scholarship after 1945 took on discernibly new dimensions.

The character of American legal thought after the Second World
War was shaped by responses to the principal philosophical dilemmas
associated with Realism. By the close of the war, we have seen, three
such dilemmas had crystallized. One involved the linkage of Realism
to moral relativism, conceded by some Realists and explicitly attacked
by polemical critics of Realism. If a Realist perspective on jurisprudence denied the capacity of law to serve as a repository of timeless moral values, how could the Realists justify their preference for
one legal sytsem (the democratic, egalitarian, and "humane" system
of America) over another (the totalitarian, autocratic, and genocidal
system of Nazi Germany)? How could one be a thoroughgoing "func-
tionalist"—eschewing what "ought to be" for what "really was"—and
yet affirm one's belief in law as a means of preserving a "free society"?

Many Realists, as noted, retreated in the face of this criticism,
principally by affirming their patriotism and modifying their insistence
that ethics and morals be separated from law.[5] That retreat implicitly
signified the renaissance in American jurisprudence of "consensus"
thought: a search for core values or basic principles around which
lawmakers might cohere. Some comparable searches had occurred at
the height of Realism's influence, but Cardozo, for example, had conceded in 1928 that using law to erect a hierarchy of values was futile

and that for every "basic" principle existed its opposite.[6] By the close of the Second World War the appeal of such fatalism had been exhausted. To be a thinking and feeling American meant to deny that totalitarian regimes could be regarded as the mere embodiment of current morality. If one could say that one "knew" the policies of the Nazis to be morally wrong, one should be in a position to affirm the sources of that conviction. Understanding the values and principles embodied in the American legal system became associated with understanding the values and principles that distinguished "free" America from totalitarian regimes.

A search for unifying principles in American law highlighted a second dilemma inherent in Realism. A principle seized upon by scholars participating in that search was rationality. American law was based on "reason" rather than "fiat": among the sources of its rationality were an obligation in lawmaking officials, especially judges, to give published justifications for their decisions; the opportunities for political checks on official decisions created by an elective system; and the separation of lawmaking powers among competitive branches of government.[7] But the identification of rationality as a core value in American law exposed a potential contradiction in Realist thought. Realists simultaneously held a faith in affirmative government as a beneficial social force and a conviction that official lawmakers were as inclined as any other humans toward irrational judgments. If rationality, either in the professional sense of intellectually defensible justifications for legal decisions or in the political sense of a power in the general public periodically to replace the decisionmakers, was a distinguishing feature of American law, how could one be fatalistic about irrational judgments? And if the common sense of the behavioral sciences required one to accept irrationality in public officials, why should one have any confidence in affirmative government?

Thus a search for core values embodied by the American legal system led to a further search for methods to insure that one such value, rationality, be preserved. Since rationality had both professional and political connotations, methods proposed by scholarly participants after 1945 sometimes focused on the obligations of politically insulated lawmakers (judges and to a lesser degree administrative agencies) to give professionally acceptable justifications for their decisions, and sometimes focused on the obligations of politically exposed lawmakers (legislatures and to a lesser degree the executive) to insure that their decisions were being adequately scrutinized by the public at large. Irrationality was checked, therefore, by a process of communication. Obligations to provide formal justifications for one's decisions or to insure that interested parties would be able to scrutinize the decisionmakers were based on an assumption that a process of exchange between lawmakers and their constituents would maintain rationality in the legal system. The existence of professional or political processes whereby lawmakers would be able to establish to constituents the rationality of their decisions became, for some scholars, a value in itself. The ultimate content of legal decisions became less important than the processes that produced them.[8]

But the identification of rationality as a core value of American law and the maintenance of communication processes to preserve rational decisions did not solve a third dilemma of Realism: a tension between the general and the particular in Realist thought. While advocates of Realism had been embarrassed by the potential affinity of moral relativism to totalitarianism, and perhaps also by a contrast between the ideal of rationality in a democracy and the irrational "fiats" of the Nazis, no element of their thought had caused them greater practical difficulties than their insistence that generalized doctrines and principles were meaningless except in their particularized application. For in that description of the relationship between the general and the particular in law Realists seemed to be denying the existence of any solid body of rules in the legal system. Generalized doctrines were merely "paper" rules, and "real" rules apparently could not be generalized beyond the immediacy of a given result.

No leading Realist went so far to deny that any general theory of legal decisionmaking could be advanced. The "functional" approach of several Realists, in fact, explicitly propounded a general theory: law was shaped by social and economic conditions. To understand a legal decision, one asked what social and economic function it performed, what "interests" in society it protected or compensated or penalized or taxed. The theory's predictive value, however, was limited, because although one could often roughly discern in advance what "interests" were at stake in a given controversy, one could not easily predict how an individual judge or legislator or administrator would "balance" those interests. Hence the Realists advocated close, detailed studies of the behavior patterns of judges and other lawmakers, so that perhaps the function of a legal decision could be ascertained in advance.[9] Such studies, while initially undertaken with enthusiasm by many advocates of Realism, proved, in their completion, singularly lacking in interest or influence.[10]

The problem was that by denying the meaningfulness of legal doctrine the Realists had abandoned the basic subject matter of the common law and, since the late nineteenth century, the primary focus of legal education. If doctrines were meaningless as general propositions, the common law had no capacity for guidance, no continuity, and no modes of common discourse. Even if guidance was a sham and continuity an illusion, a jurisprudence that could supply no alternative mode whereby professionals communicated with one another was unlikely to be well received by the legal profession. Realists sought to incorporate such modes in their functional approach. But their critics pointed out that if legal doctrines only had meaning in their particular application, the same could be said of social theories. Why, then, was a theory of law based on its social and economic functions preferable to a theory of law based on the declared content of its rules? The latter might be based on fictions, but the former might be based on unproven hypotheses.

Thus postwar legal scholars conducted still another intellectual search, whose object was a more effective integration of the levels of generality and particularity in law. The emphasis of this search was on refining professional techniques of analysis. Scholars focused on the nature of legal reasoning,[11] the different devices used by courts, legislatures, and agencies to justify their decisions,[12] and the character of craftsmanship in the legal profession.[13] They examined the effect of a crowded docket on the capacity of the Supreme Court to produce "reasoned" decisions;[14] they analyzed techniques by which the Court could postpone full-blown resolution of controversial issues;[15] they identified "steadying factors" in appellate judging;[16] and they argued that appellate courts, especially the Supreme Court, had an obligation to justify their decisions in Constitutional cases by appeal to "neutral principles" of law, which translated itself as principles of sufficient generality to divorce the decision from its particularized social context.[17]

Each of these scholarly efforts, which appeared from the 1940s through the 1960s, can be seen as attempts to integrate generality and particularity in law through a precise analysis of the level at which a given decision was intending to communicate. Such an analysis required a sophisticated awareness of the nature of rationality in law and of the institutional contexts of legal decisions.\ Judges, for example, had an obligation to give reasons supporting the results they reached, but their reasons functioned on different levels. Some reasons justified the narrow holding; other reasons generalized the result in a limited fashion (dicta); still others were added as emotional weight and their generalized significance was uncertain (obiter dicta). Legislatures had different obligations. Although the reasoning justifying statutes could be less precise, statutory language needed to be broader and wider in scope; its particularization was for a future time. If one continued this analysis throughout the legal system—asking what type of institution was making a decision and at what level the decision was communicating—one could, ideally, resolve the tension between the general and the particular in law.

As stated, the above inquiry about techniques of reasoning seemed largely descriptive: one simply asked how courts and legislatures and agencies were communicating their decisions. But normative consequences were not far from the surface. Not only was an investigation of techniques of legal reasoning founded on the assumption that rationality was a core value of the American legal system, the thrust of legal scholarship after the Second World War was increasingly toward the view that the maintenance of rationality in legal discourse required certain obligations on the part of lawmakers. Judging was more effective if results were grounded on "neutral principles"; if no such principles existed, the scope of a judicial decision should be sharply curtailed.[18] Legislating was more effective if legislators openly conveyed the purposes of legislation, so that subsequent interpreters of statutes (agencies, courts, or private parties) could tie a specific application to a generalized purpose. Courts ought to do what they could do well (reason through appeals to general principles of law) and not what they could not do effectively (balance political interests). Legislatures and agencies, likewise, should make decisions within the ambit of their competence.[19] "Craftsmanship," therefore, involved more than technical skill; it involved conforming to a tacitly assumed model of how various lawmakers in the American legal system should interact.

The orientation of this perspective toward consensual thinking is readily apparent. American society and its institutions were assumed to be capable of cohering around basic values; law could have an "inner morality." [20] An ideal of rationality and the pursuit of techniques to further its presence were affirmed in the face of the irrational dimensions of human behavior. A seemingly insoluble tension in law between abstract general guidelines and indeterminate particular decisions was alleviated by careful analysis of the processes by which decisions were made and justified. The dilemmas of Realism were "solved" by a combination of improved professional techniques and renewed attention to the common bonds of American civilization.

The refinements of Realism that occurred in the 1940s reflected a general tendency in mid-twentieth-century American thought to emphasize the continuing and distinctive features and values of American culture. Some of these features or values had been recently "discovered"; they were recognizable, in fact, as offshoots of early twentieth-century reformist thought. But by the Second World War features such as pluralism, interdependence, and social flux had come to be perceived as familiar characteristics of life in America, and the values of modern liberalism—humanitarian policymaking, professional specialization, faith in affirmative governmental action—had become orthodoxies. Historians argued that "liberalism" had been a widely shared American ideology from the founding of the Republic; [21] political scientists claimed that the task of governing in America repeatedly had been a task in accommodating the diverse interests of a pluralistic society; [22] sociologists, psychologists, and literary critics maintained that a "natural character," an American "identity," and an "archetypal American" existed. [23]

"Consensus" thinking was thus a characteristic of intellectual life in the mid-twentieth century; ascribing to law an inherent rationality and an "inner morality" and developing a spate of professional techniques of analysis consistent with those qualities were invitations to legal scholars to think consensually. But a "consensus" jurisprudence seemed quixotic for a profession whose stock in trade was advocacy and whose scholarship had regularly been expressed in argumentative modes. In Torts scholarship, especially, the development of intellectual consensus seemed strikingly lacking in promise. There was first the perceived nature of the subject. Torts, by the Second World War, had been pictured for at least a decade in casebook and treatise literature as a shapeless mass; its leading principle, negligence, as inherently variegated and fluid; its rules in a constant state of change; its boundaries uncertain. Few subjects seemed as relativistic, as susceptible to intuitive, emotional decisionmaking, or as incapable of being made orderly and coherent. Or so Torts appeared in Realist literature.[24]

Moreover, Torts scholars in the Realist years had seemingly labored to avoid consensus thinking. The gap between the intellectual assumptions of the framers of the Restatement of Torts and those of functionalists seemed unbridgeable; while Bohlen and Green shared a few common convictions, their disagreements were numerous and profound. Beyond those disagreements lay competing approaches to tort law: a doctrinal approach, personified by Bohlen and other modified conceptualists; a functional approach, personified by Green; and the origins of a third approach, hinted at in writings in the 1930s and 1940s by Charles Gregory, Albert Ehrenzweig, and Fleming James, that argued for a basic reorientation of tort theory in which negligence would play a far less central role.[25] Torts, at the close of the Second World War, seemed a field highly unlikely to be influenced by the emergence of consensus thought.

Yet in an indirect fashion the intellectual developments of the postwar years were to stimulate a scholarly reevaluation of the nature of tort law. The contribution of mid-twentieth-century consensus thought to the intellectual history of Torts cannot easily be compared to the contributions of conceptualism or Realism. The new postwar perspectives, as noted, modified Realism rather than sharply challenging it; although scholars sought to resolve philosophical contradictions in Realist thought, they did not wholly abandon its assumptions. While changes from conceptualist to Realist perspectives are dramatically apparent in Torts literature, the influx of consensus thought reveals itself more subtly. Nonetheless mid-twentieth-century consensus thought had a considerable impact on Torts scholarship.

Consensus Thought and the Purposes of Tort Law

The primary consequence for tort law of the emergence of consensus thought was a revived interest in doctrine. As doctrinal analysis came again to be regarded as a source of rationality, predictability, and continuity in tort law and other common law subjects, a basic scholarly debate over the nature and purposes of tort law resurfaced. Hints of the debate's thrust were present early in the 1930s; after the Second World War its issues became clearer. The debate's central issue would be whether tort law best functioned primarily as an instrument for admonishing currently undesirable civil conduct or whether tort law ought primarily to be a means for compensating injured people. An assessment of the ramifications of this issue and its relation to mid-twentieth-century American thought requires attention to the emergence of liability insurance as a factor in twentieth-century tort law.

Few features of the history of twentieth-century American law more clearly illustrate the triumph of reformist thought than the massive infiltration of liability insurance into the field of Torts. As originally conceived in the late nineteenth century, liability insurance was a device to indemnify employers against the risk of lawsuits from employees. It was thought of as a contractual relationship between employers and insurers that had no direct consequences for third parties. If an employee was injured during his job, he could, where common law or statutes permitted him, recover in tort against his employer. As the number of permissible recoveries increased, primarily through protective legislation, employers responded by indemnifying themselves.[26] Standard liability insurance contracts of the late nineteenth century provided that an insurer's settlement with an employer would not be made until the employer had actually compensated an employee. In the event that compensation was not made, employees were not permitted to sue insurance companies directly. The Supreme Court of Massachusetts declared in 1902, the last year of Holmes's chief justiceship, that "insurance [is] a matter wholly between the [insurance] company and [the insured] in which [third parties] [have] no legal or equitable interest." [27]

By the 1930s, however, a strikingly different conception of liability insurance had surfaced. The presence of liability insurance was now regarded as creating an opportunity to compensate injured parties in Torts suits. Several examples of this altered conception can be noted. Early twentieth-century commentators began to articulate the risk-distribution potential of tort law and to criticize court decisions that ignored the potential effects of two-party insurance contracts on third parties.[28] Some courts, through the creation of ingenious fictions, prevented insurance companies from conditioning payment on an insured's prior satisfaction of a tort claim against him.[29] State statutes mandated similar restrictions on insurance companies, and in 1925 the Supreme Court sustained the constitutionality of such legislation.[30] Louisiana and Wisconsin, the former by statute and the latter by

judicial decision, allowed injured parties to proceed directly against
insurance companies where persons who had tortiously injured them
possessed liability insurance.[31]

In 1930 a commentator speculated on such developments:

> "The 'humanitarian' social conscience of today is apparently much
> more concerned with the poor one who gets injured by our modern
> devices than was the social conscience of the Victorian period. . . .
> [T]he social concept of what is the end or purpose of law seems to be
> changing . . . as . . . judgments are given in favor of plaintiffs who
> have suffered harm through the operations and activities of other per-
> sons or groups, and who are enabled in this way to shift the burden of
> the loss incurred." [32]

That comment demonstrated a nascent awareness that a new conception of the role of insurance in tort law was tied to a changed attitude
toward the social consequences of civil injuries. Holmes had, in 1880,
identified and rejected the very attitude that had emerged. A paternalistic state, rather than letting losses "lie where they fell," was
intervening, through its lawmaking officials, to distribute losses among
society generally, with the criteria for distribution being prevailing
notions of efficiency or fairness. Liability insurance had come to be
conceived of as the principle mechanism for distributing losses in tort
law. A tort suit was no longer a two-party affair, whose costs were
imposed on one or the other of the participants, but a "three-party
affair," in which the third party was society at large. Such a conception of tort law assumed that American society was an interdependent
entity in which the misfortunes of one person affected others. That
assumption was fundamental to early twentieth-century reformist
thought.

The dramatic emergence of liability insurance in familiar areas of
twentieth-century tort law, such as accidents caused by manufacturers
or suppliers of products, would not have been possible without the
emergence of a theory that the central purpose of tort law was to
compensate injured persons. For if one began with the late nineteenth-
century assumption that civil injuries lay where they fell unless the
person committing the injury was blameworthy, one viewed the
central purpose of tort law as admonishing blameworthy persons.
Injured people normally bore the cost of their injuries unless they had
the "luck" to be injured by a blameworthy person. The notion that
injured persons could seek compensation from some general pool of

funds amassed through insurance was antithetical to the nineteenth-century ethos of injury.

But if a civil injury was something deserving of compensation rather than something fortuitous, persons injuring other persons could expect that governmental officials would find a way to compel them to compensate the persons they injured. If "blameworthiness," as reflected in the "fault" requirement of much of tort law, was the standard of conduct that triggered compensation, injurers could expect, since the compensation of injured persons was deemed a desirable social goal, that they would more regularly be found "blameworthy," or liable in tort. Accordingly they could be expected to protect themselves against the risks of having to compensate others. Liability insurance secured them this protection. But there was no need for liability insurance unless one expected oneself to be found liable for the injuries one caused, and that expectation was a function of how likely one's injury-creating conduct was to be found blameworthy.

Thus the more successful tort law was as a liability-limiting device, the less well it functioned as a compensation system and the less it needed to be infiltrated with liability insurance. Pristine nineteenth-century negligence theory, we have seen, was admirably designed to limit liability. Pristine negligence theory was also consistent with an admonitory conception of the purposes of tort law, which deterred the spread of liability insurance. And as pristine negligence theory broke down in the early twentieth century, a marvelously circular argument about tort law and liability insurance developed.

Injured people should be compensated, the argument ran, because their injuries affected society at large. Tort law was a prime means of providing that compensation, but, unfortunately, compensating one person for an injury took money away from someone else. Liability insurance, however, allowed injurers to spread or shift their losses. Thus with the emergence of liability insurance more injured persons could be compensated and the "blameworthiness" requirements of tort law could be liberalized. This argument assumed that the growth of liability insurance was a solution to the "problem" of more injuries in society, when in fact it was a response to a changed ethos of injuries.

The infiltration of liability insurance into tort law thus reinforced a judgment on the part of Torts scholars that tort law was no longer a subject dealing with two-party private relations, but one dealing with multi-party public relations. With the addition of liability insurance tort law had become primarily a compensation system designed to distribute the costs of injuries throughout society efficiently and fairly; it should no longer be regarded principally as a system designed to deter and punish blameworthy conduct. This point of view, expressed as early as the 1930s, was well established by the 1950s.[33] Leon Green summarized it at the end of that decade. "Tort law," Green maintained, was "public law in disguise." It was essentially concerned with "providing a remedy . . . for the every day hurts inflicted by the multitudinous activities of our society." [34]

Green's conclusion that tort law was "public" rather than private in its orientation had distinctly antidoctrinal connotations. Since "interests outside and beyond the interests of the immediate parties to the litigation" were "parties to every lawsuit," [35] the public policies served by tort law were far more important than its doctrines, which either masked policy considerations or were products of an older conception of Torts as a two-party private law subject. Doctrine for Green "[fed] on itself; harden[ed] into cliches and block[ed] the arteries of thought." [36] As doctrines became "crystallized," they "sometimes [could] not be dislodged until . . . lawyers . . . and their books are left behind by the transmutations of the social order." [37]

As in the 1930s, the vivid articulation of a perspective on Torts by Green precipitated an academic debate. In the 1930s the Green-Bohlen interchanges had employed "conceptualism," "functionalism," and "realism" as their charged words; in the 1960s "doctrine" and "policy" occupied comparable roles. The shift in language signified a shift in jurisprudential concerns. By the 1950s "conceptualism" had come to signify the static legal science of Langdell, and no law professor concerned with his reputation among his peers was prepared to advocate a "jurisprudence of concepts." To the extent that Realism implied an opposition to conceptualism as so defined, the overwhelming majority of legal scholars were Realists.

But "doctrine" had broader and more ambivalent connotations. The thought of legal scientists had been "doctrinally" oriented in the sense that a major goal of their work was the creation of generalized propositions (doctrines) on which classifications of legal subjects could be based. A "doctrinal" orientation, however, was not inconsistent with a conception of law as a constantly changing entity. Green's characterization of doctrine, however, invested it with qualities of rigidity. Scholars and judges enamored of doctrinal analysis could, Green argued, "become obsessed and imprisoned," and in seeking "to scale the heaven of certainty and universal justice through their doctrinal perfection" [38] forget that policy judgments inevitably lay behind doctrinal formulations.

Like their counterparts of the 1930s, scholars of the 1950s, and 1960s responded to Green's position by denying that doctrinal analysis was incompatible with creativity or innovation in the law. They also revived a complaint launched by Bohlen and other modified conceptualists against Realism: how was an examination of the "policy" dimensions of legal decisions helpful if this knowledge could not then be made the basis of a set of professional techniques through which decisions might be analyzed? "Functionalism," according to this complaint, was based on hindsight; one knew how "interests" would be "balanced" only after they had been balanced and policy preferences had thus been clarified. "Policy" analysis raised similar problems. Since important legal decisions involved choosing between competing policies, simply conveying the implications of one such choice did not help in the analysis of future choices. Doctrine, on the other hand, was conceded to be a universal professional language through which the "methods and conclusions" of one group of decisionmakers were communicated to others.[39] Doctrine therefore had elements of continuity and predictability: it was "there" for later generations to evaluate. Policy, in contrast, was as fleeting as the fashions of time.[40]

Thus alongside a jurisprudential conception of common law subjects as instruments of public policy there gradually emerged, after the Second World War, a competing conception of such subjects as repositories of evolving doctrine. The two conceptions differed in their philosophical outlooks as well as in their methodological emphasis. In Torts they made different assumptions about the nature and purposes of the field.

A belief that the central purpose of tort law was to compensate injured persons was compatible with a "policy" approach to tort issues. Compensation was itself a social policy, but it was not one expressly articulated in the traditional patterns of common law decisionmaking. Late nineteenth- and early twentieth-century judges and scholars had not talked about the proper distribution of the risks of civilly inflicted injuries in American society; they had talked about negligence, "fault," "reasonable conduct," "proximate" causation, and the like. Their articulations of doctrine thus concealed rather than exposed the policy implications of their results. But with the emergence of liability insurance the compensation function of tort law had become apparent. One could see the manner in which tort law allocated the costs of injuries between one set of persons or another even if the allocating officials declined to publicize this aspect of their work.

By reducing the role of doctrine in tort law and increasing the role of conscious policymaking one not only furthered "realism" and candor, one furthered social justice. For the "doctrinal" emphasis of Torts necessitated serious attention to established doctrine, and established doctrine reflected the nineteenth-century ethos of injuries. By deemphasizing the importance of doctrine one facilitated a shift in the central purpose of tort law from admonition to compensation. Doctrines whose purpose was to confine tortiously liable conduct to "blameworthy" conduct would lose their influence and be replaced with policies whose purpose was to secure the efficient and fair compensation of injuries.

Such was the philosophical thrust of one branch of Torts scholarship after the Second World War. The thrust of a competing branch was less overt. Scholars associated with this latter perspective sought to preserve a doctrinal approach to tort issues, but they did not concede that doctrinal analysis was inconsistent with the pursuit of social justice in tort law. They maintained that the creative use of doctrine had regularly produced just results in tort cases and that doctrine was sufficiently flexible to respond to changed social needs.

In their endorsement of creative doctrinal "continuity" in torts, however, these scholars were endorsing the corpus of tort law that a doctrinal perspective had produced.[41] The doctrinal analyses of scholars and judges in the late nineteenth and early twentieth centuries had created the modern negligence principle, with its tests, standards, and defenses; the concept of legal fault, with its consequences for the scope of tort liability; the theory of "proximate" or "legal" causation, in which tort liability was arbitrarily cut off beyond a certain point; and a whole host of associated techniques for regulating civil conduct and determining civil responsibility. A belief in the viability of doctrine in tort law was not a philosophically neutral belief. Advocates of a doctrinal approach to torts implicitly assumed that the prevailing late nineteenth- and early twentieth-century view of the primary purpose of tort law, to admonish blameworthy civil conduct, was sound.

Thus an era of "consensus" thinking in academic and professional disciplines hosted a serious debate over the nature of tort law itself. But unlike the Green-Bohlen debates of the 1930s, confrontations between mid-twentieth-century advocates of "policy" and advocates of "doctrine" did not lapse into polemics. On the contrary, the trends toward consensus scholarship that characterized postwar American intellectual life eventually resulted in a surface reconciliation of doctrinal and policy perspectives in the field of Torts. Crucial to that reconciliation were the contributions of a newly influential Torts theoretician, William Prosser.

The Contributions of Prosser

In each of the earlier phases in the history of Torts scholarship university affiliations had contributed to the development of a theoretical perspective. The creation of Torts as an independent legal subject, with its own casebooks and treatises, had been accomplished largely by scholars at Harvard. The development of a mature "science" of tort law, culminating in the 1935 Restatement of Torts, had received a major impetus from law professors at Harvard, the University of Pennsylvania, Columbia, and Northwestern.[42] The Realist critique of orthodox "scientific" theories had emerged at Columbia, Northwestern, and Yale; a counterattack had been launched at Harvard and Pennsylvania.[43] And as Realism was gradually absorbed into mid-century consensus thought, the competing conceptions of tort law that developed after 1945 could also be seen as having institutional affiliations.

Prominent in articulating a "compensation" purpose for tort law and in stressing the overriding policy aspects of Torts cases were Green, who returned to the University of Texas in 1948 after twenty years as Dean at Northwestern, Charles Gregory of the universities of Chicago and Virginia, Fowler Harper and Fleming James of Yale, and Albert Ehrenzweig of the University of California. No Harvard or Pennsylvania professor, in the years from 1945 to 1970, advocated comparable positions. And all the major advocates of renewed attention to a doctrinal perspective in Torts—Warren Seavey, Page Keeton, Robert Keeton, Roscoe Pound, and Clarence Morris—either taught at or had studied at Harvard. While these Harvard-trained scholars differed from one another in their emphases, the rough consistency of their points of view was suggestive.

The national identity of Harvard Law School had been, since the

1870s, linked to its distinctive educational approach. In the classroom, this approach emphasized the "case method" of instruction; in scholarship, it emphasized doctrinal analysis of common law subjects. The continuity of Harvard's commitment to this approach can be seen in the successive classroom use of one Torts casebook from the 1870s through the 1960s. The casebook, originally conceived by James Barr Ames, included among its authors Jeremiah Smith, Roscoe Pound, Joseph Beale, Warren Seavey, Edward Thurston, and Page and Robert Keeton. The impact of individual authors can be seen in new editions, but the basic posture of the casebook underwent remarkably few changes in nearly a hundred years. Ames's edition was broadened by Smith to include much greater emphasis on the negligence principle. Pound's edition, which had made few changes in Ames's and Smith's format, and had merely been updated by Beale, was reshaped by Seavey and Thurston to achieve an increased emphasis on the discrete case. The Keetons retained that emphasis, but modified the casebook's coverage to reflect the emergence after 1945 of alternatives to the negligence principle as standards for tort liability. Despite these changes, the doctrinal orientation of the casebook remained constant.

Legal education at Harvard thus regularly equated "professional" training in Torts with instruction in techniques of doctrinal analysis. In the 1920s, when the first glimmerings of a "functional" perspective appeared, Harvard hired Bohlen, the Reporter for the doctrinally oriented Restatement of Torts. In 1931 Pound, then Dean at Harvard, openly broke with Realism.[44] Of the four leading Torts casebooks that appeared from the 1930s through the 1950s, three exhibited a "policy" orientation; none of the three sets of authors was affiliated with Harvard.[45]

There is some evidence to suggest, therefore, that the continued seriousness with which doctrine was taken by one branch of postwar Torts scholars was a product, in part, of institutional affiliations. Academic thought, in law as in other disciplines, has been influenced by university affiliation since the university became a professional training ground during the nineteenth-century knowledge revolution. But the middle of the twentieth century produced, at least among leading American law schools, some particularly fierce institutional rivalries. It was as if a number of law schools whose early twentieth-century growth had been influenced by Harvard patterns suddenly sought to declare their independence. The leading edge of criticism of "conceptualistic" modes of teaching and scholarship came from law schools other than Harvard, and universities such as Northwestern and Chicago, whose educational goals had been modeled on those of Harvard under Langdell and Ames, became centers of a "policy" approach to legal subjects.[46] By the 1950s the perceived characters of Harvard and its principal competitors for influence and prestige in American legal education were markedly different. Law schools aspiring after "national" reputations had developed their own faculties—often recruited in part from their own student bodies—and specifically sought to distinguish their own educational programs from that of Harvard.

It is in this context that the postwar clashes between "doctrinal" and "policy" approaches to the field of Torts and between admonitory and compensatory goals for tort law become most intelligible. An admonitory emphasis in Torts and a doctrinal orientation toward common law subjects were features of orthodox late nineteenth-century "scientific" tort theory, which had been articulated principally by persons trained at Harvard. A consensual approach to legal subjects had among its goals a search for core values and overriding continuity in American thought: one could expect that advocates of that approach, in the field of Torts, would oppose polemical scholarly debate, seek to articulate common intellectual ground rules, and search for a renewed doctrinal consensus, thereby justifying the past seventy years of Torts teaching and scholarship.

Crucial to the revitalization of doctrine in Torts was an implicit communication to the legal profession that tort law was, after all, made up of intelligible general principles. Realist literature had furthered the image of Tort law as a shapeless mass, and as late as 1961 Green, citing the work of Fleming James, could assert that "there are no universal and immutable principles about which tort law can be coagulated"; Torts was, as James had put it, a "heterogeneous mass of stuff" without doctrinal solidarity.[47] Fortunately for advocates of a doctrinal perspective, they had a singular ally, whose success as a "consensus" tort theoretician was made possible by the fact that he employed a methodological approach congenial to Realism. That ally was William Prosser, who became in the 1950s the author of the nation's leading Torts treatise, the coauthor of its most widely adopted Torts casebook, and the Reporter for the Second Restatement of Torts.

Prosser was, in some respects, a curious candidate for eminence, given previous success patterns in American legal education. He had been an undergraduate at Harvard and in 1947 had spent a year on the Harvard law faculty. But he had not attended law school or practiced in the Northeast; until 1947 he had spent his entire legal career as a student, teacher, and practitioner in Minnesota. Two years after the publication of his remarkably successful treatise on Torts he left law teaching altogether; at the age of forty-eight he was a partner in a Minneapolis law firm.

Other characteristics of Prosser, however, assured his eventual success in mid-twentieth-century law teaching. In a profession where cumbersome, weighty prose of the kind supplied by Bohlen was the norm among leading scholars, Prosser's writing was clear, light, and eminently readable: he was read for enjoyment as well as for information. In a circle of scholars whose ranks were not numerous and whose contacts with one another were close, Prosser, with his capacity for humor, his restless energies, and his instincts for drama, gravitated toward the limelight. He needed companionship and acclaim; he used public roles as shields for his private feelings. In countless tall tales, trivia contests, poetry readings, and like performances Prosser developed his own legendary persona. Legends grew, prose flowed, honors came, and the cumulative effect was to make Prosser, by his death in 1972, dominant among Torts professors. "Prosser on Torts," a contemporary said that year, "has a completed sound, a belonging sound, a natural sound." [48]

As in the case of Bohlen, a high-strung temperament, manifesting itself periodically in eccentricities, underlay Prosser's scholarly energies. But whereas Bohlen was never entirely able to capture, in his serious and impassioned essays, the picturesqueness of his vision, Prosser's picturesqueness saturated every level of his writing on Torts. The same spirit that motivated Prosser to play practical jokes on his contemporaries at conventions revealed itself in numerous vivid footnotes and passages of text. [49] Not content with an abstract statement of a doctrine, Prosser conjured up striking examples of it in operation. "[I]n the absence of any reason to expect the contrary," he wrote of one facet of negligence, "the actor may reasonably proceed upon the assumption that others will obey the criminal law . . . [I]t is not reasonably to be expected that anyone will intentionally tamper with a railway track, blow up a powder machine, forge a check, push another man into an excavation, assault a railway passenger, or hold up a bowling alley and shoot a patron." [50] The fact that Prosser's citations indicated that lawsuits had resulted from each of those "unantici-patable" acts only heightened his effect.

But if Prosser's capacity for vivid, lively writing contributed to his emergence as a widely read Torts scholar, it was not the principal source of his influence. Prosser rose to scholarly prominence primarily because of his approach to the subject of Torts. In the thirty-odd years that spanned the four editions of his treatise numerous substantive changes occurred in tort law; Prosser's successive editions duly noted such changes. But Prosser's methodology remained constant. He treated tort law as a collection of doctrines, each of which was capable of being reduced to a general formula that articulated its salient features. Such formulas, however, represented only simplified aggregates of countless cases, no one of which precisely embodied all the elements of the formula. By this approach Prosser sought "to make [rules] sufficiently flexible to allow for the particular circumstances, and yet so rigid that lawyers may predict what the decision may be, and men may guide their own conduct by that prediction." [51]

Prosser's approach was thus a fusion of the insights of Realism and the countervailing demands of doctrinally oriented theories of tort law. Prosser's philosophical conception of Torts was derivative of those of early twentieth-century reformist scholars, especially Green.[52] He saw "the administration of the law" as "a process of weighing the interests for which the plaintiff demands protection against the defendant's claim to untrammeled freedom in the furtherance of his own desires, together with the importance of those desires themselves." [53] In tort law, especially, "this process of 'balancing the interests' . . . has been carried to its greatest lengths and has received its most general conscious recognition." Tort law consisted of exercises in "social engineering": it was "concerned primarily with the adjustment of the conflicting interests of individuals to achieve a desirable social result." [54] Prosser retained this conception, with its distinctively early twentieth-century flavor, throughout his scholarly career. In the 1971 edition of his treatise he repeated the identical description of the process of interest-balancing that he had made in 1940, listing as support for his assertions articles by tort scholars in the 1920s and 1930s.[55]

So clearly was Prosser's thought identified with the Realist genera-tion of legal scholars that one may wonder why he came into promi-nence at a time when Realism was on the decline. Several explanations suggest themselves. While certain features of Realism, such as its moral relativism and its skepticism toward order and predictability in law, had lost influence in the 1940s, other features had become orthodoxies. The idea of law as an instrument of "social engineering" may have been startling in the 1900s, but it was commonplace by the Second World War. "Interest-balancing" was also regarded as a familiar and generally sound description of how lawmaking officials made decisions. In conceiving of tort law as a process in social engineering in which competing interests were weighed Prosser was in the mainstream of mid-twentieth-century legal thought.

Secondly, the jurisprudential perspective on tort law that Prosser articulated did not accurately reflect his method of approaching the subject of Torts. While Prosser stated that tort law was an exercise in interest-balancing, he conceded that "most of the writers who have pointed out the process have stopped short of telling us how it is to be done." [56] Prosser, by contrast, was concerned with the mechanics of deriving general and predictable rules. He assumed that "we are to have general rules," and that rules needed to be "rigid" so as to serve as "guide[s] [for] conduct." [57] On these assumptions Prosser built his scholarship, and he did not seem to find them inconsistent with a conception of law as a process of interest-balancing. Realists believed that energy directed toward the derivation and promulgation of predictable rules was energy misspent. Prosser, however, thought that rules could be made sufficiently flexible to "allow for the particular circumstances" and sufficiently rigid to serve as guides for planning conduct.

Prosser's abstract endorsement of Realism, then, did not prevent him from making assumptions that ran counter to its thrust. Moreover, the ultimate explanation for Prosser's success came not in what he said tort scholars should try to do—his comments on jurisprudential issues, but the most part, were perfunctory and unrevealing—but in what he actually did. To explain fully Prosser's impact on his contemporaries one needs to examine his scholarship firsthand.

Prosser's treatment of the last clear chance doctrine, virtually unchanged in each of the editions of his treatise, illustrates his methodology. He began his discussion by asserting that any "doctrinal" explanation for last clear chance failed to make sense. A "proximate cause" rationale was "quite out of line with modern ideas" of that concept; a "comparative fault" rationale could "scarcely explain [cases] in which the defendant's fault consists merely in a failure to discover the danger at all." Last clear chance had been applied "with much confusion," there being "as many variant forms and applications . . . as there are jurisdictions which apply it." Given the "general . . . confusion and disagreement," Prosser maintained, "reference must of necessity be made to the law of each particular state." Last clear chance in his view was simply a manifestation of "a dislike for the defense of contributory negligence which has made the courts . . . accept without reasoning the conclusion that the last wrongdoer is necessarily the worst wrongdoer." [58]

Having exposed the fictional, inconsistent, and arbitrary nature of last clear chance, and having claimed that the application of the doctrine was as varied as the states in the union, Prosser then announced that, after all, the "situations" in which last clear chance tended to arise "may be classified." [59] His classification distinguished between three types of "last clear chance" cases: "helpless plaintiff" cases, "inattentive plaintiff" cases, and cases where the defendant's "antecedent negligence" prevented him from avoiding injury to the plaintiff even though he had exercised the "last clear chance" to prevent the accident. In his 1941 edition Prosser argued that in "helpless plaintiff" cases "nearly all courts" allowed a plaintiff to recover if the defendant had discovered the "helplessness," and many allowed recovery even if he should have discovered it.[60] By 1971 Prosser was even more categorical: "all" courts, including those "which purport to reject the whole doctrine by name," allowed recovery where the helplessness had been discovered, and "a considerable majority" allowed recovery where it should have been.[61]

In contrast were the "inattentive plaintiff" cases, where an injured party could have escaped injury but failed to notice his own danger. Here "most courts" held that a plaintiff could recover if the defendant had actually discovered his inattentiveness, but "nearly all" the courts denied recovery if the defendant merely should have discovered it. In the last class of cases it was "obvious" to Prosser that "neither party can be said to have a 'last clear' chance." [62]

Thus one could make sense of "last clear chance" cases by focusing on the state of being of the plaintiff. Or if that failed, one could focus on the character of the defendant's original "negligence." If it were of the kind that prevented the defendant from avoiding injury even after he had discovered the plaintiff's peril (failure to drive with functioning brakes), a "last clear chance" did not truly exist. Only if the original "negligence" (say speeding) did not affect the defendant's subsequent effort to avoid hitting a plaintiff did the last clear chance doctrine come into play. The most typical last clear chance case, then, was one in which a "helpless" plaintiff was discovered by a hypothetically "negligent" defendant whose original "negligence" played no part in his subsequent failure to use reasonable care to avoid injury to the plaintiff.

Prosser's classifications left a sense of tidiness and allegedly represented the views of "nearly all," or a "substantial majority" of courts, although Prosser cited only a few jurisdictions for each of his generalizations about last clear chance.[63] But the classifications were nearly useless as predictive rules. In the first place, most accidents could not be reconstructed so as to determine whether the plaintiff was "helpless" or merely "inattentive." Moreover, allowing defendants to avoid the last clear chance doctrine by showing that they had not actually seen the plight of an "inattentive" plaintiff, even though they should have, encouraged defendant testimony to that effect; in most accidents such testimony was incontrovertible. Finally, the "antecedent" negligence of the defendant, if distinguished from the conduct that resulted in the plaintiff's injury, was either "proof of negligence in the air," and thereby without legal significance, or another means by which defendants could avoid the last clear chance doctrine, since in most cases the only testimony relevant to whether the defendant's "antecedent" negligence had ceased was that of the defendant himself.

Thus the classifications of last clear chance cases made by Prosser, while they may have reflected tendencies in the courts, only served as collections of justifications courts had made for allowing a contributorily negligent plaintiff recovery for his injuries. The "helplessness" of a plaintiff, "knowledge" of that helplessness on the part of a defendant, and the lack of extenuating circumstances absolving a defendant who failed to avoid injuring a helpless plaintiff were each part of an equitable case for disregarding the defense of contributory negligence in a given accident. Taken as predictive rules the classifications led to absurdities, as Prosser himself recognized: "the driver who looks carefully and discovers the danger, and is then slow in applying his brakes, may be liable, while the one who does not look at all, or who has no effective brakes to apply, may not." [64] But the classifications were not predictive rules, only after-the-fact justifications. Prosser had conceded in 1953, after all, that "[t]here [was] no substitute for dealing with the particular facts." [65]

Why, then, did Prosser make his classifications at all? His interest in classifying a doctrinal area characterized by "irreconcilable rules" and a "lack of any rational fundamental theory" suggests that he felt a compusion not to leave his material in an undigested mass, thereby implicitly suggesting that the discrete case contained the only "rules" of tort law.[66] Prosser's approach was rather to create psuedo-rules, classifications that purported to summarize the "state of the law" in a given area of Torts, but in fact were simply devices that aided in summary and synthesis of a disparate mass of material. Unlike the classifications attempted by legal scientists, which were intended to function as working doctrinal principles, Prosser's classifications were only his efforts to wrest some surface intelligibility from the chaos of cases spread out before him.

But Prosser's technique worked so well that his classifications came to take on a doctrinal function. In his treatment of intentional infliction of emotional distress, for example, Prosser stated that "somewhere around 1930 it began to be recognized that the intentional infliction of mental disturbance by extreme and outrageous conduct constituted a cause of action in itself." [67] The "recognition," as noted, was mainly Prosser's: he had collected "mental disturbance" cases in a 1939 article, announced the birth of a "new tort," and proposed an "extreme and outrageous" standard for liability.[68] By 1948 the "extreme and outrageous" standard had been adopted by the Restatement of Torts and had begun to be applied in case law.[69] A phrase originally conceived as a synthesizing device had become invested with doctrinal significance.

In other areas of Torts Prosser made similar helpful classifications: his division of libel into libel per quod and liber per se; [70] his "discovery" of the basis of liability in injurious falsehood; [71] his exploration of "consciousness of confinement" in false imprisonment cases; [72] his amalgamation of the tort of "privacy" from four separate causes of action.[73] While Prosser's syntheses of these tort actions may only have been intended to describe some of their salient features, the effect of his scholarship was to identify the actions with Prosser's synthesis.

The impact of Prosser's classifications is all the more striking because of the general thrust of his scholarship, which was to undercut the explanatory power of generailzations about tort law, including Prosser's own. Prosser's practice in describing an area of Torts was to produce a textual narrative, succinct and vividly written, setting forth central features of the area. The narrative, whose primary purpose was to give structure to the mass of cases Prosser analyzed, was interspersed with footnotes that numbered approximately 125 for every 10 pages of text. A standard page of Prosser's *Law of Torts* treatise contained as much space devoted to footnotes as to textual matter. Prosser's footnotes were not meant to serve the role they had served in the scientists' treatises; their purpose was not to support generalizations made in the text. Rather, Prosser's footnotes dramatized the varied and contradictory applications of rules. Repeatedly Prosser would refer to the "arbitrary and illogical rules" that characterized a particular area and then give, in footnotes, examples of the bizarre results such rules produced. The examples regularly amused, but they also summoned up a vision of Torts as a field incapable of being reduced to meaningful generalizations.

In light of the explicitly Realist perspective from which Prosser viewed law and in light of the methodological thrust of his treatise, which was not inconsistent with Realism, the reactions of reviewers to the first edition of *The Law of Torts* were surprising. Prosser's treatise first appeared in 1941, when, as a contemporary later put it, "[t]he grim necessities of the threat of war demanded that we lay aside the luxury of skeptical thinking for a while, and legal realism ground to a halt." [74] Not a single reviewer criticized Prosser's stance; few, in fact, commented upon it. The reviews were numerous, almost entirely praiseworthy, and disinclined to probe Prosser's jurisprudential perspective. One found Prosser's point of view free from "dogmatic assertions about debatable points"; [75] another noted that Prosser had "profess[ed] no adherence to any particular school of thought among legal theorists," and said that Prosser had told him in conversation that his interest was in writing on tort law as it "is," letting others ponder how it "ought to be." [76] This separation of "is" from "ought" in discussions of legal subjects was a familiar Realist technique, and one that had infuriated critics of Realism in the late 1930s.[77] No reviewer found it objectionable in Prosser. No reviewer, in short, quarreled seriously with Prosser's approach; one thought "the 'social engineering' aspect" of Prosser's treatise "interesting and thought provoking." [78] The most searching criticism of *The Law of Torts* came from a mythical symposium of "The National Union of Torts Scholars" (known popularly by its initials) created by Prosser in a "review" of his own book.[79] When an author is his severest public critic, success or anonymity is assured, and Prosser was not destined to be anonymous.

|The reaction of commentators to Prosser's first edition suggested that he had accomplished, surreptitiously, what other reformist tort scholars had failed to do in their more explicit efforts.| Prosser had made Realist-inspired innovations in tort law part of the received orthodoxy of the field. His accomplishment may be traced to his strategies, conscious and unconscious, of treatise writing. He had created the impression that tort law could be synthesized and was thereby not an unintelligible mass, although the utility of his synthetic principles was undermined by the data base on which they rested. He had downplayed any polemical features of his perspective by the circumspection of his language, although the emphasis in his treatise on the constantly changing quality of tort doctrine marked his thought as close to that of the Realists. And without denying the significance or the intelligibility of doctrine, he had shown that doctrinal generalizations were dependent on the results reached in discrete cases, and that individual results, even though they did not conform to a generalization, were not to be ignored.

In his conception of tort law as an exercise in social engineering Prosser hinted that policy considerations were decisive in the decision of Torts cases; the popularity of Prosser's treatise suggested that a "policy" approach to Torts had become acceptable. But at the same time one could not endorse Prosser's treatment of the subject of torts without conceding that doctrine and doctrinal analysis were essential to its comprehensibility. Thus Prosser settled into a moderate position between advocates of policy and enthusiasts for doctrine. While he did much to preserve the viability of a doctrinal approach to tort law, his particular varieties of doctrine were intended to be less imposing and comprehensive than those of the scientists. Prosser was a conceptualist in spite of himself: his skills at classification and synthesis distinguished him from his peers, and made his reputation, but his attraction was for the anomalous, the disorderly, the absurd, and the picturesque.

The Impact of Consensus Thought on Tort Doctrines

With the emergence of Prosser as the central Torts theoretician of the years after the Second World War, consensus thinking among Torts scholars reached a high-water mark. Prosser's position on an issue, which was increasingly also that of the Restatement of Torts after 1959 when Prosser succeeded Warren Seavey as Reporter, served as a litmus paper test of the permissible range of scholarly dispute in the 1950s and 1960s. In general, tort theory in those decades moved away from a fixation on negligence to explore alternative standards of liability and moved away from stressing the distinctiveness and integrity of tort law to exploring its interaction with other legal subjects. In both these trends Prosser's scholarship served as a catalyst for change, but it also reflected the acceptable limits of novelty. Three doctrinal areas are illustrative: comparative negligence, products liability, and privacy.

Pristine nineteenth-century negligence theory, we have seen, assumed that liability for risk-creating conduct should not attach unless the person creating the risk had been "at fault." "Fault" was used as a label by which "blameworthy" conduct was admonished; the party "at fault" was forced to pay for injuries he had caused. It followed from this conception of civil responsibility that a person who was himself "at fault" should not be able to recover for his injuries, even if the risk of those injuries had been created by another blameworthy person. While blameworthy people could be required to compensate others injured by their carelessness, they did not have to compensate those others who were themselves blameworthy. Having no demands of morality to satisfy, nineteenth-century negligence could, in cases where both parties were blameworthy, let losses lie where they fell.

The absolute defense of contributory negligence was thus consistent with pristine negligence theory; such modifications as last clear chance were escapes from the rigors of its logic. But last clear chance did not challenge the assumptions of nineteenth-century negligence theory that liability be based on "fault" and that only blameworthy persons be forced to compensate others. By creating a mini-action within a negligence action, last clear chance created a new blameworthy party (he who had the "last clear chance" and failed properly to exerice it) and placed the loss on him. The other party lost his blameworthiness by being in peril and having his peril discovered.

At approximately the same time that the "arbitrary" loss-shifting aspects of last clear chance were being discovered,[80] legislative efforts to mitigate the consequences of contributory negligence appeared. These efforts were indications of an altered attitude about the primary purpose of tort law. An admonitory view of the function of tort law assumed that there was nothing unjust about the costs of injuries being borne by injured parties themselves unless the injurers had done something blameworthy. The injustice of no compensation for tort victims lay in the fact that blameworthy injurers were not admonished rather than that injured people were not being compensated. Once the situations where a blameworthy (contributorily negligent) person was deprived of compensation for his injuries came to be regarded as "unjust," a new primary purpose for tort law could be assumed. "Injustice" could now be equated with the absence of compensation for injuries rather than with the failure to admonish blameworthy conduct.

Between 1908 and 1941 various statutory modifications of contributory negligence were passed. The Federal Employer's Liability Act of 1908 [81] abolished contributory negligence as an absolute defense for actions brought by railroad employees engaged in interstate commerce and substituted an apportionment of losses, whereby recovery by an injured employee was diminished only to the extent that he was comparatively at fault. Comparable provisions were incorporated into the Jones Act (1915) [82] and the Merchant Marine Act (1920) [83] both of which covered marine employees. Meanwhile Texas, Arizona, South Dakota, Oregon, and Florida instituted comparative negligence for railroad employees in intrastate commerce or for employees engaged in "hazardous" occupations, such as lumbering or mining.[84] Eventually Mississippi, Nebraska, Wisconsin, and South Dakota enacted general comparative negligence statutes, applicable to "all persons and all property involved in all types of accidents." [85]

With the passage of South Dakota's statute in 1941 the momentum of comparative negligence legislation slowed; no other state adopted comparative negligence until Arkansas did so in 1955. Another period of relative inactivity then ensued, followed, in the 1970s, with a burst of legislation [86] and two judicial decisions [87] replacing contributory negligence with a comparative negligence standard. The last flurry of activity is outside the scope of this chapter; between 1945 and 1970 the climate in which comparative negligence was discussed was one in which the doctrine made some, though not sizable, inroads on nineteenth-century negligence theory. The question these developments raise is why, once the loss-distribution features of tort law were recognized and once its compensation features became generally accepted, the doctrine of comparative negligence did not achieve wider acceptance. While several factors may be stressed in answering this question, such as the apparent disinclination on the part of common law courts to change established doctrine radically or the relatively low priority allegedly given issues of tort law by legislatures, [88] the most striking factor was the relative lack of attention paid to comparative negligence by postwar legal scholars.

Charles Gregory observed in 1936 that "it is self-evident that the principle of . . . comparative negligence . . . furnish[es] a theoretically fairer basis for loss distribution in negligence cases than the accepted principles of the common law." In Gregory's view it required "no argument" to "establish that if two people unintentionally cause damage for which both are responsible and one of them discharges the entire obligation, the other ought to share the loss . . . in proportion to the extent to which he effected the loss." [89] That observation was supported by numerous scholars over a twenty-year period, beginning in the 1930s. Almost all the scholarly literature on comparative negligence advocated its implementation, and some commentators provided model statutes for legislatures.[90] But no scholars advocated that the change be judge-made and few expressed confidence in legislative modifications. Statutes instituting comparative negligence, Prosser maintained, were "more or less obvious compromises between contesting groups in the legislatures, remarkable neither for soundness in principle nor succeess in operation." [91]

The reformist thrust of legal scholarship, evident in numerous other areas of tort law, seemed blunted in the area of comparative negligence by the sheer complexity of the reform. Prosser, himself a reformer, alluded in 1964 to the "understandable reluctance" on the part of courts to make "so sweeping an alteration of the law, affecting so many thousands of cases." [92] In a 1953 article Prosser had endorsed comparative negligence in principle and had drafted a brief model statute. But the bulk of his article had outlined the administrative problems attendant on replacing the contributory negligence defense with some version of comparative negligence. Among these was the problem of determining a formula for loss distribution and the related problem of reducing negligence to percentages; the problem of distributing losses among multiple parties; the problem of uneven insurance coverage or insolvency in one or more of the parties; the problem of obtaining jurisdiction over nonresidents; the problem of choosing between competing treatments of negligence where the parties resided in different jurisdictions; the role of assumption of risk and the last clear chance doctrine in a jurisdiction that had adopted comparative negligence.[93] Each of these difficulties highlighted the "merits of simplicity" [94] of a system where contributory negligence was an absolute bar to recovery, and together they illustrated why nineteenth-century commentators had given, among their justifications for the contributory negligence defense, "the inability of human tribunals to mete out exact justice." [95]

The renewed sense among postwar legal scholars that in a modern interdependent society even small changes in the law had the potential to generate large and unforeseen ripples proved to be a deterrent strong enough to hold back sweeping proposals for reform of common law negligence. Those scholars had discovered the extent to which changes in legal doctrines affected numerous persons beyond the immediate scope of a given litigation; [96] the possible retroactive effects of judge-made rule changes; [97] the consequences for one institution of changes instituted by another; the necessity, in a complex society, of having intelligible general rules of law. Comparative negligence seemed capable of spawning unanticipated and perhaps insoluble complexities. The "injustice" of the common law was muted by its ease of administration.

The interest evidenced in postwar legal scholarship in the complex interactions of the "legal process" thus may have adversely affected scholarly enthusiasm for the instigation of comparative negligence.[98] By the time a major influx of comparative negligence statutes and judicial decisions did appear, in the 1970s, a change in the climate of scholarly opinion had taken place. Academicians had attacked negligence theory head-on and had suggested alternatives to the common law "fault" standard of tort liability; the rush of comparative negligence legislation of the early 1970s may be seen, in this context, as an effort to preserve negligence theory against the prosepective competition of "no-fault" theories.

The quiescent status of comparative negligence in the 1950s and 1960s was thus an ironic by-product of the intense scholarly attention given in those decades to the singular complexity of the American legal system. A sense of injustice with pristine nineteenth-century negligence theory was present, but this feeling was not effectively translated into influential appeals for reform; it lingered and festered, thwarted in its implementation by "administrative" difficulties. Here one could see two strands of Realism in opposition: a perception that tort law was "really" policy and that sound policy required emphasis on its compensation capacities, clashing with a perception that "law" was the "administration of law" and that to understand legal doctrine one had to understand the "processes" by which it was implemented. The doctrine of comparative negligence was "sound" from a policy standpoint, but the institutional processes through which it would be administered—where its "real" effect would be felt—were not easily made simple and intelligible.

If the jurisprudential assumptions of postwar scholars deterred rapid doctrinal change in the area of comparative negligence, they stimulated it in the area of products liability. In the years after 1945 an alternative to negligence theory surfaced and gained momentum to the point where, in the area of defective products, it supplanted negligence as the principal theoretical basis of tort liability. The dramatic rise of strict liability theory in defective products cases between the 1940s and 1970 furnishes a striking example of the way in which tort law has been shaped by the interactions of influential scholars and visible appellate judges.

In the 1941 edition of his treatise Prosser did not give products liability separate treatment, nor did his chapter on strict liability include more than a perfunctory discussion of defective products cases.[99] In his chapter on the liability of suppliers to third persons, however, Prosser identified "a considerable impetus" in the courts to "find some ground for strict liability" on the part of manufacturers to consumers.[100] He advanced some justifications for strict liability for product manufacturers: the ability of manufacturers to spread or shift their costs through insurance; the difficulties of proving negligence encountered by injured consumers; the insignificant role of intermediate suppliers in insuring the safety of products; the circuitous requirements of warranty law, which necessitated each party in a chain of distribution to proceed separately against his warrantor; and "the public interest" in "maximum . . . protection" for the consumer.[101]

Despite his own enthusiasm for strict liability in the defective products area and despite "the approval of every legal writer who has discussed it," [102] Prosser conceded in 1955 that "the majority of courts still refuse to find any strict liability without privity of contract"; that those "which recognize it as to food have refused to extend it to any other type of product"; and that "as to defendants other than sellers, who supply chattels under contract, there has as yet been no suggestion of any strict liability to third persons." [103] Prosser had said in 1941 that strict liability would "be the law of the future" in defective products cases," and "that the end of the next quarter of a century will find the principle generally accepted." [104] By the middle of the 1950s such developments had not come to pass. Perhaps for this reason Prosser decided to initiate his own survey of the defective products area.

Between 1955 and 1960, the year Prosser's first article on products liability appeared, Torts scholarship reflected the embryonic growth of strict liability theory in the defective products area.[105] Only Fleming James had gone on record as endorsing the adoption of strict liability beyond defective food cases, where it was already established. Other commentators maintained that food cases were unique, [106] or opposed strict liability on policy grounds, [107] or suggested a case-by-case approach.[108] James, for his part, advocated extension of liability on the basis of a warranty theory rather than through strict liability in tort.[109]

Prosser's "The Assault Upon the Citadel" took a far bolder approach.[110] His essay, in fact, was a model of how legal scholarship can serve to further doctrinal change in a common law subject. While admitting that "most of the courts which accept strict liability without privity as to food still refuse to apply it to [other] things," [111] Prosser found "cracks" in the citadel of resistance. "Seven spectacular decisions" of "the last two years" appeared "to have thrown the limitation to food onto the ash pile." [112] Seven such cases in so short a time in Prosser's view "[amounted] to a Trend." It needed "no prophet to foresee that there will be other decisions in the next few years, and that the storming of the inner citadel is already in full cry." [113] Prosser's "prediction of the extension of strict liability to products of special danger," which had unfortunately "not been realized" [114] by 1960, was perhaps on the verge of being vindicated.

Gathering seven cases together and calling them a trend was designed to stimulate momentum for change, but if vivid language was not enough, Prosser was prepared to supply some policy arguments. He claimed these arguments had "proved convincing to the courts which have accepted . . . strict liability," [115] but his normally abundant citations were thin, and he had articulated the same arguments in earlier scholarship.[116] He advanced three arguments: one resting on "public sentiment" for "maximum possible protection . . . against dangerous defects in products which consumers must buy"; [117] a second resting on the crucial role of the supplier in placing the product on the market, in contrast to the "mere mechanical" function of the retailer; [118] a third resting on the "expensive, time consuming, and wasteful" warranty theory of liability, which was "pernicious and entirely unnecessary." "If there is to be strict liability in tort," Prosser maintained, "let there be strict liability in tort, declared outright, without an illusory contract mask." [119] Prosser then ventured yet another prediction. "The public interest in the safety of products which the public must buy," he asserted, "certainly extends to a great many other things. The wedge has entered, and we are on our way . . . Ultimately . . . we may arrive at a general rule of strict liability for all products." [120]

As in so many other instances throughout his career, Prosser's timing was propitious. Six years later, in another article, he proclaimed the "fall of the citadel" and the triumph of strict liability theory in the defective products area.[121] In "the most rapid and altogether spectacular overturn of an established rule in the entire history of the law of torts," [122] strict liability had come to be applied directly against the manufacturer of a defective product in all but ten jurisdictions. Three cases, in particular, were landmarks: *Henningsen v. Bloomfield Motors,*[123] allowing an injured consumer of an auomobile to recover against the manufacturer for a defective steering gear; *Goldberg v. Kollsman Instrument Corp.,*[124] allowing a beneficiary of a person killed in an airplane crash to proceed against the manufacturer of the defective altimeter that caused the accident; and *Greenman v. Yuba Power Products,*[125] in which a person injured by a defective power tool successfully sued the manufacturer in strict liability. Unquestionable proof of the new state of affairs was provided by Section 402A of the revised Restatement of Torts, which applied strict liability theory to "any [defective] product" even when "the user or consumer has not bought the product from or entered into any contractual relation with the seller." [126] The draftsman of that section was, of course, Prosser himself.

The triumph of strict liability theory in the defective products area would not have occurred, it seems fair to say, without a tacit consensus among academicians and courts that negligence theory was not performing satisfactorily in defective products cases. The difficulties with negligence theory were not in its limited reach. Developments after *MacPherson v. Buick* had extended the duty of manufacturers to remote persons injured in a foreseeable fashion.[127] The use of strict liability as a ground of recovery did not, therefore, create a vast new class of litigants in defective products cases. Nor did strict liability help plaintiffs surmount problems of proof: courts had developed the doctrine of *res ipsa loquitur* (the thing speaks for itself) to allow plaintiffs injured by defective products to create a rebuttable presumption that their injuries had been caused by negligence merely by describing the circumstances of the injury.[128] Where negligence theory proved most inadequate was in insuring that an injured plaintiff would be able to identify the defendant accountable for his injuries. Chains of product distribution had created intermediaries between the manufacturer and the consumer. Even if an injured person, through *res ipsa loquitur,* could show that his injury would not ordinarily happen in the absence of someone's negligence, he could not easily show which of the parties handling the product had been negligent. Failure to meet that burden meant that the loss of his injury would fall on him.

Thus it is hard to conceive that strict liability would have emerged in defective products cases without the interaction of two trends: a greater interest on the part of commentators and courts in the working processes of the legal system, and an assumption that injured persons should be compensated for their injuries where possible. A shift to strict liability in defective products cases meant that consumers could identify manufacturers as prospective defendants and that manufacturers could assume that anytime their products were defective and used in an ordinary manner, they would have to pay for the injuries the products caused. Given such a predictable state of affairs, it is hard to conceive of consumers not suing manufacturers, as opposed to retailers, and it is hard to imagine manufacturers not calculating a certain amount of business costs from defective products and seeking to recover those costs through the medium of insurance, recouping the costs of their premiums through higher priced products. Efforts to streamline the processes and to expand the compensation function of tort law, then, seemed naturally to lead to expanded liability insurance; courts imposing strict liability on manufacturers increasingly seemed conscious of insurance and its loss-spreading capacities.[129]

Prosser, for his part, never warmed to the idea that the presence of liability insurance had an effect on the state of tort doctrines. In 1960, while admitting that "the 'risk-spreading' argument" was "entitled to . . . respect," he found that only one appellate court had "so much as mentioned insurance in a products-liability case," and stated that while "[l]iability insurance is obviously not to be ignored," it "is a makeweight, and not the heart and soul of the problem." [130] Six years later a few more cases had turned up that mentioned liability insurance, but Prosser still found "the 'risk distributing' theory" a "makeweight argument." [131] A year before his death Prosser claimed that "[a] dispassionate observer . . . might . . . readily conclude that the 'impact' of insurance upon the law of torts has been amazingly slight." [132] In defective products cases Prosser pointed to the thousands of opinions that had appeared in the recent past, only a handful of which had even mentioned insurance. He found this fact "at least some indication that the changes in this area of the law have not been due primarily to this one factor." [133]

Prosser was probably correct in rejecting the presence of liability insurance as the primary factor stimulating the growth of strict liability theory. Yet the growth of liability insurance was intimately related to the advent of strict liability, because both phenomena were manifestations of a changed attitude about the primary function of tort law. Liability insurance, in its modern, risk-distributing form, emerged when injuries to people came to be perceived as a matter of social concern. When leaving losses where they fell seemed philosophically sound, the burdens of compensating injured persons, which liability insurance helped meet, were not perceived of as significant. When, however, uncompensated injuries became an injustice, compensation devices emerged and a compensation theory of tort law developed. Thus liability insurance was an index of the same attitude that fostered the acceptance of strict liability theory. Strict liability was a better compensation device than negligence; liability insurance distributed the costs of compensation. It was not the presence of liability insurance that made courts inclined to extend the strict liability principle, but rather their concern that victims be compensated. Liability insurance, like strict liability theory itself, was a response to that concern.

Prosser's influence in the products liability area was either somewhat fortuitous or a tribute more to his perspicacity than to the inherent soundness of his views. To be sure, he had been an early and vigorous advocate of strict liability, but so had others: as Prosser pointed out, nearly all the scholars writing on strict liability theory since the 1930s had endorsed its extension. Prosser distinguished himself by claiming, on less than fulsome evidence, the existence of a "trend" toward acceptance of the strict liability principle; by reminding courts of some arguments for its continued use; and then by claiming that in defective products cases strict liability had prevailed. This sequence was a good example of how to impress by sleight-of-hand techniques, but it did not establish Prosser as a creative architect of strict liability theory. Only his bold stroke of stripping strict liability from its "illusory contract mask" and declaring its status as a tort doctrine ranked as a genuinely creative effort. There Prosser's technique was reminiscent of the scientists who had liberated assumption of risk from "waiver" doctrines in contract.

In another major locus of doctrinal change in postwar tort law, however, Prosser's contribution can clearly be called creative. The "tort" of privacy, which has had a remarkable history since 1945, was in some respects Prosser's own invention: he gave privacy a doctrinal unity and continuity that it had not previously possessed. Commentators, including Prosser,[134] have traditionally identified the "origins" of the tort of privacy with the appearance in 1890 of an article by Samuel Warren and Louis Brandeis in the *Harvard Law Review*.[135] In that article Warren and Brandeis protested against the appropriation by newspapers and magazines of private information about socially prominent persons and suggested that tort law might provide some relief. While Warren's and Brandeis's presentation was skillful, the recognition that invasions of privacy could be thought of as tortious activities had actually occurred when privacy became a significant value in American society, beginning in the latter part of the nineteenth century. Privacy became important when America became more heterogeneous, crowded, urbanized, and socially mobile: it was a respite from the pressures of living in a complex world. Brandeis's and Warren's article did not invent privacy; it signified its emergence as a common concern.

Doctrinally, the emerging tort of privacy faced some difficulties. With the exception of cases where someone had appropriated a feature of another's private life that had unquestioned commercial value, the sting of the tort seemed to be in the emotional distress it caused. Emotional harm was, we have seen, slow to be recognized by the courts, and its recognition was essential for privacy to develop. As late as 1955 Prosser still believed that "[w]hen the 'new tort' of the inten-

tional infliction of mental suffering becomes fully developed and receives general recognition, the great majority of the privacy cases may
very possibly be absorbed into it." [136] Yet privacy cases very regularly
raised complaints that would not have been redressed through an
action in intentional infliction of emotional distress. A standard
privacy case involved circumstances in which a person was upset by
the unauthorized disclosure by another of information about his or
her private life. While the information might not have been embarrassing to the average person, it was embarrassing to the person bringing the action. For recovery to be allowed for intentional infliction of
emotional distress, the claimant would have to show that the defendant's disclosure amounted to "extreme and outrageous" conduct. The
mere publicizing of some private information—such as the fact that
a bookkeeper had once been a child prodigy as a mathematician—
would not meet the "extreme and outrageous" standard.[137]

In its early history privacy was merely a residual category of tort
law, covering cases where the harm was emotionally based, where
the information revealed was true rather than false, and where the
revelation of private information, while offensive to the claimant, was
not sufficiently offensive to others so as to give rise to a claim for
intentional infliction of emotional distress. As such, privacy was a
"miscellaneous" tort, which drew its identity from its residual capacity,
and in his 1941 edition Prosser treated privacy in this way.[138] By the
1960s, however, privacy had not only become a tort with its own
identity, it had become a constitutional right, whose existence symbolized the possibility of redress for "affront[s] to human dignity." [139]
The story of the rapid rise of privacy was one in which Prosser had
played no inconsiderable part.

From its beginnings the residual category of "privacy" had encompassed different types of complaints. One type, emphasized by Warren
and Brandeis, was the appropriation of another's name or image for
commercial purposes: "appropriation" privacy issues dominated most
of the early twentieth-century cases.[140] A second type of action involved intrusions into one's home or one's personal possessions, or
merely persistent prying into one's personal affairs. Appropriation and
intrusion privacy were quite different kinds of torts. The "privacy"
protected in the former was akin to a copyright on one's name or like-
ness, which was not itself secret but which could be publicized only
on consent of the owner; the privacy protected in the latter was not

freedom from publicity but freedom from invasion into the ambit of one's personal "space."

In 1931 a California case highlighted a third type of "privacy" action, unauthorized public disclosure of "private" information.[141] A former prostitute and defendant in a murder trial had rejected her past, married, and was living at the time she initiated suit a life of apparent respectability. A motion picture producer made a movie about her life, using her actual name. She sued, claiming emotional harm. The case could not be brought as defamation since the facts were true; the defendant's conduct was not sufficiently extreme to make out an emotional distress action. In finding against the defendant the California Supreme Court gave dramatic impetus to the tort of "disclosure" privacy.

By 1941 Prosser had distinguished the above three types of privacy claims, asserting all the while that those privacy cases that could not be subsumed under intentional infliction of emotional distress occupied a "limited area," which existed primarily because "no other remedy is available." [142] In 1955 he added a fourth category of privacy, "putting the plaintiff in a false light in the public eye." [143] Examples of the last type were attaching a photograph of a person to an article with whom the person had no connection [144] or attributing an opinion to a person who had not voiced it.[145] In the thirty years that spanned Prosser's treatise "false light" privacy cases escalated, it seemed, even beyond his control. In 1941 he had not recognized false light privacy at all; in 1955 he saw false light cases, as well as other types of privacy claims, as "only a phase of the larger problem" of protection against infliction of mental distress; [146] but by 1964 he expressed concern that false light privacy was "capable of swallowing up and engulfing the whole law of defamation." [147] In general, the residual category of privacy had become "a concept sufficiently broad to include almost all personal torts." [148] Prosser was at least partly responsible for the dramatic expansion of the tort of privacy. He personally had wrested it from its residual status and declared it to be a separate tort—"a complex of four distinct wrongs"—in the 1955 edition of his treatise.[149] In 1960, in a law review article, he identified "the law of privacy" with that complex of wrongs, which he saw as making up "an independent basis of [tort] liability." [150] And in 1971 he maintained that "as yet no decided case allowing recovery" in privacy had occurred "which does not fall fully within one of the four categories" [151] that he had developed. The familiar Prosser pattern had emerged. A classification made seemingly for convenience (1941) had been expanded and refined (1955), hardened and solidified (1960 and 1964, when the "common features" of privacy were declared), and finally made synonymous with "law" (1971). Prosser's capacity for synthesis had become a capacity to create doctrine. One began an analysis of tort privacy by stating that it consisted of "a complex of four wrongs," and implicitly, *only* those wrongs.

In searching for the sources of Prosser's influence as a Torts theoretician one recurrently comes upon his capacity to synthesize; his persistence in maintaining and refining his classifications so that they hardened into doctrine; his skill in preserving doctrine he had helped create. To those qualities one must add prescience. In 1960 Prosser announced that the assault on the citadel of proof in products liability was under way; six years later he could claim that the citadel had fallen. In 1960, again, Prosser worried about some of the "dangers" of an expanding law of privacy. He spoke of the possible abolition of "the defense of truth"; of "the requirement of special damage"; and of other "jealous safeguards thrown about the freedom of speech and the press." [152] By 1970 the Supreme Court had involved itself in tort privacy cases, under the guise of concern for First Amendment principles, so extensively that privacy law had become nearly "constitutionalized." Of particular concern to the Court were protection for true statements that presented persons in a false light [153] and protection against trivial claims not based on a showing of "actual injury." [154] In major cases between 1965 and 1975 the Court, citing Prosser as an authority on privacy, partially vindicated his concerns.[155]

Prosser and the Legacy of Consensus Thought

Other scholars were writing on Torts in the 1950s and 1960s, and some of their writings exhibited a perspective on tort law, particularly as a compensation system, that was more probing and reflective than that of Prosser.[156] Not one to trumpet publicly his influence, Prosser compared himself to "a packrat," who was "at best a collector; and the most that can ever be said for him is that he sometimes chooses well." [157] But Prosser was nonetheless the significant theoretical force in Torts scholarship from the Second World War to the opening of the 1970s. His position of significance illuminates the intellectual climate of those years. Prosser's methodology, as author of casebooks, treatises, articles, and the Restatement, was essentially constant. He classified and simplified doctrine; he buttressed his classifications with compendious footnotes, which, if examined, revealed his classifications to be far more preliminary than they seemed. He raised policy issues and debated them, but rarely with passion and sometimes wearing the mask of the "dispassionate observer." His principal interest was in facilitating the orderly processes of the American legal system. In this effort he made sure to keep his writing clean, bright, and lively: when a doctrinal area was "in hopeless confusion" Prosser's portrait of the chaos was clear enough, and when administrative difficulties muddled the thrust of legal reforms, Prosser cataloged the difficulties with dispatch. He did not abandon traditional doctrinal categories, nor did he make a fetish of insurance; on the other hand his most influential scholarship was in areas where the negligence principle either did not apply or was being supplanted.

If the direction in which Torts scholarship moved after World War II was toward a more explicit recognition of the compensatory features of tort law, Prosser moved with the trends. His lukewarm endorsement of comparative negligence underscored the difficulties with pristine negligence theory as a compensation device, and his work in products liability helped encourage the growth of strict liability theory, which allegedly distributed risks and allocated losses more efficiently than negligence. His transformation of privacy from a miscellaneous residual category to an expanding new tort opened up another vast potential means of redress for emotionally injured persons. Yet in none of these ventures did Prosser seriously propose an alternative to established tort theory. His comparative negligence proposals stopped short of outlawing contributory negligence as a defense. He maintained that the risk-distribution arguments of strict liability theory were "makeweights," and that public safety was its principal rationale. And he expressed concern over too broad an expansion of the ambit of privacy.

In his position as an intermediary between those who would retain the dominance of negligence theory and those who proposed alternatives to negligence, and in his focus on process, sometimes at the expense of substance, Prosser symbolized the "consensus" intellectual posture of legal scholarship in the 1950s and 1960s. The consensus that he implicitly articulated was that common law subjects were capable of doctrinal analysis, that they changed constantly but incrementally, that they resisted radical modifications, and that their analysis was best left in the hands of professionals. In the 1971 edition of his treatise Prosser listed, as he had in every edition since the first, the "factors affecting tort liability." These were the "moral aspect of the defendant's conduct," the "convenience of administration," the "capacity to bear loss," the "prevention and punishment" of future harm, and the "historical development of tort law." [158] Having listed those factors, Prosser then got to the business at hand: classifying and cataloging cases, with scant reference to his list.

One might have the impression, from reading the organization of Prosser's four treatise editions, that tort law had changed only slightly from the 1940s to the 1970s. That was, of course, the impression Prosser wanted to create: the same bundle of factors allegedly affected tort liability in 1971 that had affected it thirty years earlier. And yet all the areas in which Prosser had made scholarly contributions had exhibited trends that suggested that a basic change in the conception of tort law was taking place. An idea of Torts as a public law subject, concerned primarily with the adjustment of risks among members of the public so as to achieve fairer and more efficient means of compensating injured persons, was replacing an idea of Torts as a private law subject, concerned primarily with deterring and punishing blameworthy civil conduct.

To conceive of tort law as "public law in disguise" had its heretical aspects, since the conception suggested that tort doctrines were, and perhaps always had been, exercises in public policy. That being so, there seemed nothing wrong with legislative invasions of common law areas, such as comparative negligence, with sweeping doctrinal change if public sentiment demanded it, or with the transformation of Torts into a subject, like administrative law, that used private disputes as a basis for making public rules. Prosser's synthesis did not openly acknowledge any such transformation in the way that tort law was conceived. Rather, Prosser took pains to retain the doctrinal superstructure of an autonomous private law subject, whose changes came from within.

But nonetheless the change seemed to have come. Making an assumption that tort law was now a "compensation system," a number of scholars, beginning in 1970, began to revive theoretically oriented analyses of the field of Torts that were reminiscent of the early undertakings of Holmes and his peers in the 1870s. With Torts seemingly defined as a "public" field, a search was instituted for new theoretical perspectives on its public issues. The result was a striking renaissance of creative scholarship in Torts and a fragmentation of the surface coherence that Prosser had helped secure. Before considering scholarly developments in the 1970s, however, this narrative takes up the contributions of a judge who emerged as an influential torts theoretician in the same years that Prosser emerged as the preeminent torts scholar of his generation. Prosser and Roger Traynor were friends and often intellectual allies: their partnership was a significant event in the intellectual history of torts in America.

6

The Judge As Twentieth-Century Torts Theorist: Traynor

Only two years elapsed between the last year of Cardozo's judicial tenure and the first year of Roger Traynor's: but for Cardozo's sudden illness the two men's careers might have overlapped. Even so the universes in which the two men functioned were barely comparable. Cardozo began as a judge in 1916; Traynor retired in 1970. Cardozo's tenure on the New York Court of Appeals took place in a period when Torts was conceived of as a private law subject dominated by the negligence principle. During Traynor's thirty years as associate justice and chief justice of the Supreme Court of California the "public" implications of tort law were increasingly perceived and alternatives to negligence were given serious attention. Both Traynor and Cardozo had a keen sense of the intellectual climate of their tenures and each operated within the tacitly appropriate limits of his perceived role as judge. But Traynor, like Cardozo, is singled out for attention in the intellectual history of Torts because he did not simply work within the prevailing theories of his time and place, but made theoretical contributions of his own, thereby influencing the direction of twentieth-century tort law.

Traynor's Conception of Judging

The context of Traynor's tenure alone dictated that his opportunities would be different from those of Cardozo. By the early twentieth century New York was a mature commercial state, its jurisprudence a rich panoply of the legal themes associated with urban and industrial life. California, by comparison, was in the infant stages of its growth and diversification. California's massive growth occurred after 1930, a significant fact because "problems" and "solutions" associated specifically with rapid growth had come to be addressed in new ways. In particular, the role of government as a paternalistic agent had come to be approved. In California this meant legislation designed to alleviate the human costs of growth; it also meant legislation designed to achieve minimum standards of health, security, and education for California's vast and heterogeneous population.

Traynor's career thus took place in a time when California judges confronted an increasingly detailed legislative apparatus that threatened to usurp their lawmaking powers. Moreover, Traynor did not have the established base of common law jurisprudence with which Cardozo had worked. Within the ambit of his common law powers Traynor arguably had more room to innovate; Cardozo, on the other hand, had not, for most of his career, operated in an age of social legislation by a paternalistic state. The different contexts suggested that Traynor would need to define his lawmaking role vis-a-vis that of the legislature more carefully than had Cardozo. On the other hand Traynor would not need to spend as much time confronting the established opinions of his predecessor judges.

Perceptions of the nature and function of tort law had also changed from Cardozo's tenure to that of Traynor. Cardozo had not exhibited much awareness of the potential of tort law as a device for spreading and shifting losses. His infusion of standards of mortality into the law of fraud and his preservation of status categories in the area of landowner duties, for example, were consistent with an admonitory conception of the purposes of tort law. While Cardozo was not unsympathetic to the plight of the disadvantaged, there is little indication that he assumed, as a judge, that society had a responsibility to compensate injured persons. By 1940, when Traynor was appointed to the California Supreme Court, literature on the compensation functions of tort law had appeared and the primacy of a nineteenth-century ethos of injury had at least been shaken. Traynor and his contemporary judges had to contemplate seriously the notion that tort law was primarily a compensation system.

The most central factor distinguishing Traynor's tort decisions from those of Cardozo, however, was Traynor's conception of the role of a judge. That conception was reflected in three special concerns of

Traynor: a strong interest in academic literature as source material; an effort to preserve, where possible, the lawmaking power of courts; and a search for a harmony of result and doctrine in his opinions, so that "an interest in a particular result" appeared as "no more than the final step toward a reasoned judgment." [1]

In *State Rubbish Association v. Siliznoff* [2] Traynor seized upon an opportunity to establish a "new tort" in California. The tort was the one Prosser had discovered in 1939: intentional infliction of emotional distress. John Siliznoff, a prospective rubbish collector in Los Angeles, had refused to join an association that controlled the city's rubbish collection business. Members of the association threatened to beat him up, to damage his truck, and to "put [him] out of business completely." [3] In the face of this threat he promised to join the association, but subsequently became ill, was absent from work for several days, and ultimately failed to pay promissory notes connected to his joining the association. The association sued him on the notes, and Siliznoff counter-claimed, arguing that the notes had been obtained under duress and that the association members' threats had caused him mental suffering. The association countered by arguing that California did not recognize suits for emotional distress alone.

Traynor, for the Supreme Court, concluded that a cause of action in tort was established "when it was shown that one . . . intentionally subjects another to the mental suffering incident to serious threats to his physical well-being, whether or not the threats are made under such circumstances as to constitute a technical assault." [4] To buttress his conclusion Traynor introduced a series of academic authorities, including Prosser and the 1948 Supplement to the Restatement of Torts, which allowed recovery for emotional distress alone. Citing these authorities, he advanced a series of arguments for recognizing the "new tort." Mental suffering was allowed as a major element of damages in "slight-impact" cases; it was "anomalous to deny recovery" because the defendant's conduct "fell short of producing some physical injury." [5] The common experience of jurors was an adequate check on feigned claims.[6] And "administrative difficulties" resulting from the granting of relief in emotional distress cases were not a justifiable reason for not recognizing the action.[7]

The *Siliznoff* pattern was common: in nearly every instance where a Traynor decision represented a departure from precedent or a revision of established doctrine he relied heavily on academic sources to lend support to his position. Traynor felt that academicians could "differentiate . . . good growth from rubbish," and "mark . . . the diseased anachronism for rejection" by courts. A law professor at Berkeley before becoming a judge, Traynor was particularly conversant with academic literature and notably adept in its use. A commentator in 1965 declared that Traynor had "the best taste in legal citation of any contemporary judge": [9] while Traynor's scholarly citations strengthened his argument, they never overwhelmed it or distracted from it. Traynor used academic sources to create an impression of varied and knowledgeable support for a position he was advancing. The contributions he cited were treated respectfully, but they were nonetheless grist for the mill of Traynor's central argument. More than anything else, Traynor brought academic sources within the range of cognizable authorities for a court—they were for him the equivalent of past decisions. This in itself went far toward establishing the authoritative professional dimensions of legal scholarship and underscored the symbiotic relationship between twentieth-century legal scholars and judges. Academicians, noting Traynor's respect for their work, responded in kind: one commentator said that "we professors prefer Judge Traynor's clear, analytic approach"; [10] another called him "a law professor's judge." [11]

The value that he placed on educated opinion and the fact that he was conspicuously educated may have given Traynor a sense of self-esteem as a judge. [12] In any event he appreciated his lawmaking powers and sought to guard them against potential infringements by other lawmaking bodies. Mid-twentieth-century judges have had two principal competitors as lawmakers in the decision of torts cases, legislatures and juries. The latter competitor's presence has been primarily an offshoot of the growth of the negligence principle; the former's presence has been augmented with the emergence of alternatives to negligence theory.

As the tests of negligence ("reasonable" conduct and "due care under the circumstances") were increasingly conceived of as exercises in scrutinizing the discrete conduct of individuals, the role of juries as lawmakers in torts cases potentially loomed large. Holmes, as noted, disliked the unpredictability of jury lawmaking and sought to design tests that would avoid jury participation where possible, but nonetheless recognized that the kinds of situations that give rise to negligence actions do not tend to repeat themselves in any precise way. [13] "Scientific" late nineteenth-century tort theory, recognizing this problem and sharing Holmes's assumption about the anarchic consequences of jury lawmaking, attempted to avoid jury participation by establishing rigid, universal defenses, such as assumption of risk, and by making proof of their violation a matter of law. Under this approach judges could often find that a defense was absolute and dismiss the case before it was sent to the jury.

As negligence theory was modified in the early twentieth century to encompass a more "relational" definition of civil duties, one might have expected more jury participation, since the "relation" between a given plaintiff and a given defendant often involved special, non-duplicative circumstances. But, as Cardozo's opinions illustrated, early twentieth-century judges increasingly used the concept of "duty" to analyze the relation parties bore to one another, and considered the existence or nonexistence of duties to be questions for courts to resolve. One rationale, in fact, for subsuming legal causation questions in questions of duty was the uneven and unpredictable effects of making proximate cause an issue to be determined by juries.

Nonetheless by Traynor's tenure juries remained a potentially powerful lawmaking force in negligence cases, because every time the question of a defendant's negligence turned on an evaluation of his conduct in discrete circumstances, the jury emerged as a prospective evaluator. As Traynor put it in a 1944 decision: "In the field of negligence it is common practice for the jury to determine not only the facts but the standard of conduct to be applied within the compass of the rule that the conduct prescribed must be that of a reasonably prudent man under the circumstances. To determine whether given conduct should impose liability or bar a recovery is to make law." [14]

The scope of the jury's lawmaking power, however, could be controlled by the court. If a court had formulated a standard of reasonable conduct, the jury's only responsibility was to determine whether the defendant had violated that standard. Traynor saw this determination as a "factual" one. If, on the other hand, a court had not formulated a standard, the jury could do so. The message of Traynor's view of the court-jury partnership in negligence cases was thus clear enough: if a court wanted to retain lawmaking power for itself, it needed to set standards of care through specific jury instructions.

An illustrative case for Traynor was *Startup v. Pacific Electric Railway Co.*[15] A three-car train struck an automobile at a grade crossing. The railroad used wig-wag signals as devices to warn drivers crossing its tracks. The grade crossing where the accident occurred had multiple tracks, and when the driver of the automobile approached the crossing, the signals began to move and he stopped. Two trains then passed the crossing on separate tracks. The signals then stopped, and the driver, without looking further, proceeded to cross the tracks. As he did, a third train struck the automobile. A passenger in the car sued the railroad, claiming that the company was negligent in the maintenance of the signals.

A majority of the California Supreme Court held that the questions of the railroad's negligence in maintaining the signals and the car driver's negligence in crossing the tracks were for the jury. Traynor wrote a separate opinion in which he disputed the holding on the car driver's negligence. The majority had said that "it is ordinarily a question for the jury whether the precautions taken by the driver of the automobile are sufficient in view of all the circumstances." [16] Traynor, however, felt that the question of the car driver's negligence was a question of law to be determined by the court. "A jury," Traynor argued, was "in no better position than [the] court to answer this question. There is every reason why this issue, often raised in practice, should be settled by this court and not left to the oscillating verdicts of juries." He then cited Holmes's remarks about juries in negligence cases in *The Common Law* and proposed that "the court . . . should determine the standard of reasonable conduct" [17] in cases where drivers entered grade crossings after signals had ceased to move. In Traynor's view drivers who had stopped when a signal began to move and crossed after it had ceased were not negligent as a matter of law, even if they failed to look before crossing.

Traynor's position in *Startup* was especially notable because he conceded that the question of the car driver's negligence was irrelevant.[18] The plaintiffs in the suit were passengers; their driver's negligence was not imputable to them. Thus, if the railroad was negligent in failing to maintain signals, any contributory negligence on the part of the car driver would not defeat recovery by passengers. Given this fact, Traynor's exegesis on setting the standard of conduct for the car driver took on the quality of advisory comments. He appears to have regarded *Startup* as an opportunity for articulating his views about the proper division of lawmaking power between courts and juries in negligence cases. Those views, with their focus on the unpredictability of jury decisions, paralleled ones held by Holmes.

Traynor was no more anxious to concede lawmaking power to

legislatures than he was to concede it to juries. A case in point was *Clinkscales v. Carver,*[19] in which Herman Carver failed to stop at a stop sign and collided with an intersecting car, thereby killing Richard Clinkscales. The stop sign had been authorized by a county ordinance that had never become effective because of "defects in publication." [20] The trial court had instructed the jury that Carver's running of the stop sign, being a violation of the ordinance, was negligence as a matter of law (negligence *per se*), and if they found that it caused Clinkscales's death, they should find against Carver. On appeal Carver argued that since the ordinance was defective, its violation could not be negligence *per se,* and therefore the question of his negligence was a matter for jury determination.

Traynor's opinion advanced a theory of the effect of criminal statutes on negligence cases. Where criminal statutes, such as stop sign ordinances, provided no civil penalties, Traynor argued, their effect on negligence cases was merely that of possible standards of civil liability. The decision to convert the statutory standards of conduct to standards relevant to negligence actions rested with the court: "the standard formulated by a legislative body . . . in a criminal statute becomes the standard to determine civil liability only because the court accepts it." [21]

In *Clinkscales* the effect of Traynor's theory was to affirm the trial judge's finding that Carver's failure to stop at the stop sign constituted negligence *per se*. Traynor accepted the statutory standard: "failure to observe a stop sign," he maintained, "is unreasonably dangerous conduct whether or not the driver is immune from criminal prosecution." [22] But the theory gave an appellate court an option not to apply a statutory standard to a negligence case: the court could treat a violation of a statute as wholly irrelevant to the determination of civil liability. This gave courts a good deal of autonomy, especially in those cases where the purpose of the statute seemed directed at the kind of accident that had occurred. While Traynor gave no indication in *Clinkscales* that he would ignore standards of conduct established by relevant safety statutes, his language gave him that option. A dissenting opinion in *Clinkscales* called the question of Carver's negligence "a question of fact for the jury," and maintained that Traynor's opinion had reinforced a "manifestly prejudicial" [23] withdrawal of the issue from the jury.

In short, Traynor's approach to the role of statutes in negligence cases had a two-fold purpose: increasing lawmaking power in appellate courts vis-à-vis legislatures and increasing lawmaking power in appellate courts vis-à-vis juries. The twin goals of the theory were made manifest in Traynor's long concurring opinion in *Saterlee v. Orange Glen School District*.[24] That case involved a collision between a car and a school bus at an intersection where there was sharply controverted testimony as to which vehicle had entered the intersection first. A statute provided that drivers entering an intersection from a "different highway" had the right-of-way over those continuing on the same highway, and that vehicles entering an intersection on the right had the right-of-way over vehicles entering on the left. The bus was entering the intersection from a "different highway" and was on the right of the car.

The trial judge, after instructing the jury about the relevant right-of-way statutes, then said that one who had the right-of-way could abuse it: there was no "absolute right to barge through ignoring any danger to the other motorist[s]." "In other words," the trial judge said, "the test is [w]hat would a reasonably prudent person do under the same or similar circumstances." [25] A majority of the Supreme Court found this instruction erroneous because it allowed the jury to excuse entirely violations of the right-of-way laws. Violation of the statute, the majority maintained, created a presumption that the violator was negligent; that presumption had to be rebutted and could not be cast aside in a general "reasonableness" inquiry.

Traynor's concurrence went further, finding that the car driver's violation of the right-of-way statutes was negligence in itself. His theory of the case was based on two assumptions: that the applicability of the statute to the negligence action was to be determined by the court, and that once the court had decided that the statute was applicable a jury, if it found that the statute was violated, could not make an independent judgment about "reasonableness." In *Satterlee* findings of fact were sharply disputed. The jury had to determine whether the bus or the car had entered the intersection first, or whether the bus had exceeded the speed limit in attempting to be first into the intersection. Those findings were crucial to the result, but once they were made the jury had no power to excuse their violation if it found that one or another of the litigants had violated the right-of-way rules.

Thus Traynor was arguing in *Satterlee* for discretion in appellate courts to adopt or disregard criminal statutes in negligence cases and also for a check on "uncontrolled discretion in the jury" to disregard those statutes. Such an argument could be based only on a sense that an orderly disposition of negligence issues required the formulation of tests and standards by courts rather than by other prospective lawmakers. Nowhere in the corpus of Traynor's decisions can one find an explicit rationale for this intuition. Yet it is clear that he intended, where potential competition surfaced between judges and other decisionmakers in common law cases, to retain decisionmaking power in judges.

The basis for Traynor's faith in the judiciary as a lawmaking force —his activist theory of judging was maintained intact during decades where judicial "self-restraint" was a popular posture among judges and commentators [26]—was his conviction that rationality could be achieved through enlightened judging. A faith in rationality had returned with the emergence of "consensus" attitudes in legal thought after the Second World War, and Traynor was in this sense representative of his age. In Traynor, unlike Cardozo, there was a strong sense that by simply going about the business of judging one would achieve rational results. Absent from Traynor's opinions was any of the soul-searching of Cardozo when a result seemed anomalous or harsh, or the assertiveness of Holmes when elaboration led one to sticky places. Traynor simply began his arguments with certain premises, gathered from the pronouncements of others, and let them lead to results. The creative qualities of his opinions were downplayed; the common sense of the opinions was allowed to speak for itself.

Traynor never departed from his belief that rationality was an achievable judicial goal. His extrajudicial writings were laden with evidence of that belief. Judges were "uniquely situated to articulate timely rules of reason." They were free from "adversary bias" and from "political and personal pressures"; they worked in an "independent and analytically objective" atmosphere; [27] they sought to "rise above the vanity of [their] stubborn preconceptions"; they understood that it was "essential [to] be interested in a rational outcome." [28] So long as judges took the time and care to justify their decisions in their reasoning, their motivation in reaching particular results became unimportant. The reasons themselves justified the result: if the reasons were plausible and persuasive, given current values and analytical standards, that was enough.

The charge of being an activist judge never disturbed Traynor, for he believed a judge was only as powerful as his reasons were persuasive. Traynor had no difficulty infringing on juries' traditional power to decide questions of fact,[29] or undertaking substantial review of the decisions of administrative agencies,[30] or deriving common law rules from statutory analogies,[31] or filling in gaps in legislative coverage,[32] or openly making policy choices,[33] or adjusting the retroactive effect of judicial decisions,[34] or creating new common law actions.[35] Since he took seriously the obligations of judges to be "analytically objective" and reach "rational outcome[s]," he never assumed that judicial activism might become an exercise in arbitrary power.

Here one sees how closely Traynor's conception of judging identified itself with the prevailing drift of mid-twentieth-century thought. The assumption that "objectivity" was realizable, either by detached scholars or disinterested judges, and the assumption that rational outcomes would somehow emerge from the deliberations of officials each invested objectivity and rationality with an independent weight that now may seem implausible. Understanding the currently approved techniques of scholarly analysis in a profession or a discipline does not make one more objective; in judicial decision making, especially, those techniques become aids in reaching a result about which one is not indifferent. "Rationality" can be reduced to current notions of plausibility; it does not seem to be a timeless construct that is simply "there" to be grasped and articulated. So unless one regards Traynor as naive—a trait that his career belies—one is inclined to conclude that his exaltation of objectivity and rationality was a version of homage to the prevailing canons of his time. It seemed, in the postwar years, that to deny the possibility of achieving an objective stance toward one's work or to caricature one's ability to reach reasoned outcomes was to threaten some basic faiths of the American creed.

Traynor as Torts Theorist: Negligence

Traynor, then, foreswore agonizing about either the legitimacy of his power or the hard policy choices he was required to make and got on with the job. His opinions minimized his own presence to concentrate on the logical momentum of his arguments. His effort, like that of Cardozo in his innovative decisions, was to create an impression that results flowed naturally from a canvass of available sources and arguments; that one had only to think the problem through and one would arrive at the solution. Since several of Traynor's decisions also represented innovations in the common law of California, there has been some tendency to consider him a "reformist" or a "liberal" judge and to assume that he was regularly aligned on the side of doctrinal change. In torts, however, Traynor's pattern was much less easily characterized. He was perhaps the leading judicial innovator of his contemporaries in the field of products liability, and his career may be most remembered for his accomplishments in that area. But in negligence cases his opinions were far more cautious and doctrinaire, and his results limited liability as much as they extended it.

A revealing set of Traynor's negligence decisions involved cases defining the liability of landowners. This area has been persistently dominated by the categorizing impulses of late nineteenth-century negligence theory and even by "status" conceptions of tort liability that had preceded the rise of modern negligence. Liability in land-owner cases has turned on the status of the person injured and the requisite duty owed to him by the landowner. In orthodox classifications, landowners owed no duty to trespassers, a limited duty to licensees, and a more extensive duty to invitees, especially those invited for a "business purpose." [36] While courts carved out exceptions, especially for child trespassers and "social" invitees whose presence on the land was beneficial to the landowner, the categories persisted in all jurisdictions until very recently.

Traynor's approach to landowner cases, especially in light of his reformist tendencies in the area of products liability, was relatively preservationist. Landowner accidents seem a fertile field for the presence of liability insurance, since, especially where the landowner-ship is a business enterprise, they occur with some regularity and are difficult to prevent. The acquisition of liability insurance has become common among landowning business enterprises. In products liability Traynor used the presence of insurance among product manufacturers as a rationale for the imposition of strict liability. In landowner cases, however, Traynor not only persisted in employing negligence, he regularly used the existing status categories as devices to bar injured persons from recovery.

Traynor's first landowner opinion came in *Neel v. Mannings, Inc.,*[37] where a woman struck her head against a ceiling board while going up a stairway in a restaurant. The restaurant was crowded and the woman apparently moved to her left to avoid persons descending the stairway, striking her head in the process. A majority of the California Supreme Court sustained a jury verdict in the woman's favor, finding that she was an invitee, that the restaurant owed her a duty of reasonable care to keep its premises safe, and that its maintenance of the stairway amounted to negligence. Traynor, in dissent, argued that the danger of the stairway ceiling was "so apparent that the visitor [could] reasonably be expected to notice it and protect himself." [38] Since there was no basis for concluding that the injured woman "did not have adequate notice of the condition of the stairway," Traynor maintained, there was no basis "for concluding that [the restaurant] violated any duty owed to [the woman]." [39]

In the context of landowner cases at that time, Traynor's view was not striking: the Restatement of Torts did not expand the scope of landowners' duties toward "obvious" hazards until the late 1950s. [40] Traynor's opinion was nonetheless interesting in light of his conclusion two years later that a manufacturer of soft drinks should be liable to a consumer to which it owed no duty, since the consumer's injuries had been caused by an exploding bottle whose explosion could not have been prevented through the use of ordinary care. [41] In 1948, Traynor again found no liability in a landowner case, in this instance where a homeowner failed to protect a domestic employee against injuries from a fall when a defective railing gave way. [42] In this case, *Devens v. Goldberg,* Traynor maintained that the employee was an invitee and that homeowners had no duty to protect invitees against latent defects. [43] The defect in the railing, Traynor argued, could not have been detected except by a trained building inspector, and to hold a homeowner to an expert's standard of care was to extend the duty of landowners beyond its hitherto recognized limits.

The most significant of Traynor's landowner opinions came in *Knight v. Kaiser Co.,* [44] where a ten-year-old child was asphyxiated when a sand pile on which he was playing collapsed. The majority found that the child was a trespasser and was owed no duty of care unless the sand pile constituted an "attractive nuisance," which might entice child trespassers. It further found that sand piles were not attractive nuisances, analogizing them to cliffs or bodies of water. [45] The majority opinion's reasoning was strained to the point of ineptitude and provoked a searching Traynor dissent.

Traynor began by quoting a section of the California Civil Code, which appeared to enact a universal duty of care owed to all the world by all the world.[46] He then stated that the section augured the coming of a time when a choice would seem necessary between its provisions and established California cases that held that landowners owed no duty of care to trespassers. Reviewing the "better considered cases," however, Traynor concluded that they too had implicitly adopted a standard of liability based on "the reasonableness and propriety of [the landowner's] conduct, in view of all surrounding circumstances and conditions." [47] In the *Knight* case the defendant had tolerated children trespassing on his property, should have known that sand piles were dangerous to children, should have known that children would not know of the dangers consequent on playing in sand piles, and could have easily and cheaply erected barriers. Traynor would have made the defendant liable, but, more significantly, he would have resorted to "the customary rules of ordinary negligence cases" [48] in deciding child trespasser cases.

Looking back at the sequence of decisions from *Neel* through *Knight,* it is possible to argue that Traynor had never taken the landowner categories seriously. He may have been persuaded in *Neel* that the plaintiff had simply not looked where she was going, given the fact that the restaurant had been open for several years, that about 300 to 400 persons patronized it daily, and that no like accident had previously occurred. His statement about a landowner's lack of responsibility for obvious hazards, in this vein, merely buttressed his intuitions. In *Devens,* similarly, Traynor's conception of the landowner's duty seemed to square with his sense of the equities (a homeowner could hardly be expected to discover a latent defect in a railing) rather than with existing rules about the obligations of landowners. Finally in *Knight,* provoked by a labored, mechanical majority opinion, he jettisoned the categories altogether in child trespasser cases and substituted the "reasonableness" standard that he had been employing all along.

This reading of Traynor's landowner cases has the advantage of hindsight, since in 1968, in an opinion in which Traynor was with the majority, the California Supreme Court abandoned status categories in landowner cases and substituted a reasonableness test.[49] The case went beyond *Knight* in that it involved an adult "social guest" rather than a child trespasser. Likewise analogizing to the California Civil Code, the opinion stated that "everyone is responsible for an injury caused to another by want of his ordinary care of skill." [50]

While Traynor's *Knight* dissent may have foreshadowed the eventual abandonment of status categories in the landowner area, it is too much to say that Traynor had that result in mind all along. His pattern of decisions in landowner cases typified general trends in his tenure: a cautious, even mechanical beginning, where his decisions were not distinctive; a growing interest in his middle years in searching for a "rational" basis of common law rules and in discarding the rules if he could not find such a basis; and a confident, activist posture in his later years, in which he made rules and drew lines with apparent ease. The landowner sequence nonetheless shows Traynor not inclined to depart from negligence theory to investigate an "enterprise liability" rationale. Even though he did not find the status categories binding or invariably helpful, he felt that the "customary rules" of negligence should govern.

All twentieth-century common law judges with an interest in developing a comprehensive approach to negligence have had to formulate a theory of legal causation. Cardozo had chosen to approach causation issues through the rubric of "duty" analysis, which transferred the difficult questions from those pertaining to "causes" to those pertaining to the existence and violation of duties. "Independent," "intervening," "concurrent," and other comparable labels for "causes" were abandoned by Cardozo's analysis, which focused on the "interests" at stake in a case and the extent to which a plaintiff's interests should be cognizable to a defendant. Traynor adopted a similar approach. Where possible, he avoided legal causation questions by subsuming them in his analysis of duties.

Richards v. Stanley [51] is a case in point. There Mrs. Manfred Stanley left her car on a public street, where it was stolen. The thief subsequently collided with Robert Richards, a motorcyclist. Richards sued Mrs. Stanley, arguing that her act in leaving the keys in her car created a foreseeable risk that motorists such as he would be injured. Mrs. Stanley countered by arguing that even if she had been "negligent" in leaving the keys in the car the theft constituted an independent intervening cause relieving her of liability.

Traynor was confronted in *Richards* with a statute making it a misdemeanor to leave keys in a car parked on a public street, and with cases in other jurisdictions holding that car owners owed a duty to injured third persons in such situations. Nonetheless, he found that

Mrs. Stanley was not liable to Richards. Traynor disposed of the statute by noting that it was not intended to have any bearing on civil actions and therefore had not been enacted for the protection of injured third persons. The purpose of the statute was apparently to protect owners of cars only from their own carelessness.[52] He next turned to the question of a common law duty. He noted that at common law a person who voluntarily entrusted his car to another was under no duty to protect third parties from the other's carelessness unless the car owner knew in advance that the person to whom he had entrusted his car was incompetent to drive it. The question in *Richards* was whether a car owner who had not intended to "loan" his car to a thief should be responsible if the car, at the hands of the thief, injured third parties. In the absence of a statute designed to create such responsibility, Traynor found the imposition of liability on defendants such as Mrs. Stanley anomalous.

The risk of negligent driving created by Mrs. Stanley's act of leaving her keys in her car, Traynor argued, was less than the risk she would create by voluntarily lending her car to another. She owed no duty to third persons in the latter case. Moreover, the legislature had provided that owners who voluntarily entrusted their cars to "financially irresponsible persons," although those persons' negligence would be imputed to them, would have their liability limited to $5000 for personal injury and $10,000 for property damage. To allow recovery in *Richards* would mean that persons who had not willingly loaned their cars could be subject to unlimited liability. Consequently Traynor concluded that Mrs. Stanley's "duty to exercise reasonable care in the management of her automobile" did not "encompass a duty to protect [third persons] from the negligent driving of a thief." [53]

Other California cases had held, however, that the negligent driving of a third person was not an "unforeseeable" intervening cause so as to relieve the original defendant from liability.[54] Traynor's ruling in *Richards* enabled him to bypass those cases altogether. The car owner owed no duty to the motorcyclist, he argued, because of the "remoteness" of their relationship. And since "no . . . duty exists, "no problem of intervening causation arises." [55]

Richards was reminiscent of *Palsgraf* in that duty analysis supposedly eliminated any speculation about the spatial or temporal limits of "proximate" causation in such cases. Under the *Richards* standard the car owner apparently would not be liable to a person who was injured chasing the thief as he or she drove away. No duty to third persons meant no duty. And yet implicit considerations of remoteness and foreseeability had affected the result in *Richards*. That fact became clear in another stolen vehicle case, *Richardson v. Ham*,[56] where Traynor found that the owners of a bulldozer who had left it unlocked were liable to persons injured by two men who had broken into the bulldozer, started it, and then were unable to stop it. The *Richardson* case was an obvious one in which to impose liability. Two bulldozers had been left out overnight on top of a mesa, one without adequate locks. A bulldozer can be started without ignition keys, hence failure to lock one of the bulldozers meant that any passerby could start it. Bulldozers are not easily operated without special knowledge; in the *Richardson* case the two men who started the bulldozer eventually had to abandon it, pointing it in the direction of a canyon. After they abandoned the bulldozer it plowed over the edge of the mesa, crossed a freeway, traveled through a house, collided with a house-trailer and a car, and finally was stopped when it crashed into a retaining wall and a utility pole.

Given this scenario, the question was only what rationale could be employed to compensate the victims of the bulldozer's sortie. That question was somewhat complicated by the broad language in *Richards*, which intimated that persons who inadvertently allowed others to use their vehicles owed no duty to third parties injured in the process. Counsel for the defendants in *Richardson* argued that the *Richards* case relieved them from liability.

Traynor had several options in *Richardson*, including focusing on the obligation of vehicle owners not to make their vehicles available to others whom they suspected of being incapable of managing them. That was arguably a much larger prospective class of persons where bulldozers were concerned, arguing for stricter vigilance over bulldozers. Traynor chose, however, to focus on the unusual and "attractive" nature of bulldozers, their "enormous" potential to do harm, and the relative ease ("a simple but effective lock") by which they could be protected.[57] He thus concluded that the owner of the bulldozers owed "a duty to exercise reasonable care to protect third parties from injuries arising from [the bulldozers'] operation by intermeddlers." [58]

Having established a duty, Traynor had resolved any legal causation issues. The bulldozer's owner had argued that even if he owed a duty to protect third persons from injuries caused by the operation of the bulldozer by intermeddlers, the fact that the intermeddlers' acts were intentional constituted a "superseding cause" that relieved him from liability. To this argument Traynor merely quoted the Restatement of Torts, which stated that if "the realizable likelihood that a third person may act in a particular manner" was the very risk that made the bulldozer owner negligent, it was irrelevant whether the risk occurred through a third party's innocence, negligence, or intentional act.[59] In other words, the same "duty-risk" analysis that resulted in the bulldozer owner owing a duty to those injured by the bulldozer eliminated all issues of "superseding" causation. The very risk that the owner should have foreseen had occurred, causing injury; it was irrelevant how the injury was caused.

It is hard to imagine that Traynor was wedded very seriously to the implications of his causation analysis in *Richardson*. Suppose in the process of its sortie the bulldozer crashed through a shed in which dynamite was stored, setting off an explosion which knocked down a birds' nest on an adjoining farm. It was highly unlikely that the owner of the birds could successfully sue the owner of the bulldozer. Yet the damage to the shed was foreseeable if the bulldozer was let loose, and the dynamite explosion was foreseeable once the bulldozer invaded the shed. If damage to adjoining property (the birds) was a foreseeable risk of allowing the bulldozer to be loosed, was it irrelevant how the property was damaged?

Richards and *Richardson,* taken together, suggest that Traynor, like Cardozo, was disinclined to grapple with the metaphysics of causation. He tended to convert causation questions to "duty" questions and to determine the existence of duties through interest-balancing. When interests were balanced the claim of the injured persons in *Richardson* took on considerably more weight than that of the motorcyclist in *Richards*. The foreseeability of harm from a moving bulldozer was far greater than from a moving car; the potentially serious nature of the harm, given the comparative weights of the vehicles, also was far greater for bulldozers; the cost of preventing the theft of a bulldozer, like the cost of preventing the theft of a car, was relatively minor. Beyond that simple exercise the *Richards* and *Richardson* opinions could not be said to stand for much, since their broad language seemed limited in its application.

The search for order and predictability characteristic of Traynor's stance as a judge cannot be said to have come to fruition in his negligence opinions. The status categories of landowner cases afforded a certain predictability, if rigidity, but Traynor's opinions never adhered to them faithfully and finally abandoned them for a test—due care under the circumstances—which invited individualized treatment. In the area of causation Traynor's approach ended up being a process of interest-balancing which, as the *Richards-Richardson* sequence illustrated, could confine the breadth of Traynor's own generalized pronouncements.

The most interesting feature of Traynor's negligence opinions was their relatively traditional cast. Cardozo's relational approach to negligence and duty-risk analysis of causation issues were innovative for his time, but by Traynor's tenure they had become standard formulas, sanctioned by the *Restatement of Torts*. At no time in his landowner opinions did Traynor raise the possibility of alternative approaches, such as a strict liability standard for latent defective instrumentalities on a landowner's premises, that he had pioneered in the defective products area. He did not suggest, for example, that a bulldozer would be regarded as an "abnormally dangerous" instrumentality, or that industrial enterprises could insure against the possibility of injuries to children from substances on their land. There is the hint in his negligence decisions of a sympathy for victims of industrial enterprises as distinguished from victims of private persons, but even this pattern is not clearly apparent.

Why did Traynor regard the area of defective products as somehow inadequate for treatment by negligence theory and peculiarly suited for strict liability? An effort to answer this question strikes at the heart of Traynor's motivations as a judge. But a full response to the inquiry must await consideration of Traynor's remarkably innovative and activist set of opinions in the area of products liability.

Traynor as Torts Theorist: Strict Liability

Escola v. Coca-Cola Bottling Co.[60] was Traynor's most famous opinion. Like *MacPherson,* it was one of those moments in the history of Torts when a judge is given an opportunity to assemble some emerging ideas and apply them to an actual case in a manner that results in significant doctrinal change. In *Escola* the emerging ideas were associated with a theory of strict liability for defective products cases. Traynor, as we shall see, did not originate any of the ideas. He applied them, however, to a case in which they seemed to make good sense, and then used that case to advance arguments for their general use. His contribution was in the collection of insights made by scholars and in the transformation of those insights into common law doctrine.

In *Escola* a waitress was injured when a soda bottle exploded in her hand as she was carrying it from its case to a refrigerator. Soda bottles were tested by the bottle manufacturer before being shipped to the defendant company, which then filled them with soft drinks and distributed them to retailers. The waitress stated that she had handled the bottle carefully and did not know how it had exploded. The trial court allowed her the benefit of the doctrine of *res ipsa loquitur* (the thing speaks for itself), thereby compelling the Coca-Cola company to come forward with evidence to rebut a presumption that it was not negligent. The defendant showed that it regularly checked the pressure in the bottles and made visual inspections for defects in the glass, but the jury found for the plaintiff. On appeal a majority of the Supreme Court held that the waitress could receive the benefits of *res ipsa loquitur* and was entitled to recover. Traynor concurred separately.

A comparison of Prosser's 1941 treatise with Traynor's *Escola* concurrence illustrates the heavy reliance placed by Traynor's opinion on academic literature. In his 1941 edition Prosser had, as noted, catalogued reasons why strict liability was an attractive theory for defective products cases. Prosser had maintained that "the consumer is entitled to the maximum of protection at the hands of some one, and . . . the producer, practically and morally, is the one to provide it." [61] "Public policy demands," Traynor said in *Escola,* "that responsibility be fixed wherever it will most effectively reduce the hazards to life and health inherent in defective products that reach the market." [62] The producer, Prosser had argued, was "best able to distribute the risk to the general public by means of prices and insurance." [63] "[T]he risk of injury," Traynor pointed out, "can be insured by the manufacturer and distributed among the public as a cost of doing business." [64] "Even with the aid of *res ipsa loquitur"* Prosser had claimed that difficulties of proving negligence existed for the injured consumer.[65] "An injured person," Traynor asserted, "is not ordinarily in a position to . . . identify the cause of the defect . . . even by the device of *res ipsa loquitur.*" [66]

A "series of warranty actions carrying liability back through retailer and jobber to the original maker" produced "wastefulness and uncertainty," Prosser had argued.[67] Warranty procedure for Traynor was "needlessly circuitous and engender[ed] wasteful litigation." [68] Warranty cases extending liability to the consumers were noteworthy, Prosser felt, for "considerable ingenuity in evolving theories," including a theory that warranties ran with the goods; that dealers assigned the warranties of their producers to consumers; that "a third party beneficiary contract" was "made with the dealer for the benefit of the consumer"; and that the manufacturer was allegedly negligent.[69] "In the food products cases," Traynor noted, "the courts have resorted to various fictions to rationalize the extension of the manufacturer's warranty to the consumer: that a warranty runs with the chattel; that the cause of action of the dealer is assigned to the consumer; that the consumer is a third-party beneficiary of the manufacturer's contract with the dealer. They have also held the manufacturer liable on a mere fiction of negligence." [70]

Warranty was, however, "originally a tort action," Prosser had pointed out, and "a return to the tort theory is still possible." It seemed "far better to discard . . . warranty and impose strict liability outright in tort as a pure matter of social policy." Prosser quoted a 1912 New York decision with approval: "[t]he remedies of injured consumers ought not to be made to depend upon the intricacies of the law of sales." [71] "An action on a warranty 'was, in its origin, a prior action of tort,' " Traynor argued, and the proper view was that "the warranty of the manufacturer to the consumer in the absence of privity of contract rests on public policy . . . The right of a consumer . . . does not depend 'upon the intricacies of the law of sales.' " [72]

Finally, Prosser placed two qualifications on his espousal of strict liability: "the liability should . . . extend only to normal injuries, and the injured plaintiff must still trace the defect to the defendant." [73] Traynor, at the close of his *Escola* opinion, stated that "the manufacturer's liability should . . . be defined in terms of the safety of the product in normal and proper use, and should not extend to injuries that cannot be traced to the product as it reached the market." [74] The striking parallel between the two sources was completed by their use of authorities. Prosser based his advocacy of strict liability in part on the fact that it had "met with the approval of every legal writer who

has discussed it," [75] citing articles by Rollin Perkins,[76] Lindsey Jeanblanc,[77] Lester Feezer,[78] Edwin Patterson,[79] and George Bogert and
Eli Fink.[80] Traynor's battery of academic citations in *Escola* included
each of those articles. And both authors argued the relevancy of criminal statutes prohibiting the manufacture of defective food or drugs.
Prosser stated that such statutes "generally have been construed to
impose an absolute . . . liability in a tort action by the injured consumer"; [81] Traynor stated that "[s]tatutes of this kind result in a
strict liability of the manufacturer in tort to the member of the public
injured." [82]

Traynor relied particularly on Prosser's work in his opinions; the
strong parallels between *Escola* and Prosser's 1941 treatise should not
be taken as an effort to diminish the significance of Traynor's accom-
plishment. It was one thing for Prosser to collect authorities, marshall
reasons, and argue for strict liability in the abstract; another for
Traynor to show, through an impressive synthesis of case law and
academic writing, the apparently obvious advantages of strict liability
treatment for defective products. Traynor's *Escola* opinion came at a
time when strict liability theory was in an embryonic state; he gave it
a model for practical application. Like *MacPherson, Escola* was one
of those cases that helped recast thinking about an entire area of tort
law. Traynor's opinion shifted inquiries from the proper theory of
liability in the defective products area—the logic of strict liability in
tort overwhelmed that of negligence or warranty—to inquiries about
the limits of the strict liability principle. As a consequence of his
Escola concurrence Traynor became identified as the leading judicial
strict liability theorist of his time.

Five years after *Escola* another exploding bottle case came before
Traynor's court, and again he concurred separately. In the case,
Gordon v. Aztec Brewing Co.,[83] a proprietor of a cafe was trans-
ferring a beer bottle from its case to a refrigerator when it exploded,
blinding him in one eye. He sued the bottler. The majority again invoked *res ipsa loquitur* to sustain a jury verdict for the proprietor.
Traynor thought that the facts of the case did not sustain the use of
res ipsa against the defendant, since there was considerable evidence
that the bottle may have been weakened by warehousing operations
after it left the defendant's control. He felt that the use of *res ipsa*
amounted to "hold[ing] [the bottler] strictly liable not only for defects
in its bottles when they leave its control but also for defects that

develop in the normal course of marketing procedures." [84] If so, Traynor would impose strict liability "openly and not by spurious application of [res ipsa] rules." [85]

Employing strict liability analysis, Traynor saw the *Gordon* case as an extension of *Escola*. In *Escola* the bottler was also the distributor, thus no question of the liability of a manufacturer for the acts of others in the chain of distribution was raised. In *Gordon,* however, others in the distribution process had handled the bottle, and the question was whether the bottler was strictly liable for defects traceable to them. Traynor concluded that the bottler should be liable: "public policy demands that the bottler's responsibility must be measured in terms of the normal risks attendant upon the handling of bottled beverages." [86] The bottler could not "shift the responsibility to provide a product that will be safe in the hands of the consumer by routing his products through others." [87]

Thus far in defective products cases Traynor had announced strict liability as his governing principle and included within that principle's reach the acts of agents in the chain of distribution. He had not, however, persuaded a single member of the California Supreme Court to endorse his approach. In the next case in the sequence, *Trust v. Arden Farms Co.,* [88] *res ipsa loquitur* was again considered by a majority of the court, which this time found it inapplicable where one Ruth Trust had set down a half-empty milk bottle on a drainboard. The bottle broke, cutting her wrists. A majority found that she had not produced sufficient evidence to show that any defect in the bottle had occurred before she received it. The majority distinguished *Escola* and *Gordon* on the ground that the milk bottle had remained in Trust's refrigerator for four days after it had been delivered, and the defect might have been caused by it being handled in that interval. Trust had sued both the bottle manufacturer and the milk company; the majority dismissed her case against both.

Traynor, in a separate opinion, agreed that there was no evidence that the bottle was defective when it left the manufacturer's control, given that several months had elapsed between the time the bottle was delivered from the manufacturer to the milk company and the time that it was delivered to Trust. [89] He did not regard the milk company as part of a chain of glass product distribution, since the company was in the milk business, not in the business of making glass products. Traynor would, however, have applied strict liability against the milk company, since he felt that the impact under which the bottle broke was "mild," that there was no evidence that any other person in Trust's family had handled the bottle (the bottle contained skim milk, which only she drank), and that therefore the bottle was defective when delivered by the milk company to Trust.[90] He repeated his reasoning in *Escola* and *Gordon:* enterprises should "incur an absolute liability when an article that [they] have placed on the market, knowing that it is to be used without inspection, proves to have a defect that causes injury to human beings." [91]

Traynor was again the sole proponent of a strict liability approach in *Trust.* But four years later, in *Greenman v. Yuba Power Products,*[92] he imposed strict liability on a manufacturer of a defective power tool with the unanimous consent of his associates. The triumph of Traynor's views was in part a function of personnel changes: three new justices sat on the *Greenman* court. Three others, however, joined Traynor's position where they had shown no previous inclination to do so. Their shift may have been a result of the significant publicity given by Prosser and other scholars to the supposed "trends" toward judicial extensions of strict liability for the benefit of injured consumers in defective products cases.[93] In his *Greenman* opinion Traynor said that, "[w]e need not recanvass the reasons for imposing strict liability in the manufacturer. They have been fully articulated," [94] and then cited, in addition to cases in other jurisdictions, Prosser's 1960 article "The Assault Upon the Citadel," Harper and James's treatise, and his *Escola* concurrence.

In *Greenman* Traynor gave a clue to the core of his attraction to strict liability in the defective products area. Noting that the liability did not arise out of contractual relations but was imposed by law, thereby making notice requirements inapplicable, Traynor quoted a distinction made by Prosser between ordinary commercial relationships and the standard consumer products liability case. "As between the immediate parties to [a] sale . . . notice requirements [were] sound commercial rule[s]"; "as applied to personal injuries, and . . . to remote seller[s]," they became "booby-trap[s] for the unwary." [95] The purpose of strict liability in consumer defective products cases, Traynor felt, was "to insure that the costs of injuries resulting from defective products are borne by the manufacturers that put such products on the market rather than by the injured persons who are powerless to protect themselves." The "powerlessness" of the untrained consumer was as vital a part of the rationale for strict liability as the efficiencies achieved through spreading losses.

Reflecting on Traynor's products liability sequence, every case in which he advocated the imposition of strict liability can be viewed as a case in which the injured person was "powerless": incapable of discovering the defect himself, inclined to assume that such products would not be defective, unacquainted with the procedures whereby the products were tested, and unaware of the process by which the products reached him.[96] The manufacturer, on the other hand, either knew or was in a position to know about each of those features of his product. If soda bottles regularly broke at the warehouse, as a witness for the defendant in *Gordon* testified,[97] the manufacturer was in a position to know of that fact and to choose whether to subject the bottles to further tests before distributing them to consumers. Persons using soda bottles, on the other hand, were unlikely to know of the fate of bottles in warehouses. In general, manufacturers of products saw them in mass: they were in a position to become cognizant of defects that occurred or pitfalls that were attendant upon their distribution. They were therefore better able to assess their potential for dangerousness than were consumers. They could even insure themselves against regularly recurring risks if such developed. Consumers often only knew that they came in contact with a product and became injured in so doing.

Equal access to information about risks thus emerges as a central principle distinguishing Traynor's products liability cases from his landowner cases. While both sets of cases involved enterprises that were in a position to spread or shift their liability costs through insurance, parties injured by landowners were in some instances as cognizant of the risks as were the landowners. A patron of a restaurant would be as aware of the risks of an overhanging ceiling as the restaurant owner; neither a landowner nor a domestic employee would have any information about the riskiness of a stair railing with latent defects. A construction company using a sand pile in its excavation, however, would be better informed about the risks inherent in such an object than a ten-year-old child. The general negligence standard that Traynor finally settled on in the landowner area allowed for the consideration of access to information about risks: "interest-balancing" involved such a consideration. Strict liability analysis, on the other hand, supposedly abandoned interest-balancing, thus it is possible that when Traynor employed strict liability analysis he assumed that access to information about risks was essentially available only to the defendant.

Traynor's strict liability decisions after *Greenman* are suggestive in this regard. In *Vandermark v. Ford Motor Co.*[98] a new car driven by Chester Vandermark suddenly swerved sharply to the right, veered off the road, and hit a light post, injuring Vandermark. Vandermark produced expert testimony, which suggested that the swerving was caused by a failure of one of the pistons in the car's master cylinder that affected the brake fluid and caused the car's brakes to malfunction. Vandermark had bought the car from a dealer, Maywood Bell Ford, which made final inspections and adjustments before delivering the car to consumers. Vandermark sued both Maywood Bell and the Ford Motor Company.

After *Greenman,* the case was a straightforward one, with Traynor holding Ford Motor Co. strictly liable for the injuries caused by the defective piston and Maywood Bell also strictly liable because it was "an integral part of the overall producing and marketing enterprise that should bear the cost of injuries resulting from defective products." [99] The defendants could "adjust the costs of [protecting injured consumers] between them in the course of their continuing business relationship." [100] Contractual disclaimers made by Maywood Bell to Vandermark were immaterial, since Maywood Bell's liability was in tort. The significance of the case was principally in opening up claims against members in the chain of a manufacturing enterprise when a defective product had passed through their control. This made it easier for injured consumers to bring lawsuits in the defective products area.

Vandermark was a clear instance where the manufacturer's and dealer's access to information about the risks of a defective piston were greater than that of the consumer. Vandermark had in fact noticed the car pulling to the right on another occasion and had apparently called the incident to the attention of one of Maywood Bell's representatives. Vandermark was, Traynor assumed, in no position to know that the car's pulling to the right on that occasion suggested a defective piston that ultimately would cause it to veer off the road. Ford and Maywood Bell, on the other hand, were in the business of manufacturing and servicing cars.

The next Traynor opinion, *Seely v. White Motor Co.,*[101] involved another defect in an automobile. But Traynor regarded the case as distinguishable from *Vandermark* and inappropriate for strict liability treatment. One Daniel Seely, whose business was heavy-duty hauling, purchased a truck manufactured by the White Motor Company. The truck developed a tendency to bounce violently and was repeatedly returned to the dealer for corrective repairs. Over an eleven-month period sixteen different types of alterations were made to the truck, but the bouncing continued. On one occasion the brakes failed and the truck overturned, causing about $5,000 worth of damage to the truck. Seely, who was not hurt in the accident, eventually stopped making payments on the truck, which was repossessed by the dealer and resold.

Seely sued the dealer and the White Motor Company for damages from the accident, damages related to the purchase price of the truck, and profits lost when the truck was out of service. His suit was based both on express warranties and on strict liability in tort. The trial court dismissed Seely's claim against the dealer without prejudice and found White Motors responsible for the price of the truck and lost profits under a warranty theory. The trial court found that Seely had not shown that the bouncing caused his accident, and thus could not recover damages related to it.

Traynor's opinion on appeal was as activist and broad-ranging as any in his career. He agreed with the trial court that White Motors had made express warranties of fitness and merchantability on the truck, even though Seely believed that the warranties had been made by the dealer.[102] He found that lost profits were contemplated by the warranty remedies of the Uniform Commercial Code and that the damages were not excessive.[103] He denied recovery for physical damage to the truck in the accident, finding no causal connection between the defect in the truck and the brake failure.[104] He then considered a strict liability theory of recovery, even though it was now unnecessary to the decision of the case, and found that strict liability developments in California had not supplanted the law of sales in cases where defective products had caused economic loss rather than personal injury.

Traynor's discussion of strict liability appeared to spring from an interest in clarifying the relationship between the *Escola-Vandermark* sequence of products liability decisions and the Uniform Commercial Code. If so, *Seely* was not the best case in which to attempt such a clarification, since express warranties existed and a strict liability rationale was not necessary for recovery. A dissenting judge said that Traynor's comments on strict liability had been made "unnecessarily and gratuitously," and that they amounted to an "advisory opinion." [105] Moreover, Traynor addressed some issues, such as the applicability of strict liability to physical injury to property, which had been disposed of on other grounds. The general effect of *Seely* was to expose Traynor's interest in boldly venturing into unsettled areas of products liability law and "cleaning them up." That capacity for boldness, which had produced a classic opinion in *Escola,* caused Traynor some discomfort in *Seely*.

Traynor first argued that "the history" of strict liability in tort indicated that the doctrine "was designed . . . to govern the distinct problem of physical injuries." While each of the cases in the *Escola-Greenman-Vandermark* sequence had involved physical injury, nothing in Traynor's opinions in those cases focused on the necessity of separate doctrinal treatment for physical injuries. The two rationales repeatedly expressed in those opinions were the ability of product manufacturers to spread the costs of injuries and the "powerlessness" of consumers with respect to information about the risks of defective products.

The next set of arguments advanced by Traynor for limiting strict liability treatment to physical injuries was that "although the rules of warranty frustrate rational compensation for physical injury, they function well in a commercial setting." [106] He maintained that Seely was in the business of hauling and that the economic losses suffered by businessmen ought to be adjusted by the law of sales and the "practical construction" of sales agreements. But while Seely used his truck in his business, he did not own a fleet of trucks or buy them regularly. Traynor's assertion that he "could have shopped around until he found the truck that would fulfill his . . . needs" [107] would apply to any consumer of automobiles. Thus Traynor was apparently suggesting in *Seely* that a salesman who used his car for business purposes could not recover lost earnings if a defect in his car had damaged it and made it impossible for him to work.

Most troublesome of all, perhaps, was Traynor's suggestion that had Seely been able to show that the bouncing tendencies of the truck had caused it to overturn, he would have been able to recover in strict liability for damage to the truck. "Physical injury to property is so akin to personal injury," Traynor claimed, "that there is no reason to distinguish them." [108] This left him with a bewildering set of rules regarding defective products. Suppose that a rug contained a hidden defect in its fibers. If a consumer who invested in rugs bought that rug from a dealer, and the rug began to unravel, he could not recover for the loss of his prospective investment unless the dealer had expressly warranted the rug to be free from defects. On the other hand, if the defect in the rug made it combustible, and it ignited, injuring the consumer, he could recover in strict liability in tort. Moreover, if the flames from the rug destroyed a chair in the consumer's house, he could recover for the value of the chair.[109] Traynor claimed that his suggested rules did not "rest on the 'luck' of one plaintiff in having an accident causing physical injury," [110] but they seemed to rest on just that fortuity.

Despite Traynor's overreaching in *Seely,* the case is a good one to illustrate his efforts to restrict strict liability to those areas where a true inequality of access to information about the risks of defective products existed. Traynor regarded the plaintiff in *Seely* as someone other than a "powerless" consumer. He knew the nature of his business and the demands hauling made on his trucks; he could select trucks with that in mind. To the extent that long-distance hauling put unusual stress on trucks, the plaintiff in *Seely* was arguably as conversant with the risks such stress induced as was the truck manufacturer. The plaintiff in *Seely* thus was distinguishable from the plaintiff in *Vandermark,* whose use of the Ford made no special demands on it and could not have been expected to be aware of the risks of a defective piston. *Seely* therefore fits Traynor's pattern of reserving negligence or warranty treatment for those cases where a rough parity of risk anticipation existed, and promoting strict liability analysis in those cases where an injured person was truly "powerless."

Locating Traynor in Time

Traynor's career as a Torts theorist produced a distinctive blend of activism and traditionalism. With Traynor we see the field of Torts in its mid-century phase: a blend of private relationships and public concerns, in which the duties of private citizens could be imposed by public policy and the relationship between manufacturers and consumers could be regarded as a matter of public concern.

We see also in Traynor the maturing of a judicial stance that took for granted the significance of academics as lawmakers and openly based results on "extrajudicial" considerations. Whereas Cardozo, even in cases arbitrarily limiting the liability of municipal water companies for losses due to fire,[111] never mentioned insurance, as if to do so would disturb the integrity of the common law, Traynor remarked that "the consuming public [should not] pay more for their products so that a manufacturer can insure against the possibility that some of his products will not meet the business needs of some of his customers."[112] Whereas Cardozo's academic citations were dwarfed by his use of more orthodox materials, such as common law precedents, Traynor rarely extracted principles from case analysis and very regularly found them in academic literature.

Yet another characteristic of Traynor was his impatience with doctrinal confusion, with "oscillating" jury verdicts, and with overlap between the spheres of influence of common law subjects. Like Cardozo, he had an urge to mark out the governing principles of an area of Torts in a clear and orderly fashion; like Cardozo as well this urge sometimes led him to overly broad pronouncements that could be perceived as unnecessary and gratuitous. Cardozo's anxiousness to clarify a confused area of tort law can be traced to his own yearning for certainty and his tendency toward dogmatism; with Traynor a comparable anxiousness can be traced to his confidence in the ability of properly educated judges to make rational decisions.

Only Traynor's firm confidence in the objective nature of rationality "dates" him as a judge. In his activist conception of judging he was one of the pioneers of his time and one of the precursors of a "policymaking" role for judges in tort cases that is now much more commonly acknowledged, if not universally supported. Traynor was, in some respects, the state court equivalent of a "Warren Court" judge, committed to using his powers as fully as possible to promote social policies in which he believed and to reorient the common law of California in directions he thought rational and desirable. While social attitudes in the nation have changed since the tenure of the Warren Court, judges have shown no disinclination to abandon their role as activist policymakers. Nor does that role seem inconsistent with prevailing conceptions of how judges ought to comport themselves, a current absence of confidence in public officials notwithstanding.

Traynor's conception of tort law as a hybrid of "private" and "public" issues seems also to have retained its relevance. There was a recurrent tension in Traynor's tort decisions between comprehensive, policy-oriented, "public" solutions to tort issues, of which strict liability theory is an example, and ad hoc, doctrinally oriented, "private" solutions, exemplified by negligence theory. That tension is a defining feature of current tort law; Traynor's inclination to let the two types of solutions coexist is still a viable, though not uncontested, approach to contemporary tort theory.

Where Traynor appears, to this observer, as a man of "his time," as distinguished from "ours," is in his belief that the "primary internal characteristic of the judicial process" was that it was "rational." [113] One may argue, of course, that if Traynor's decisions were motivated by his reading of the equities or his sense of fairness, those feelings were irrelevant once he put words on paper and the doctrinal superstructure of his opinions was made manifest. But it is one thing to accept the fact that judges cannot always articulate all their reasons for arriving at a result—some reasons, one senses, are better for public consumption than others—and another to claim that the process of judging is somehow inherently rational, and further that the legal system in America is based on an inexorable rationality. That type of claim suggests that for every problem there is a consensual rational solution and that educated people will sooner or later arrive at it.

To make such a claim, in my view, is to blink the numerous official decisions of the past decade that were not made through any deliberative consensus and, with hindsight, reveal themselves as the end products of highly challengeable notions of what is "best" for American society. It is also to invest in persons who happen to hold judicial office qualities of disinterestedness, impartiality, and wisdom that make them a singular collection of human beings. I am not uncomfortable with judges as policymakers, and there is surely nothing wrong with judges *trying* to make rational decisions and to find effective reasons for their results, but there is nothing about the people selected to be judges or the process of judging itself that suggests to me that the judiciary has a greater hold on "rationality" than the rest of us.

A theme of this study is that the "consensus thought" of the 1950s, with which I have identified Traynor, has decisively broken down in the 1970s, and that the current wave of creative theoretical scholarship in tort law is an effort to articulate some new consensus, or at least to identify some new starting philosophical assumptions from which legal subjects can be approached. While Traynor's views of

judging or of the legal stystem as a whole may no longer be representative of attitudes in the 1970s, his contributions to tort law can be seen
as raising issues central to Torts scholarship in that decade, issues
that will now be considered in a concluding chapter.

7

The 1970s: Neoconceptualism and the Future of Tort Law

For those inclined to adopt a cyclical view of history, the course of scholarship in tort law over the past hundred years might furnish a source of stimulation. We have seen, emerging in the late nineteenth century and cresting in the early twentieth, impulses toward the conceptualization of the subject of Torts and the espousal of overarching theories of tort law; and then, beginning in the early years of the twentieth century and becoming dominant in the 1930s and 1940s, a reaction against conceptualism, an atomizing of the subject of Torts, and a resistance to comprehensive theorizing. One can also see, beginning irregularly in the 1960s and gaining considerable momentum in the 1970s, the rebirth of conceptualist perspectives. Literature that can fairly be called neoconceptualist has begun to dominate recent Torts scholarship, and while the theoretical offerings of contemporary scholars bear little resemblance as manifestos of social policy to the offerings of Holmes and his nineteenth-century contemporaries, they represent a distinct break with the intellectual assumptions of the Realists and the consensus thinkers of the 1950s. Comprehensive, abstract, generalized theory has reappeared in Torts literature.

The Emergence of Neoconceptualism

If, as this study suggests, the most fundamental assumptions of prevailing intellectual thought at various times are not seriously open to verification or to challenge, individual theories propounded by Torts scholars may come under attack in this decade, but the impulse to theorize will be taken seriously. While the late nineteenth-century conceptualists were eventually to settle on a dominant theory for Torts—the negligence principle—their modern counterparts have shown no comparable ability to coalesce. The significance of neoconceptualism in Torts literature thus far lies in its reaffirmation of the value of abstract theorizing itself, not in the seminality of any of the theories its proponents have advanced.

It seems worthwhile, therefore, to give some attention to the characteristics and possible sources of neoconceptualism before addressing the substance of individual contributions. The distinguishing feature of neoconceptualist literature, both in Torts and in other legal subjects, is its relentless preoccupation with abstract theory. The contrast between typical law review articles of the 1950s and those of the 1970s is striking. Scholarship from the former period was narrow in its focus, modest in its goals, and saturated with the conventional patterns of approved professional reasoning of the time, which stressed careful distinctions between fact situations, explicit attention to logical analysis, and a thorough marshalling of relevant arguments. Case analysis was the nub of an article: the scholar appeared as the balanced voice of reason.

In contrast, contemporary law reviews are filled with articles whose methodologies are remarkably diverse, whose subject matter is wide-ranging, and whose focus is often broad and abstract. The articles are loosely unified only by their regular interest in stating and advancing a theoretical perspective. At times the perspective comes from a discipline other than law, such as economics or another of the social sciences, and in the course of presentation a focus on methodology may surface. But the methodology employed is often not the conventional legal analysis of the 1950s, but that of the "foreign" discipline: graphs or tables or charts may replace the dissection of cases.

Nor are authors in "typical" 1970s articles inclined to suggest that their analyses ought to be confined to the narrow range of materials they are investigating. Rather than applying an approved general methodology to a particular area of law, as the "typical" article of the 1950s did, legal scholars of the 1970s often seek to apply an unorthodox methodology to a broad area of legal relationships. Their claim is that this application can produce fresh perspectives, which may ultimately lead to a new theory of a field of law. Their interest seems less in tracing the theory through its particularized applications than in stimulating others to consider the perspectives of the theory itself.

These contrasts may be overdrawn or stereotyped, but the shift in scholarly focus is readily observable. It appears as if the inclination of legal scholars in the 1950s to assume the omnicompetence of a shared professional methodology has given way to efforts to refurbish the methodology of legal scholarship with insights from other professions and disciplines. A "consensus" on what proper professional analysis consists of has broken down. Further, the object of scholarship in the 1950s was less to develop new or original theoretical perspectives in law than to reinforce the versatility of a common professional methodology. By contrast, the new directions of scholarship in the seventies are advanced in the service of theory: one looks to economics or psychology or sociology or history because there purportedly lie new sources of theoretical insight about the law. When "process" dominates substance, the influence of Realism is apparent; when theory dominates data, conceptualist impulses have surfaced.

The search in contemporary legal scholarship for illuminating perspectives from other disciplines, then, seems more than an academic excursion. It appears to rest on an inarticulate conviction that the traditional professional methodologies of legal scholarship have become barriers to the development of an adequate theoretical perspective in legal subjects. This conviction flows, of course, from a belief in the value of theory itself, and the sources of that belief remain to be explored.

For reasons that are not altogether clear, especially to one living in the seventies, a loss of consensual values in contemporary American society has stimulated a concern with personal values. A skepticism toward previously unifying cultural values, such as patriotism, "decency," or "equal opportunity," seems to have fostered a strong interest in identifying one's own personal convictions and in sharing them with others. It is possible that the revival of theoretical perspectives in academic literature has some affinity to this trend. The interest in articulating new scholarly theories may be an extension of the broader interest in generally expressing ideas that stimulate one and in which one believes. A theoretical focus, in this vein, becomes a form of communicating a personal statement of values to others. In the absence of any overriding social or professional consensus about what values should prevail, one theory may seem as attractive as another; the effort seems to be less to insure that the theory is authoritative than to express it as forcefully as one can.

There are thus some parallels between the neoconceptualism of the

1970s and the conceptualist impulses of the late nineteenth century. In both instances a perceived breakdown in solidifying cultural values contributed to the proliferation of theory in academic literature. Nineteenth-century theories sought to develop organizing principles to order a universe that could no longer be explained by religious dogma. The function of recent twentieth-century theories is less discernible, but, at least in legal scholarship, the proliferation of theory seems to be linked to some tacit protest against the confining effects of an orthodox "lawyer-like" approach to intellectual issues, an approach which has equated "thinking like a lawyer" with precise speech, "inductive" logical reasoning, skepticism about unsubstantiated value premises and—curiously, in the eyes of many law students—clarity of expression under pressure.

Uneasiness with the state of higher education has also marked both periods. In the late nineteenth century, conceptualism became linked to reformist trends in legal education: the casebooks of the scientists not only extracted principles, they altered the mode of classroom teaching. No comparably close link has yet appeared between neoconceptualism and educational reform in contemporary law teaching although dissatisfaction with the "case method" has surfaced.[1] It is clear that if theoretical perspectives on law continue to be based in the thoughts of other disciplines, "foreign" material will have to be learned in the classroom, and orthodox "legal" methods of acquiring knowledge, such as case analysis and socratic dialogue, may not be well suited to the examination of such material.

Finally, conceptualist impulses in both periods have generated new patterns in legal scholarship. The late nineteenth-century scientists reoriented legal literature and established law professors as lawmakers through their casebooks, law review articles, and revised treatises, which amounted to novel modes of communication. Contemporary law professors, in addition to writing more explicitly theoretical law review articles, have taken to publishing monographs, in the mode of academicians in the liberal arts and sciences. The rise of monographic communication may have profound effects on both the audience reached by legal scholars and the teaching of law. Monographs are designed to reach a wider audience than journal articles and to deal with broader topics: their presence may be seen as reinforcing a concern with theory. Monographs, unlike casebooks, are not designed for socratic teaching. They seek to answer questions rather than to ask them and they assume that "learning law" is not entirely synonymous with developing powers of logical reasoning.

In previous chapters a characterization of intellectual trends in legal and other scholarship has been followed by discussions of the impact of those trends on tort literature and subsequently on tort law itself. A chapter on contemporary developments must necessarily omit the third of these themes. While the relationship between academic literature and judicially created doctrinal developments in tort law has been characterized as symbiotic, academic syntheses have generally preceded judicial innovations. In the case of neoconceptualist trends in contemporary Torts scholarship, moreover, the contributions have tended to be so markedly broad and abstract that their precise application to the doctrinal state of tort law, while clear enough in the mass, is more elusive in the individual case. Thus the following portions of this chapter do not address recent case law developments. Rather, an analysis of the impact of neoconceptualism on Torts scholarship is followed by a theoretical discussion of the future of tort law in an age where conceptualist impulses are taken to be powerful creative forces.

The Impact of Neoconceptualism: Recent Torts Scholarship

An index of the current preoccupation with theory in legal scholarship, and a testament to contemporary efforts to broaden the range of "legal" inquiry, is the fact that the principal distinguishing feature of new Torts casebook editions in the seventies does not involve, strictly speaking, an area of traditional tort doctrine at all. The novel quality of recent casebooks is their tendency to speculate broadly on the functions of tort law as a whole, especially when evaluated against alternative compensation systems, such as no-fault insurance schemes. This speculation has been informed by two perspectives not common to previous Torts casebooks, that of welfare economics and that of moral philosophy. A selection of prefaces from recent editions of casebooks illustrates the tendency. One refers to "the emerging issues of economic theory and behavioral analysis that increasingly will confront lawyers into the next century"; [2] another calls for a "critical examination of fundamental ideas underlying tort liability and alternative systems for compensation"; [3] a third, most explicitly, speaks of "fundamental disagreement about the proper orientation toward [the] subject matter [of tort law]," and identifies three competing perspectives: that of "corrective justice," that of compensation, and that of economic theory.[4]

A casebook emblematic of recent trends, whose long history vivifies contrasts among its successive editions, is the 1977 edition of Page and Robert Keeton's *Cases and Materials of the Law of Torts*. That casebook, we have seen, stretches back to James Barr Ames's original Torts casebook in 1874 and has included among its authors Jeremiah Smith, Roscoe Pound, Joseph Beale, Edward Thurston, and Warren Seavey. The 1957 and 1964 editions of the Keeton casebook were striking in their strong emphasis on numerous discrete cases, heavily edited, and in their relative absence of conceptual order or theoretical perspectives. The message of those editions was essentially that conveyed by Thurston's and Seavey's 1942 edition, which, as noted, abandoned previous subject matter organizations for an unstructured presentation of diverse, but artfully grouped, appellate cases.[5] While the editors of the 1957 and 1964 editions had become more conscious of the "study of the legal process in tort cases"[6] and accordingly presented some cases where courts contrasted their role as lawmakers with that of legislatures, their intent was clearly to teach methodology as much as substantive doctrine and to avoid any explicit theoretical overview of the subject of Torts itself.

In 1971 a new edition appeared, and the editors announced that they had "substantially reduce[d] the emphasis heretofore given to negligence law and increase[d] the attention focused on alternatives." They referred specifically to "the strong impact of economic considerations on tort doctrine" and the rising interest among legal scholars in "the influence of . . . economic factors" and "the potential usefulness to judges . . . of theories and methods of analysis current among economists."[7] By 1977 their comparatively narrow consideration of economic theory as it related to no-fault automobile insurance programs had broadened to a discussion of the "moral, economic and social premises"[8] of compensation systems generally. The discussion referred to choices, in a decision to compensate one person at another's expense, "between individual-entitlement and social-calculus premises—between criteria of justice founded on a social cost-benefit assessment."[9] Excerpts from works on moral philosophy and economic theory were presented, to identify "contrasting perspectives that may help to explain influences in tort law beyond those that are explicitly examined in judicial opinions."[10]

Given the history of the Keeton and Keeton casebook, a concession that tort law could be influenced by nonlegal theoretical perspectives and further that such perspectives had always been implicit in judicial opinions, was striking. The basic thrust of earlier editions of the casebook had been that the corpus of tort law, its doctrines and policies, could be found in judicial opinions, and that by developing an effective methodology for analyzing those opinions one could pierce to the core of the subject. This most recent statement by the Keetons now implies that some sources of tort law can *not* be found in judicial language and can be understood only by "a search for unarticulated premises of decisions." [11] That search can be aided, the editors suggest, by familiarity with literature from outside the law altogether.

To be sure, the Keetons' attention to "premises" of tort liability takes up only a small portion of an otherwise traditional common law casebook, and even this limited discourse was intended, from a pedagogic standpoint, to be introduced relatively late in a Torts course. But the notion that tort doctrine was influenced by inarticulate prevailing theories of how society ought to be organized involved an analysis of tort cases that paid little attention to traditional legal analysis. If a judge, in a case where an elderly person was injured in a fall on an unshoveled sidewalk, began his analysis by implicitly assuming that injured people ought to be compensated and then grounded his opinion in various "duties" owed pedestrians by landowners, the significant feature of his opinion might be his original assumption rather than his doctrinal treatment of landowner duties. Yet nothing in his opinion illuminated that assumption; the judge's language, indeed, minimized it. No light on the validity of the judge's assumption could be shed by other comparable opinions advancing other doctrinal propositions; the light came, somehow, from outside the traditional materials of tort law itself.

It is possible to see, in this relatively confined feature of one recent Torts casebook, the germs of an approach to tort law highly subversive of traditional conceptions of the subject. From its origins as a discrete area of law Torts has been identified by a common doctrinal base whose concepts—negligence, contributory negligence, causation, assumption of risk, and so on—were understood as entities; their shape could change but their collective existence provided a common vocabulary for the subject. Even the attack on tort doctrine launched by Realists, while it had alluded to concealed value judgments in opinions and had stressed the malleability of doctrinal concepts, had not advocated a search for the "true" grounds of tort law decisions outside law itself. While some Realists spoke of the psychological dimensions of judicial decisionmaking, abstract theorizing about law ran counter to the thrust of Realism, whose proponents ultimately seemed interested in narrower and more penetrating analyses of individual cases. By contrast, an inquiry into the unarticulated premises of tort law leads one away from case analysis to the realm of social theory.

It is doubtful that many contemporary Torts scholars would be inclined to press a view of their field that reduced to insignificance its traditional source materials. But it is suggestive that much of the recent scholarship on tort law has not focused on case analysis, or doctrinal synthesis, but on the formulation of theoretical approaches to the entire field of Torts. Two theoretical perspectives are evident in the recent literature, one based on economic theory and one on notions of "corrective justice."

The most striking feature of the recent literature on Torts that has emphasized economic theory has been the way that it revises existing approaches to tort law as a public law subject. Tort law, seen as "public law in disguise" by theorists of the 1950s and 1960s, had a regulatory and distributional character: that is, its decisions were viewed as policy judgments about shifting or spreading the costs of injuries. Traynor's sequence of products liability decisions, for example, can be regarded as efforts by a judge to use tort doctrines to redistribute losses imposed on "powerless" consumers by more powerful enterprises. In such a capacity the judge, backed by the Restatement of Torts, becomes a regulator of the market for dangerous or defective products. An apparent assumption made by Traynor in performing this regulatory role was that a "market" approach to defective products, whereby producers and consumers define their own legal rights and responsibilities through contractual relations or customary practices, is not entirely appropriate for cases where the producer and the consumer do not have equal information about the risks of a given product.

Economic theory, as it appears in recent Torts scholarship, begins with a radically different assumption. Its proponents assume that the system of tort law can be made more efficient by providing persons with good information about the prospect of being saddled with the costs of injuries, and then either letting market factors determine who chooses to bear those costs or creating tort doctrines designed to identify and to place the prospective costs of injuries on persons who can most cheaply avoid those costs by modifying their behavior. This perspective is either hostile to or indifferent to a distributional role for tort law and regards tort law, ideally, as a "private law" field in which civil wrongs arise primarily from transactions between knowledgeable parties with good information about risks.

But we have seen that the principal basis for emphasis on the compensatory features of tort law, for the revival of strict liability in such areas of defective products, and for the idea that tort law could serve as a regulatory and distributive agent was a perception that the typical tort claim arose out of an interaction between persons with unequal power, no previous contractual relations or customary dealings, and imperfect information about risks. Early and mid-twentieth-century tort scholars identified tort claims as having those features and argued that in an interdependent society the costs of injuries were everyone's responsibility. The public law dimensions of tort law grew from this perception of social interdependence.

The thrust of recent Torts scholarship emphasizing economic theory, then, is seemingly to return tort law to a deregulated, nondistributional state whose doctrines are intended to harmonize with and to facilitate private interactions. Richard Posner, for example, has argued that the essential purpose of late nineteenth-century negligence theory was "to maximize the joint value of . . . interfering activities," [12] and that, through its use of contributory negligence as an absolute defense, it achieved that purpose rather well. The prospect of a negligence suit, Posner maintains, created incentives on the part of enterprises to make their activities safer, up to the point where the cost of safety did not exceed the cost of satisfying tort claims. Similarly, the defense of contributory negligence created incentives for enterprises to avoid damage to their activities, up to the point where the cost of avoidance exceeded the cost of damage. Thus the activity of enterprises tended to be safer, freer from damage, and consequently worth more. The "dominant function" of negligence was "to generate rules of liability that [would] bring about . . . the efficient . . . level of accidents and safety." [13]

Moreover, Posner argues, negligence theory was not only compatible with the efficient use of resources, it was more compatible than was strict liability. Where a strict liability standard governed interactions between "interfering activities," the injured party had no incentive to avoid damage to his enterprise, since he would not be barred from recovery by a contributory negligence defense. Only one enterprise—the one inflicting the damage—had incentives to increase safety and reduce accidents; the other had only the incentive to avoid voluntary and knowing exposure to the risk of being damaged. If "an important . . . social value" was "the efficient use of resources" [14] a negligence standard in tort law was preferable to a strict liability standard.

Posner's approach is a good example of the subversive effects of neoconceptualist theoretical approaches on traditional doctrinal analysis in tort law. Under Posner's formulation the only prerequisites for effecting theorizing are acceptance of Posner's assumption that efficiency is an important social value, a rule of tort law that a finding of negligence on the part of an injuring party shifts the costs of his victim's injuries to him, and a rule of tort law that a finding of contributory negligence on the part of the injured party prevents this shift from taking place. With those prerequisites established, Posner can avoid all other doctrinal complexities: the status of the injurer and the injured party, the "duties" imposed on one or another by tort law, questions of "legal" causation, questions of immunity, and so on. The theory is marvelously simple and seemingly cuts through the obscurities of doctrinal analysis.

But for Posner's theory to serve as a standard for assessing tortious conduct the majority of people involved with the tort system have to act as Posner's theory assumes they will. That is, they have to be aware that investments in safety will rebound to their legal advantage and accordingly respond to negligence rules by increasing their investments in safety. They have to make "rational" analyses of the costs of preventing accidents and the costs of injuring or being injured. And they have to be inclined, in the aggregate, to prefer "efficient" interferences to inefficient ones. But while some enterprises are drawn into the system of tort law with sufficient frequency so that they have some realistic basis upon which to weigh the costs of preventing accidents they cause against the costs of paying tort claims, Posner himself concedes that safety advances in industries do not primarily come in response to the rules of tort law.[15]

Moreover, there are numerous tort litigants with no familiarity with negligence or its rules, no consciousness of accident prevention, and perhaps not even any interest in "utility maximization." It seems quixotic to think of such persons as rational planners, weighing the costs of being injured and barred from recovery in a negligence action against the costs of accident prevention. A characteristic of tort law since at least the late nineteenth century has been that its cases involve random interactions between strangers rather than planned inter- actions between persons with exchange mechanisms. The suggestive- ness of Posner's theory is counterbalanced by its highly questionable starting assumptions.

A perspective from economic theory is also explicit in the approach of Guido Calabresi, who finds, in contrast to Posner, that efficiency analysis reveals the superiority of strict liability over negligence as a general standard for tort law. The primary reason strict liability analysis is more efficient, for Calabresi, is that it conditions liability not on a showing of "fault" in a discrete case but on the nature of an "injuring" enterprise. If an enterprise is the kind that is in a good position to avoid the costs of accidents cheaply (purportedly by mak- ing its products safer), then it would presumptively be strictly liable for accidents it caused unless, for some reason peculiar to the circum- stances of the accident, it was not in a position to implement its cost- avoidance.[16]

Under Calabresi's approach tort law assumes some regulatory role, since most of the decisions about loss allocation in tort cases are made before the cases are litigated. Courts (or legislatures) develop categories of "cheap cost-avoiders" who are in good positions to deter- mine and minimize the accident costs of their products. Such enter- prises can assume in advance that they will have to pay for accidents they cause; thus (if certain assumptions about behavior are made) they have an incentive to reduce the number of accidents traceable to their products. When an accident does occur, and litigation ensues, courts have only two inquiries: which of the interacting enterprises was the cheaper cost-avoider, and whether that enterprise was actually in a position to avoid accident costs in the given accident. By this focus Calabresi's approach allegedly avoids the arbitrariness of a negli- gence standard, which makes judgments about loss allocation only on the basis of a showing of fault in a given litigated accident. An enter- prise "at fault" one time might not be another time: no "statistics which are meaningful at the category level" can be compiled in a negligence system.

Were the decision about cost-avoidance capable of regularly being made in advance of litigation, Calabresi's approach would seem to have the advantage of reducing the involvement of the courts in accident cases. But the approach is not entirely consistent with Calabresi's stated goals. For example, as Posner points out, a blanket decision to impose liability on one party (say the manufacturer of a lawn-mower) rather than another (a consumer injured using it) creates a disincentive for consumers to use lawnmowers safely and is accordingly inefficient.[17] Those cases that are litigated tend to be ones in which despite the superior cost-avoidance potential of one party, it is not clear that that party should be liable, either because the circumstances of the accident prevented him from exercising his potential or because the other party significantly contributed to the accident (such as by exposing himself to danger).

Calabresi's approach is heavily dependent on a determination that the cheapest cost-avoider was actually in a position to make use of his advantage in the accident that occurred. This determination seems to raise the same difficulties that Calabresi associates with negligence: an "arbitrary" decision is made in a discrete case with no guidelines for future cases. An enterprise being held strictly liable in one case may be inclined to make its product safer, but in the next case the enterprise may feel that the person its product has injured altered the product's composition or otherwise increased risks to himself, and want to litigate again. Calabresi is thus placed in the following dilemma. If certain categories of enterprises (classes of cheap cost-avoiders) are presumptively liable for the injuries their products cause, then persons injured by them have no incentive to avoid the costs of their own accidents. That absence of incentive reduces efficiency, the rationale on which Calabresi's approach is based. If, however, enterprises that are cheap cost-avoider can escape liability by showing that in a given case they were not able to exercise their potential, a "balancing" process occurs, comparable to that in negligence cases, and no reason is given for preferring the strict liability calculus to that of negligence. One reason that could be advanced—that a strict liability standard deters litigation—is inapplicable in the class of cases where "balancing" occurs.

A more fundamental difficulty with Calabresi's approach is his assumption that economic theory can be used to formulate standards of tort liability because "utility-maximization" can best describe the aggregate behavior of persons in the tort system. Again, there may be

some instances where such an assumption appears plausible. Manufacturers of products, for example, would seem likely to want to make
their products safer if their products were regularly injuring consumers and they were having to pay the costs of those injuries. By
making their products safer, they would reduce their costs of doing
business and maximize the value of their products. But what about
automobile drivers who injure other drivers or pedestrians in accidents? Would they be inclined to drive more safely if they had to pay
the costs of those whom they injured? Here we have moved from the
realm of regularized business operations to the realm (in most cases)
of the uncommon event. Most drivers are not in the business of offering their cars to a "consumer" public, hoping that the public will use
them safely. Safe driving is a psychological as well as an economic
state, and the association of a past accident with incentives for safety
is much less easily made. A driver may even want to drive more safely
after having been in an accident but be physically or mentally incapable of so doing. The notion that an automobile driver would "avoid
all accidents worth avoiding" and "have only those accidents not
worth avoiding" assumes a "perfect" rational "foresight" that Calabresi himself has called "wonderful" and "fantastic." [18]

The question raised by Posner's and Calabresi's theories of tort
law is whether any perspective that assumes such a uniformity of
thought and conduct among the human participants in the tort system
is not flawed at the outset. Even if efficiency is taken to be a paramount social goal, problems remain. I take it that neither Posner nor
Calabresi would suggest that persons choosing to be inefficient should
invariably be punished for the choice: there would concededly be
times when efficiency considerations would yield to other values. That
being so, there would be situations resulting in tort litigation to which
Posner's or Calabresi's theories might not apply. But since neither
Posner's nor Calabresi's approach provides any criteria for determining when efficiency should yield to other values, one is supposed
to assume that a decision for efficiency has presumptively been made.
But if one is concerned about the validity of that decision itself or
about how comprehensively an efficiency standard should be applied,
or whether economic models adequately characterize the bulk of tort
cases, Posner's and Calabresi's theories provide no help.

Perhaps in response to these last concerns, two additional approaches to tort liability have been proposed that explicitly reject the

applicability of economic theory to the tort system and emphasize the importance of "corrective justice" in an individual tort case. While these approaches insist that justice be measured out on a case-by-case basis, they propose general standards of tort liability and generalized criteria for their application.

George Fletcher argues that "justice" in a tort case should be equated with justice between the parties, not with broader conceptions of the welfare of the community. Fletcher believes that individuals are entitled to live in society free from being exposed to the risks of being injured, and that those who expose others to risks have an obligation to compensate those others who are injured.[19] He would have a general standard of tort liability turn on the "reciprocity" of risks between parties in a tort action: the party subjecting the other to the greater risk of injury must compensate him.[20] If the risks are "reciprocal," or roughly equal in magnitude, no liability attaches.[21] Moreover, certain creators of nonreciprocal risks can be "excused" from having to compensate their victims, if, for example, they can show that they created a nonreciprocal risk through "compulsion" or "unavoidable" ignorance."[22]

While Fletcher denies that his "paradigm of reciprocity" is the equivalent of a strict liability standard, only limited inquiries are made into the "reasonableness" of a defendant's risk-creating act, and the simple statement that a defendant's creation of a nonreciprocal risk caused a plaintiff's injury is sufficient to make out a case for liability. Fletcher largely rejects notions of "foreseeability" both in the area of determining liability and in causation. "The paradigm of reciprocity," he states, "requires a single conclusion, based on perceptions of similarities, of excessiveness, and of directness."[23] Perhaps Fletcher's test for liability is the equivalent of older notions of tort liability based on "direct" injuries. Where one creates a "nonreciprocal" risk to another, one acts at his peril.

Fletcher maintains that his approach to tort law is "noninstrumentalist." He rejects the weighing of social costs and social benefits and the use of tort disputes as media "for furthering social goals."[24] But a determination of the reciprocity of two risks, which Fletcher concedes to be essential to his analysis, seems to invite appeal to considerations of social policy. For example, Fletcher posits the case of two persons, one who owns a dog and the other a cat, and suggests that were the two animals to injure each other's owners the risks would "presumably offset each other." [25] His example embodies a judgment based on the perceived comparative worth of dogs and cats in society, not on the entitlements of the two owners. If the dog in question were rabid and the cat were not, would the risks be reciprocal? Do judgments that call for a dog-cat interaction to be treated differently from an interaction between a bicycle and a bulldozer rest on justice between the parties? Or is "justice between the parties" defined in terms of current social assumptions about the value of various activities?

In one sense Fletcher's determination of the reciprocity of risks does not differ significantly from Calabresi's determination of whether the cheapest cost-avoider was in a position to avoid costs effectively in a given case. While Fletcher uses the language of moral philosophy and Calabresi that of economic theory, both approaches, at some point, require a weighing of the "interests" of the parties at stake in a torts case, based on current conventions about the "value" (in monetary or nonmonetary terms) of those interests. There are differences, of course, between the two approaches,[26] and for present purposes some of these differences are significant. Of all the approaches thus far considered, Fletcher's comes closest, in my view, to capturing what seems decisively to influence judges in tort cases, the rough scale of equities between the two litigating parties. Fletcher's notion of reciprocity of risk can be taken as an expression of equitable balance between tort litigants. In a subject not marked by recurrent and predictable litigation, the balance of equities between a discrete plaintiff and a discrete defendant has regularly been important.

Fletcher's most germane contribution to the perspective advanced in this study appears in an observation incidental to his central argument. In discussing the state of tort law before the triumph of the negligence principle, Fletcher cautions against the "unanalyzed assumption that every departure from the fault standard partakes of the strict liability expressed in the maxim 'a man acts at his peril'." [27] A number of points on a continuum between act-at-peril and negligence can be located, he claims, including making all "direct" injuries actionable; excusing a direct injury in a given case; excusing direct injuries in principle but not excusing the particular injury complained of; and allowing "reasonableness" to justify a direct injury. This statement comports closely with the argument advanced in Chapter One that it is erroneous to speak of tort law as having a "standard" of liability prior to the emergence of modern negligence, since the subject of Torts had not been conceptualized and courts and commentators simply did not think in terms of broad overriding standards of liability.[28]

A final significant set of theoretical insights into tort law has recently been made by Richard Epstein. While disassociating itself from Fletcher's, Epstein's perspective has some similarities with it.[29] He endorses "corrective justice"[30] as the principal goal of tort theory, rejects "utilitarian" approaches to tort law, and "does not regard economic theory as the primary means to establish the rules of tort liability."[31] The principal divergence between Fletcher and Epstein comes in their treatment of cases where both parties are injured, but the risks they have created are "reciprocal." Fletcher would not impose liability in such a situation. Epstein, who believes that "the liberty of one person ends when he causes harm to another,"[32] argues that "even if two risks were reciprocal, it does not follow that neither party should have his action when injured."[33]

Epstein is explicit in wanting to use the system of tort law to "protect . . . individual liberty and private property" and to "police civil conduct" by "rectifying changes in entitlements brought about by impermissible means," measures that he identifies with "corrective justice."[34] His strategy for achieving these goals is to describe tort law, in some ideal state, as a complex system of pleadings and presumptions, roughly resembling the earlier writ system. Like the writs, Epstein's pleadings are intended to serve as substantive rules of tort law: failure to plead successfully defeats one's claim. The failure, however, comes under Epstein's system not from technical deficiencies in language but from judgments on the substantive worth of a given "plea," which is the equivalent of a claim or a defense. Pleadings, in Epstein's theory, apparently serve as heuristic devices for introducing his substantive arguments.

Epstein's standard of tort liability is strict, most akin to acting at one's peril. He justifies this standard by arguing that one presumptively has a tort claim when one can show that another has caused him injury, since people have a right not to be injured. While some conduct causing injuries can be excused, it cannot be justified through "balancing" considerations of social utility; hence strict liability is the fairest standard. In defining "cause" Epstein does not refer to "legal" or "proximate" causation, nor to the traditional "but for" test for factual causation. He attempts to use cause in a way that combines notions of factual reasonableness and sound policy. Proof of causation is made out on a showing that a defendant used force directly on a plaintiff, frightened a plaintiff, compelled another to use force or to frighten a plaintiff, or exposed a plaintiff to "dangerous conditions." [35] These "paradigms" of causation for Epstein avoid the factual absurdities of the "but for" test, where literal application would produce excessive causal links, and also avoid the need for an arbitrary concept like proximate cause, whose purpose, Epstein feels, is only to limit liability by confining the ambit of "but for" causation.

Having established that a defendant has caused him harm by invoking one of the paradigms, a plaintiff creates a presumption in favor of his recovery. A defendant can then assert various defenses. Some defenses—necessity, compulsion, insanity, infancy, "best efforts," and mistake—Epstein regards as insufficient, since they represent efforts by the defendant "to shift the costs of his own problems onto the shoulders of the plaintiff." [36] The plaintiff, Epstein argues, is not responsible for the defendant's problems; it is not fair to use those problems as a basis to deny him recovery. Other defenses—causation, assumption of risk, plaintiff's trespass—Epstein regards as sufficient, either because they demonstrate a plaintiff's contribution to his own injury (causation and assumption of risk) or because the protection of a defendant's property can sometimes override the protection of a plaintiff's liberty (plaintiff's trespass). The defenses are not absolute: a plaintiff can show that some causal connections are weaker than others, or that joint causation is possible, or that he was compelled to assume the risk by the defendant, or that he was invited to come on the defendant's property.

In Epstein's ideal tort system a plaintiff asserts that a defendant has caused him harm, employing one of the paradigms of acceptable causation. A defendant pleads a defense; if all his defenses are dismissed as insufficient, the plaintiff wins. If one or more of his defenses is sufficient to rebut the plaintiff's presumptive recovery, the pleadings continue. The plaintiff then may plead that the defendant's defenses, while sufficient in principle, are insufficient in this instance because of additional factors (compulsion, invitation, etc.). By doing so the plaintiff reestablishes a presumption of recovery on his behalf, and the defendant again tries to rebut it, by showing, for example, that the plaintiff could have reduced his own injuries.

Epstein's theory is not simply designed to include the kinds of cases that traditionally have been treated by recourse to a negligence or to a strict liability standard. He also argues that intentional torts can be anlayzed through his approach. Intentional torts appear in the "third stage" of Epstein's ideal system of pleadings, where the intent of the defendant is used by the plaintiff to reply to the defendant's defense against causation. In an example given by Epstein, a defendant hits a plaintiff (a presumptive case for recovery by the plaintiff is established); the plaintiff hits the defendant back (a defense); the plaintiff shows that the defendant intended to hit him (a reply). The introduction of intent into the pleadings invites further stages: a defendant can counter that he was justified in hitting the plaintiff in order to defend himself; a plaintiff can argue that even though privileged to use self-defense, the defendant used excessive force; a defendant can contend that he used the minimum force he could to protect his own interests.[37] Through these staged pleadings, Epstein argues, the issues at stake in case are narrowed and joined.

The probable purpose of Epstein's system of pleading, as noted, is to serve as a heuristic technique for exposing the extent to which a negligence standard of tort liability lumps together a whole series of elements, giving no particular weight to any of them, under the heading of "reasonableness." Epstein is concerned that a reasonableness standard delegates too much power to judges to make decisions involving individuals on the basis of a calculus of social values. His system of pleading allows one to isolate (rigidly) the different elements in a tort action, to gain some sense of their relative importance, and to make more precise judgments about them. From this perspective, Epstein's approach is a valuable corrective to the tendency of tort law to formulate doctrines and tests notable for their vagueness.

But for all of Epstein's rigor and precision, his analysis is not able to avoid the kinds of "balancing" among social interests that he criticizes in negligence theory. In the case of a homeowner who severely injures a social guest in ejecting him from a party, for example, Epstein's system converts a tort claim by the guest into precise, measured stages, separating the causation issue from the intent issue, that issue from the issue of self-defense, and the self-defense issue from the issue of how much force is permissible in defense of oneself. But ultimately such cases turn on a social judgment of how much leeway society wants to grant to homeowners to protect their property. A social interest in prohibiting the intentional infliction of violence on others confronts a social interest in preserving the autonomy of landowners. "Intent," "consent," "excessive force" and other terms of art relevant to such cases are merely devices for permitting the interests to be balanced. Epstein's system does not eliminate this balancing, it merely rearranges it into orderly "stages."

Moreover, Epstein's system of pleas can at times contain its own inarticulated balancing, as his discussion of child trespasser cases reveals. Epstein argues, sensibly in my view, that infancy cannot be regarded as a complete defense in tort law since a person injured by an infant's torts is in no way responsible for the infant's diminished capacities.[38] But then Epstein argues that infancy should not be a justification for being exposed to dangerous substances in child trespasser cases.[39] Where strict liability serves as a comprehensive standard for tort law, no question of "duties" or their absence exists: an injured child can create a presumption of recovery once harmed. That presumption, under Epstein's system, would be rebutted by a landowner's showing that the child trespassed. The child would then establish his infancy, which Epstein would disregard. But why? It is one thing to refuse to allow one's diminished capacities to constitute a defense to an injury to an innocent and another to refuse to allow them to obviate what is in effect an assumption of risk defense. If a child does not possess the capacity to expose himself knowingly to risks, why should that fact be ignored? It seems that Epstein would ignore it because of his belief in the autonomy of landowners: a trespasser violates that autonomy. But by ignoring infancy in child trespasser cases Epstein is making his own social judgments, doing his own "balancing." He also is apparently violating his own principle that "the liberty of one person ends when he causes harm to another." [40]

To summarize, I find the principal theoretical contributions of Torts scholars in the 1970s ample testament to the intellectual capacities of those scholars but flawed as comprehensive approaches to tort law. My difficulties with professors Fletcher and Epstein are perhaps less severe than those with professors Posner and Calabresi. The former pair of scholars has not convinced me that their approaches adequately respond to the problems with negligence theory that they identify. Fletcher avows that his approach is noninstrumentalist, but then ends up with an analysis whose crucial step seems to be a determination of the reciprocity of risks. That step seems to leave considerable room for instrumentalist considerations to come into play. Epstein fears excessive "social-calculus" decisions by judges, but does not leave me sanguine about the prospects for such decisions being eliminated by his system of pleading, which is, after all, to be administered by the judiciary. Moreover, Epstein's notion of "corrective justice" may not be everyone's (witness the child trespasser cases), and he has not convinced me that his system provides a means for achieving "corrective justice" without some policy judgments. Epstein, I take it, would not claim that liberty and autonomy never compete with one another. When those values do compete the reconciliation of their competing claims often involves more than corrective justice in an individual case.

In my opinion it is not enough to say of the approach adopted by Posner and Calabresi that it "has not yet developed any straightforward set of rules consistent with its own initial premises to govern even routine cases of harm," or that its implementation would apparently require the use of an "incredibly complex mathematical apparatus." [41] I simply believe that the assumptions made by economic theory about the motivations of humans are gleaned from a world that does not resemble the world of tort claims. It is all very well to fashion a set of legal rules designed to reflect the "reality" of utility maximization and promote the ideal of efficiency if most everyone affected by the rules accepts that reality and believes in that ideal. But the theory reduces human judgments to a singlemindedness that seems to me unattainable. If the "cheapest cost-avoider" will not invariably seek to avoid his costs, a search for him becomes somewhat awkward. Even granted that economic models will function smoothly in a world of rational maximizers with perfect information, such a world seems light years away from the universe of tort law.

The Past and The Future: A Summary

If the modes of our time are neoconceptualist, there is a burden on commentators to theorize, especially if they have been critical of the theories of others. Theory in this study is inextricably related to history in the sense that my observations about the current state of tort law are designed to complement the themes that have surfaced in the course of the historical development of Torts in America. A place to start this concluding section, then, is with a recapitulation of some central themes.

Perhaps the central feature of the history of American tort law has been its tendency to serve as a testing ground for currently dominant intellectual theories. Tort liability did not become synonymous with fault, for example, because, as some early twentieth-century commentators argued, a fault standard gave greater prominence to moral judgments than an act-at-peril standard.[42] Fault and tort law became linked at a certain time in American history for reasons that had little to do with morality. The growth of negligence theory was produced by pressure for some theoretical superstructure for tort law, given the conceptualist tendencies of late nineteenth-century educated thought, and by the congeniality of negligence with limitations on tort liability, which accorded with late nineteenth-century preferences for letting losses lie where they fell.

While the scientists assumed that tort law should have comprehensive standards of liability, tort actions had existed for hundreds of years without such standards. Here the prevailing cast of intellectual thought was again a crucial influence. In an age where standardless legal subjects were considered unacceptably chaotic, it was fitting that Torts should define itself through the development of some central theory of tortious conduct, which was converted into a standard of liability. The fact that the theory that was developed happened to be negligence was fortuitous in the sense that negligence was congenial to a distinctive intellectual attitude of the late nineteenth century. Once one posits the existence of that attitude, however, the development of a comprehensive standard, and the emergence of negligence as that standard, become highly likely.

A broadening of the ambit of tort law from a "private" to a "public" law subject, and a shift in the thrust of tort liability from admonition to compensation were likewise brought about by changes in social thought. Torts was originally a subject that was not easily represented as "private" or "public," since the boundaries between those separable forms of conduct were not distinct. Many "tortious" activities, such as assault, battery, or defamation, were punished as much for their offensiveness to the general public as for their harm to individuals. The granting of punitive damages in tort actions, similarly, signified a public dimension of tortious conduct. In the late nineteenth century Torts became increasingly conceived as a private law subject, not because it was inherently so suited, but because a sharp line between "private" and "public" activity was consistent with prevailing social wisdom. The emergence of an "objective" standard of liability in negligence suggested, however, that private actions in a tort suit were being evaluated with reference to existing public standards of social conduct. Those who sued in tort, unlike those who sued in contract, could not limit the measure of their damages: a tort suit was never a wholly private affair.

The conception of tort law as "public" law that surfaced in the early twentieth century, then, did not signify a dramatically expanded ambit of the subject of Torts. That conception's significance came more from an associated belief that tort law should function primarily as a compensation system. But it was not inevitable that tort law should be concerned with compensating victims of civil injuries; compensation had probably not been its original purpose and was certainly not thought to be its central purpose by those who began to teach Torts as an autonomous common law subject. The compensatory features of tort law came to be seen as significant, however, once American society came to be perceived of as an interdependent entity whose members were responsible for one another. If the lives of injured persons affected the lives of others, so that injuries were a social "problem," then compensating people for injuries became a paramount policy goal. The tort system was one existing compensation device; it had the virtue of having survived over time and of allegedly conditioning compensation on proof of blameworthiness; it was "there" to be made into a more effective compensation system through liability insurance and other techniques for spreading and shifting the costs of injuries. The emergence of tort law as a compensation system was thus largely fortuitous.

Finally, tort law need not have been thought of as a coherent body of law at all. The field of "Torts" was originally merely a collection of writs whose common features were "discovered" by late nineteenth-century scholars and grouped together into the loose category of civil wrongs not arising out of contract. In that capacity Torts entered legal education and became a discrete subject. Soon it was highly organized, with a philosophical and analytical structure, but that organization had come from scholars. In the early twentieth century, much of that organization broke down as the prominence of a negligence standard came to be undermined and a more diffuse reading of tort "principles" emerged. The atomization of Torts, however, was also a product of trends in scholarship. Now a new characterization of the subject of Torts is developing that resists atomization and seeks to reformulate general guidelines for tort law. But nothing about the subject matter of civil wrongs not arising out of contract compels one organization of the field or another. Tort law could just as well be an incoherent mass as a tightly knit subject whose elements are arranged in a "philosophically continuous series." Prevailing conceptions of Torts have little to do with the nature of the subject itself.

In short, none of the principal features of the currently dominant conception of tort law—an emphasis on alternatives to the negligence standard, an interest in the compensation function of tort law, an insistence that Torts be considered a "public law" subject, a search for comprehensive theories of tort liability—is essential to the subject. Radically different features have been emphasized at other times, while the material of tort law has remained relatively stable. Thus proposals for emphasizing one or another feature of tort law do not have to reckon with some inherent tendency in the subject to lend itself to one theory of liability or another. They have to reckon, rather, with the prevailing intellectual wisdom of the time. *relate to pragmatism*

It may be that the momentum of neoconceptualism is sufficiently advanced that the short-term future of tort law will necessarily be associated with the formulation and refinement of some comprehensive theory of liability, whose role in twentieth-century history may be analogous to that of the negligence principle in its years of dominance. A theme of this book has been the power of ideas as causative agents, and I should not want to minimize the potential capacity of neoconceptualism to reshape the subject of Torts. But if it is not too late, I should like to resist such a tendency. My reasons, which can only be given brief treatment here, cluster into three categories. The first category relates to the tendency of conceptualist thought toward unitary theories of liability; the second to the interaction of neoconceptualism and a compensation premise for the tort system; and the third to the role of academics as lawmakers in a "conceptualized" legal subject.

My view is that Torts is not a unified subject but a complex of diverse wrongs whose policy implications point in different directions. There is first a class of "routine" unintentional injuries (some automobile accidents, some injuries from defective products, some occupational injuries, and the like) whose causes are not complex, whose victims and perpetrators often have liability insurance, and whose presence in the tort system stems from a search for compensation on the part of the injured party. There is then a class of "nonroutine" unintentional injuries whose settlement is a more difficult process. Examples are injuries that are very severe and longstanding and whose cost is therefore very high, or whose causes are highly complex, or which present genuinely difficult questions about liability. Such "nonroutine" injuries are the type that most often end up in appellate courts and produce cases reported in casebooks.

There are at least three other classes of tortious wrongs. One is composed of injuries that are intentionally produced; a second of injuries that affect the mental well being or dignity of the victim rather than his physical state. In the first of these classes are the intentional torts (assault, battery, and the like); in the second, and overlapping class, are such torts as privacy, defamation, false imprisonment, and infliction of emotional distress. Finally, there is a class of civil wrongs arising out of business relations where the litigants are not contracting parties, such as misrepresentation, unfair competition, and interference with contractual relations.

It should be clear that the basis for tort litigation in these separate classes of injuries is not always similar. A plaintiff in an intentional or a dignitary tort case may be able to show only minimal damages, but may seek to punish the defendant for the humiliation the plaintiff has endured. The "injury" suffered by a plaintiff in a business relations case may not be compensable through liability insurance. The purpose of the lawsuit may be different in each case, and the litigants may be conceiving of the tort system in different ways.

If this is so, it seems that unitary theories of tort liability run the risk of a uniform treatment for very different kinds of civil actions. Under Fletcher's approach to tort law, for example, the reciprocity of the risk determines liability, without regard to how the risk was created. But what if the risk were trivial, and the injury nominal (a stolen kiss), but the risk was intentionally created and the tort system was asked to admonish? Should that case be treated precisely like the case of a defective power saw that maims a consumer? Fletcher would undoubtedly distinguish the cases, but is their distinguishing feature the reciprocity of risk? Or is it that they enter the tort system with different purposes, seeking different kinds of redress?

Epstein finds that his system of pleading, if strictly followed, eliminates recovery for the so-called "prima facie tort" of intentional interference with economic relationships.[43] The reason, for Epstein, is causation: defendants in such cases have not inflicted force on, frightened, or exposed plaintiffs to dangerous conditions; nor have they compelled plaintiffs to do anything against their will. They have merely induced others to breach their business relationships with the plaintiffs. To maintain the integrity of his theoretical structure, Epstein is forced to declare these cases not properly within the system of tort law. Plaintiffs in such cases are using the tort system for a twin purpose, to recover economic losses and to punish offensive conduct. Making certain interferences with economic relationships "tortious" is a way not only of compensating persons injured by the interferences but of imposing sanctions on the conduct complained of. To sacrifice the opportunity to sanction such conduct in order to preserve the purity of a theory of Torts seems a misplacement in priorities.

Beyond that, it seems unnecessary. Why should different classes of tort actions not be treated differently, despite the conceptual difficulties that arrangement creates? In my judgment standards of tort liability should roughly approximate the different classes of tort actions. For "routine" unintentional injuries, I would impose a standard of no liability: in other words, I would remove such cases from the tort system altogether. This result is accomplished by no-fault systems of liability, where victims are compensated by their own insurance in exchange for forgoing tort claims. No-fault plans traditionally have limits on recoverable amounts, which tend to return cases of substantial serious injuries to the tort system. I see no difficulty in extending the no-fault principle from work-related and automobile accidents, where it is established, to "routine" defective product injuries, provided such injuries are sufficiently routine to build a statistical base for insurance purposes. I suspect they may be, and I suspect that the reason why many "routine" defective product cases now tend to be litigated is the existence of a strict liability standard in the defective products area which, as Posner points out, creates little incentive for consumers to use products carefully.[44]

It is, of course, not easy to separate the "routine" from the "non-routine" unintentional accident, and the seriousness of an injury complained of, as measured by the amount of the tort claim, is a crude method for making that distinction. But since the injured person who opts for tort litigation runs the risk of no compensation at all, and the defendant runs the risk of a substantial judgment against him, one might surmise that cases where liability, or its absence, is quite clear will not be litigated. This suggests that the truly complex case, from the point of view of tort doctrine, may be preserved for the tort system.

It is difficult to say how much reduction in tort litigation would result from the implementation of this proposal. I suspect that few cases where liability or its absence is clear are litigated at present, and I doubt that many cases where claims are insubstantial are litigated. The proposal is not designed to reduce court dockets, although that would be desirable. It is rather designed to reserve a costly, slow, wearing, and sometimes arbitrary and unjust injury-compensation system for those accidents that are, by rough measurement, serious and substantial, and for which responsibility is sharply disputed. Other types of accidents seem better disposed of by first-party insurance, which, is, after all, advertised as designed for such a purpose.

My proposal reserves the tort system, then, for "nonroutine" unintentional injuries and for all types of intentional and dignitary injuries. This means, of course, that the achievement of a unitary theory of tort liability will be difficult and that tort law will serve purposes in addition to that of compensation. Both those results are consistent with my assumptions about the proper role of tort law.

It seems to me that any theory of tort liability—even an "act-at-peril" theory—involves in its application some balancing" of variables that transcend the immediate interests of the parties in "corrective justice." Assume, for example, that a bystander at a construction site is injured by a cement mixer whose safety equipment did not include an automatic back-up horn or large sideview mirrors.[45] If the bystander can show that the cement mixer was "defectively" designed, he can recover, in some states, even though he might have been contributorily negligent in standing in the mixer's path. Strict liability theory governs, but is its application simply a matter of corrective justice? The crucial point for determination is the "defectiveness" of the mixer's design: "defectiveness" inquiries involve consideration of the relative safety of the industry, the costs of effective design, the social value of cement mixers, their hazardousness, and the other variables that go into social judgments of this kind. A strict liability standard does not end such judgments; it merely shifts their focus from the "reasonableness" of the mixer's driver to the "defectiveness" of the mixer's design. There may be other instances, however, where strict liability appears to foreclose such balancing. Take the case of a newspaper that mistakenly reports a person to be a professional gambler when in fact he is a clergyman. Strict liability might allow the clergyman to recover if he could simply show that the mistake had occurred.[46]

My view is that the particular standard that governs an area of tort law is less important than the retention of opportunities to balance the equities in a given case. Negligence, especially comparative negligence, can lend itself to balancing; so, on occasion, can strict liability. A standard that makes tortious conduct turn on "intent" may not seem to allow balancing, but it actually does, through the device of punitive damages. Intentional torts, in a sense, constitute a balancing of the social undesirability of the defendant's conduct against the perceived seriousness of the plaintiff's injury. The "extreme and outrageous" test used in the area of intentional infliction of emotional distress captures the balancing process by insisting that, since emotional distress without accompanying physical injury is perceived of as less of a tangible "hurt," the conduct creating the hurt be perceived of as very objectionable.

Much of the "balancing" under multiple standards of tort liability would involve issues not relevant to compensation, and would be undertaken by judges. Some scholars have found the "admonitory" function of tort law old-fashioned, and others have feared entrusting social policy judgments to judges. It seems to me, first, that there is something to be said for using tort law as a device for censure and punishment. Many Torts cases involve actions deliberately intended to violate the sanctity or privacy of other people or to cause them suffering. When such actions fall short of criminal conduct, there is little victims can do to acquire some feeling of recompense except forcing those who have injured them to pay them money. Compensation is not always a satisfactory remedy in such cases and sometimes it appears to be ludicrously unsuited, as where a person with a notorious past has his or her "privacy" violated by a newspaper and seeks relief. The privacy is irreparably lost: the victim may become rich, but can no longer preserve his or her privacy from friends and associates. But in such cases the tort system is primarily using compensation as a censure device; its central purpose is to admonish. While such admonitions may not deter other potential violators, there is something to be said for a society declaring, through its legal system, that it finds certain noncriminal conduct reprehensible.

Second, I am not overly concerned that under the present system judges are making most of the policy judgments implicit in tort decisions. There may be certain areas (comparative negligence and charitable immunities come to mind) where the immersion of judges in traditional common law doctrine binds them to outmoded positions. When judicial activism is in vogue, however (as it currently is), even the self-imposed professional restraints of judges will not bar them from making wholesale doctrinal changes themselves.[47] It seems to me that since the application of standards of tort liability in a given case ("doctrinal" analysis) inevitably involves policy judgments, judges are better acquainted with the intricacies of common law subjects than most other people and no more inherently incapable of making sensible policy decisions than other groups of persons. Indeed, the alternative to judicial lawmaking in torts seems to me to be not legislative lawmaking, although some new legislation has recently appeared,[48] but academic lawmaking. Lawmaking by academicians raises some difficulties that I will presently pursue.

My interest in retaining a significant admonitory function for tort law is premised on a belief that there is a value in using law to sanction or to censure undesirable civil conduct, but it also follows from a sense of the unhappy consequences of an interaction between conceptualist pressures in intellectual thought and a compensatory role for tort law. Conceptualist impulses, as the late nineteenth-century experience demonstrates, create pressure for intellectual classification systems based on comprehensive principles. A standardless tort system offended against the thrust of late nineteenth-century scholarship; little by little that system was transformed into one whose central purpose was the admonition of "unreasonable" conduct and whose governing principle was negligence. A comparable conceptualization of late twentieth-century tort law might occur, but in that conceptualization the primary purpose of tort law would more likely be regarded as compensation than admonition and the governing principle more likely to be strict liability or "no-fault" than negligence.

We have come rather far from the nineteenth-century ethos of injury, and it is doubtful that letting losses lie where they fell would be a proposition carrying much current favor. Nonetheless I do not believe that the tort system is a particularly efficient or fair compensation device. I would prefer to remove some claims for compensation from tort law rather than to strengthen its compensatory capacities. Making compensation the primary goal of tort law fully converts Torts to a public law subject, encourages the proliferation of liability insurance, and generally minimizes the goal of corrective justice in the individual case. I am not certain that I would want corrective justice always to predominate in tort law, but it seems to be largely lost in a comprehensive compensation system, since such a system encourages decisionmakers to think in terms of classes of risk-bearers rather than to focus on the equitable claims of discrete litigants.

The strict liability principle likewise encourages the spread of liability insurance, since those in the business of manufacturing "abnormally dangerous" or "defective" products have to seek some means to protect themselves against the risk of crippling lawsuits. Comprehensive strict liability would seem to me to encourage large recoveries, thereby increasing insurance rates and consequently the cost of products, and also to encourage users of products to regard tort law as their primary means of redress from injuries. The result of heavy reliance on tort law as a means of redress might well be congested dockets, delayed compensations, and the normal run of difficulties associated with the process of adversary litigation. Some of these problems have been aired in critiques of the negligence principle; I find little reason to believe they would be "solved" by a strict liability alternative.

As for no-fault, while I endorse the concept with respect to some "routine" tortious injuries, I have grave doubts about its effectiveness as a comprehensive alternative to tort liability. For one thing, no-fault plans assume the eradication of a fault standard, and I have argued that fault, especially when used in a moral sense, is an essential ingredient of an admonitory conception of tort law. One cannot convert the law of intentional torts to a no-fault standard and retain its punitive function; neither can one make a comparable conversion with respect to dignitary torts. And if no-fault is not intended to include those areas, or to affect claims whose dollar amounts exceed a fixed figure, it is hard to regard no-fault as anything more than a remedial device intended to facilitate compensation for those tort claims where issues of punishment and deterrence do not seem at stake. I have no objections to no-fault being used in that capacity, but think its proponents have far wider ambitions,[49] and I cannot reconcile no-fault as a comprehensive principle with my interest in using tort law as a device for censure and punishment.

The triumph of a comprehensive theory of tort liability is not, of course, a necessary consequence of nonconceptualism in legal scholarship. At the height of the influence of negligence, pockets of act-at-peril liability remained. The law of defamation and privacy has been recently "constitutionalized," as the relevance of First Amendment concerns to those cases has been realized, and one effect of constitutionalization has been the obliteration of preexisting strict liability standards for libel and slander.[50] But my concern is not so much that a unitary standard of liability will emerge. It is rather that pressure toward comprehensive theories of tort liability will eradicate the diverse treatment of different classes of wrongs that I see essential to a sensible resolution of tort issues. Conceptualism, as a mode of thought, is impatient with an ad hoc treatment of legal issues, with competing theories of liability, and with multiple purposes for an area of law. I think, however, that tort law more closely resembles a shifting mass of diverse wrongs than a tidy, conceptually unified subject. Multiple purposes for tort law, multiple standards of tort liability, and individualized determinations of tort claims reflect the innate character of the field.

The late nineteenth-century experience also suggests that one of the consequences of the triumph of conceptualist modes of thought in the legal profession is the emergence of academics as lawmakers. A primary goal of conceptualism is the promulgation of general principles of law, which are "extracted" from the ordinary materials—appellate cases and, more recently, statutes—of orthodox lawmakers. The extraction and promulgation tends to be done by academics, although some appellate judges regard an articulation of general principles as part of their function. The principles, of course, are created by the extractors: to the extent that an extracted principle retains some vitality and authority, its extractor has functioned as a lawmaker. When the authoritativeness of extracted principles is taken sufficiently seriously that efforts are made to reorient common law subjects in accordance with such principles, academics have the opportunity to become full-blown lawmakers. An example is Section 402A of the Second Restatement of Torts, articulating the principle of strict liability for defective products. The draftsman of that section was Prosser; his advisers, for the most part, were also academicians. Since the appearance of Section 402A several courts have conceived of the section as a standard that they regard as applicable to defective products cases. Some courts have not accepted the standard in every particular, but many have taken it as a starting point for analysis of the defective products area.[51]

When a standard of liability for a common law subject is supplied by academics, the architects of the standard are making law in a very full sense. If, because of trends in legal thought, comprehensive standards and principles are regarded as desirable in a common law subject, opportunities for academics to make law are increased. There is nothing inherently invidious about academics acting as lawmakers. They purportedly have time to reflect on the broad dimensions of a subject and to concentrate on detailed knowledge of one area of law without having to consider a number of others in the ordinary course of their business, as is the case with judges. One could even say that academics, being housed in a university environment, are more acquainted with current intellectual developments than, say, judges or legislators. Finally, one could argue, hopefully not entirely seriously, that the barriers for entry into the profession of law teaching are sufficiently formidable that academics tend to be thoughtful and articulate people whose chances of being enlightened lawmakers are somewhat better than those of the average citizen.

All these arguments, however, minimize the fact that law is an authoritative force in American society; that the exercise of authority, in a democracy, is supposedly consonant with accountability; and that academics have almost no accountability to the persons who will be effected by the laws they make. The absence of judicial accountability has been a theme of recent literature, but when judges are appointed or elected, people expect that they will be lawmakers, regard them as public officials, scrutinize their conduct, and in general treat them as persons who will be occupying positions of power and prominence and whose theories of law may become influential.[52] The prospective appointment of legal scholars is not comparably regarded. The principal reason that almost no one talks about the "accountability" of law professors is that almost no one expects that they will be functioning as lawmakers. On the contrary, many people regard an appointment to a university professorship as the equivalent of the abandonment of one's opportunities to exert influence in the "real world."

This study has suggested, however, that doctrinal changes in tort law have to an important extent been created by academicians. The influence of academics on tort law has ranged from direct and immediate examples (appellate court use of the Restatement of Torts, a treatise or a law review article as the source of a standard or test of liability) to more indirect and long-range ones (the evolution of an extracted "principle" of tort law to prominent doctrinal status in the

242

courts). But academic influence has been regular and profound, shaping basic conceptions of civil liability. To say that academics who propound theories, create doctrines, or extract principles of tort law are not functioning as lawmakers is to equate lawmaking solely with the status of the officials charged with that task. But if lawmaking, especially the judicial variety, is an exercise in persuasion as much as a declaration of the power of one's office, the sources of persuasion are important features of the exercise. If included among those sources are the works of academicians, the academicians cited have contributed to lawmaking.

In periods where conceptualist modes of thought are influential, as noted, opportunities for academic lawmaking are expanded. New comprehensive theories are sought; efforts are undertaken to unify and synthesize fields of law; appeals to broad principles are made. A difficulty can occur in such times. If the tendency of professionalization to narrow and refine the corpus of "approved" academic scholarship unites with the tendency of conceptualist thought to elevate scholars to prominence as lawmakers, a small and self-reinforcing class of persons may exert a disproportionate degree of influence. Such appears to have been the case in the late nineteenth century, when the subject of Torts was restructured by a strikingly small number of persons.

Professional training in contemporary American life seems inherently susceptible to the selective approval and disapproval of various intellectual approaches to the subject matter of one's profession. "Learning the law" not only means being exposed to a body of knowledge but to a set of purportedly authoritative judgments about what features of that knowledge should be stressed and how that knowledge should be acquired. Implicit in such judgments are value premises about becoming educated and living in society generally. It seems inevitable that such collective premises should exist, since becoming a "professional" in American life has become synonymous with specialized ("approved" and selective) thinking. But it does not seem inevitable, and it seems somewhat troublesome, for the value premises of professional academicians to affect decisively the contents of laws that persons outside professional communities are intended to follow. Academic life can be seen as a narrowing experience: one gains the time and freedom to think in exchange for the price of having one's thoughts evaluated by small, self-selected, and self-reinforcing groups of one's "peers." That is a choice one makes on deciding to become a "professional" academician. But accountability to one's peers is not the same as accountability to the public at large. The expectations of the public about lawmaking can hardly be said to include the idea that their lives will be affected by some law professor's theory of tort liability.

That such an effect nonetheless occurs has been regularly commented upon in this book, but a documentation of the influence of academics on tort law should not be taken as a plea for an expansion of the lawmaking role of scholars. On the contrary, part of the reason I am not unhappy with the current "chaotic" state of tort law, with its multiple standards for liability, its diverse jurisdictional rules and doctrines, and its absence of scholarly consensus about theoretical perspectives, is that I find such chaos an antidote to the tendency of conceptualist thought to elevate scholars to positions of undue prominence.

I close by noting that for all the impressive scholarly energies directed at the unification, simplification, and ordering of tort law, the field seems to have an inherent capacity to lapse into disorderliness, inconsistencies and complexities. It seems to me that the recurrent urge among scholars and judges to make tort law comprehensible, and the recurrent capacity of the subject to retain its incomprehensibility, is symbolic of a more basic interaction between law and human behavior in American society. Repeatedly in times of crisis, when consensual values seem to have disintegrated and the core of American civilization to have vanished, appeals have been made to law as a cementing and ordering force. But law is no more, or less, capable of achieving order and consensus than those who make it. So long as tort law, or any other area of law, deals with human problems and is made and enforced by humans it will embody dissonances and absurdities; it will resist orderliness and it will regularly defy comprehensibility. The capacity of law in America to resist serving as an orderly system of social control is at least as strong as the impulse of legal theorists to make it so serve.

Notes

Introduction

1. For examples, see L. Friedman, *A History of American Law* 261–64, 409–27 (1973); M. Horwitz, *The Transformation of American Law, 1780–1860* 85–99 (1977); Gregory, "Trespass to Negligence to Absolute Liability," 37 Va. L. Rev. 359 (1951); Roberts, "Negligence: Blackstone to Shaw to?: An Intellectual Escapade in a Tory Vein," 50 Cornell L. Q. 191 (1965).
2. See, e.g., the founding of the University of Chicago Law School in F. Ellsworth, *Law on the Midway* 54–73 (1977); the transformation of Columbia under William Keener in J. Goebel, Jr., *A History of the School of Law, Columbia University* 136–58 (1955); and the influence of "Harvard methods" at Northwestern under John H. Wigmore in W. Roalfe, *John Henry Wigmore* 35–62 (1978).
3. See T. Kuhn, *The Structure of Scientific Revolutions* (2d ed., 1970). See also D. Hollinger, "T. S. Kuhn's Theory of Science and Its Implications for History," 78 Am. Hist. Rev. 370 (1973), and four monographic studies on individual disciplines: M. Furner, *Advocacy and Objectivity* (1975); B. Karl, *Charles E. Merriam and the Study of Politics* (1974); T. Haskell, *The Emergence of Professional Social Science* (1977); and B. Kuklick, *The Rise of American Philosophy* (1977).
4. See *infra*, Chapter Two.
5. In addition to the works cited in note 4, see B. Bledstein, *The Culture of Professionalism* (1976); R. Wiebe, *The Search for Order, 1877–1920* (1967); D. Calhoun, *Professional Lives in America* (1965).
6. See *infra*, Chapter One.

Chapter 1

1. Blackstone's *Commentaries* had separate chapters on trespass and nuisance and referred to Torts as "all actions for trespasses, nuisances, defamatory

words, and the like." 3 W. Blackstone, *Commentaries on the Laws of England* *117 (1771 ed.) The general classification system of Blackstone's *Commentaries* is discussed in note 10, *infra*.

2. 1 F. Hilliard, *The Law of Torts* (2 vols., 1859) (1859) See L. Friedman, *A History of American Law* 409 (1973).

3. See *The Centennial History of the Harvard Law School* 29 (1918).

4. J. Ames, *A Selection of Cases on the Law of Torts* (1874). See Rothenberg, Book Review, 23 U.C.L.A. L. Rev. 373, 377 (1975).

5. See, e.g., L. Friedman, *supra*, note 2, at 262, 409; M. Horwitz, *The Transformation of American Law, 1780–1860* 85–99 (1977); Gregory, "Trespass to Negligence to Absolute Liability," 37 Va. L. Rev. 359, 368, 377–79, 382 (1951). See also Roberts, "Negligence: Blackstone to Shaw to ? An Intellectual Escapade in a Tory Vein," 50 Cornell L.Q. 191, 204–05, 213 (1965).

6. This generalization has received widespread support in the historical literature. See, e.g., R. Welter, *The Mind of America, 1820–1860*, 117–22, 141–56 (1975) [citing sources]; Appleby, "The Social Origins of American Revolutionary Ideology," 64 J. Am. Hist. 935 (1978).

7. See A. Kaul, *The American Vision* (1963), who traces this theme in the writings of Cooper, Hawthorne, Melville, and Mark Twain.

8. Andrew Jackson personified these tendencies. See M. Meyers, *The Jacksonian Persuasion* (1957); J. Ward, *Andrew Jackson: Symbol for an Age* (1955).

9. J. Higham, *From Boundlessness to Consolidation: The Transformation of American Culture, 1848–1860*, 6 (1969).

10. Blackstone's *Commentaries* had divided "the Laws of England" into "the rights of persons" (e.g., sovereign immunities, master-servant, domestic relations), "the rights of things" (real and personal property), "private wrongs" (e.g., trespass, nuisance, equitable remedies, and civil procedure), and "public wrongs" (criminal law and procedure). This four-fold division constituted the four volumes of his commentaries.

11. N. Dane, *A General Abridgment and Digest of American Law* (1823–1829).

12. See, e.g., T. Parsons, *The Law of Contracts* (2 vols., 1857); E. Washburn, *A Treatise on the American Law of Real Property* (1860–1862). Washburn's treatise was written between 1856 and 1860. See *The Centennial History of the Harvard Law School, supra,* note 3, at 356.

13. See Kennedy, "Form and Substance in Private Law Adjudication," 89 Harv. L. Rev. 1685, 1725–27 (1976).

14. 2 T. Parsons, *supra,* note 12, at 265.

15. Ibid. at 266.

16. See W. Houghton, *The Victorian Frame of Mind, 1830–1870* (1957).

17. See Brown, "Modernization: A Victorian Climax," 27 Am. Q. 533 (1975); Meyer, "American Intellectuals and the Victorian Crisis of Faith, ibid. at 585.

18. H. Adams, *The Education of Henry Adams* 225–26 (1918). For a collection of essays on the influence of evolution in America, see S. Persons, ed., *Evolutionary Thought in America* (1950).

19. Cowley, "Naturalism in American Literature," in *Evolutionary Thought in America, supra,* note 18 at 300, 304.

20. L. Sullivan, *The Autobiography of an Idea* 255 (1934).

21. 2 J. Fiske, *Outlines of Cosmic Philosophy* 467–68 (1892 ed.).

22. Other recent scholarship has perceived a similar unity in the pattern of reasoning in post-Civil War treatises and judicial decisions. The pattern has principally been characterized by the term formalism. See, e.g., Horwitz, "The Rise of Legal Formalism," 19 Am. J. Legal Hist. 251, 255–57, 261–62 (1975); Kennedy, *supra,* note 13 at 1728–31 (using the term "Classical individualism"); Nelson, "The Impact of the Antislavery Movement Upon Styles of Judicial Reasoning in Nineteenth Century America," 87 Harv. L. Rev. 513, 514–16, 560–66 (1974). But see Scheiber, "Instrumentalism and Property Rights: A Reconsideration of American Styles of Judicial Reasoning in the 19th Century," 1975 Wis. L. Rev. 1 (criticizing Nelson for oversimplifying changes in styles of judicial reasoning).

23. 2 L. Ward, *Dynamic Sociology* 539 (1883). Ward had begun work on *Dynamic Sociology* in 1869. See R. Hofstadter, *Social Darwinism in American Thought* 69 (1944).

24. For an analysis of the philosophical contributions of another member of the Club, Charles Peirce, see Note, "Holmes, Peirce and Legal Pragmatism," 84 Yale L. J. 1123 (1975). On the Metaphysical Club, see Wiener, "Peirce's Metaphysical Club and the Genesis of Pragmatism," 7 J. Hist. Ideas 218 (1946).

25. See [Holmes], Book Review, 5 Am. L. Rev. 340, 341 (1871). See also Frank, "A Conflict With Oblivion: Some Observations on the Founders of Legal Pragmatism," 9 Rutgers L. Rev. 425, 434 (1954).

26. In a discussion of proximate causation, Green called the phrase "natural and proximate consequence" a "stereotyped [form] for gliding over a difficulty without explaining it." N. Green, "Torts Under the French Law," *Essays and Notes on the Law of Tort and Crime* 71, 82 (1933) [hereinafter cited as *Essays*]. The *Essays* are reprints of notes and unsigned articles and book reviews which Green published in the *American Law Review,* in the eighth edition of Joseph Story's *Commentaries on the Law of Agency,* which Green edited, and in two volumes of criminal law cases entitled *Criminal Law Reports.* All the material in the *Essays* was written between 1869 and 1876. Ibid. at v.

27. N. Green, "Slander and Libel," in *Essays, supra,* note 26, at 49, 69–70.

28. Ibid. at 53.

29. N. Green, "The Liability of a Principal to Third Persons for the Torts of his Agents and Servants," in *Essays,* at 127.

30. N. Green, "Proximate and Remote Cause," in *Essays,* at 1, 16.

31. N. Green, "Insanity in Criminal Law," in *Essays,* at 161, 166.

32. N. Green, *supra,* note 27, at 70 (emphasis in original).

33. N. Green, "The Liability of a Master to his Servants," in *Essays,* at 131, 137.
34. N. Green, *supra,* note 30, at 9.
35. The interdisciplinary character of conceptualism is discussed in M. White, *Social Thought in America: The Revolt Against Formalism* (1949).
36. The impact of Green on Holmes is discussed in Frank, *supra,* note 25, at 434–44. Frank argues that "in several notable respects" Green was "Holmes' precursor" (Ibid. at 442).
37. See generally M. Howe, *Justice Oliver Wendell Holmes: The Proving Years* (1963); M. White, *supra,* note 35 at 71–75. For a discussion of Green's interest in history, see Frank, *supra,* note 25, at 439–40.
38. Cf. L. Friedman, *supra,* note 2, at 531–32 (discussing Langdell's belief that law is a science).
39. [Holmes], *supra,* note 25, at 341.
40. See, e.g., L. Friedman, *supra,* note 2, at 340–46; R. Millar, *Civil Procedure of the Trial Court in Historical Perspective* 52–53 (1952); A. Schlesinger, *The Age of Jackson* 329–33 (1945).
41. See R. Millar, *supra,* note 40, at 54–55.
42. See L. Friedman, *supra,* note 2, at 340–43, 351–53; A. Schlesinger, *supra,* note 40, at 330–33.
43. Nelson, "The Reform of Common Law Pleading in Massachusetts, 1760–1830: Adjudication as a Prelude to Legislation," 122 U. Pa. L. Rev. 97 (1973).
44. Ibid. at 112–15.
45. Ibid. at 119.
46. N. Green, "Some Results of Reform in Indictments," in *Essays, supra,* note 26, at 151.
47. For a description of writ pleading in Massachusetts, see Nelson, *supra,* note 43, at 98–116.
48. Dane's *Abridgment* was organized around existing forms of action. N. Dane, *supra,* note 11.
49. See Nelson, *supra,* note 43, at 112–16.
50. See M. Bloomfield, *American Lawyers in a Changing Society, 1776–1876,* at 83–88 (1976); P. Miller, *The Life of the Mind in America* 251–54 (1965).
51. P. Miller, *supra,* note 50, at 161.
52. [Holmes], Book Review, 5 Am. L. Rev. 359 (1871): reviewing *The Code of Procedure of the State of New York, as Amended to 1870* (10th ed., J. Townshend, 1870).
53. 1 F. Hilliard, *supra,* note 2, at v (emphasis in original).
54. Ibid. at vi.
55. Ibid. at vi–vii.
56. Ibid. at vii (emphasis in original).
57. Another factor possibly prompting mid-nineteenth-century American lawyers to reassess the worth of the writ system was a growing consciousness of the image of their profession. See M. Bloomfield, *supra,* note 50 at 136–90.

58. 1 F. Hilliard, *supra,* note 2, at x (emphasis in original).
59. [Holmes], *supra,* note 25, at 341.
60. Ibid.
61. Ibid.
62. In 1870, Green, in his preface to Charles G. Addison's *Law of Torts,* wrote that Torts was "the law of those rights which avail against persons generally, or against all mankind." Green noted that Torts was "usually treated of under the titles of the various forms of action which lie for the infringement of such rights." He felt that such a treatment tended "to confuse those fundamental principles which should be kept distinct in the mind of the student." Green, Preface to C. Addison, *Law of Torts* at iii (1870). Holmes reviewed the book in the *American Law Review.* See note 25, *supra.* Others working on the reorientation of Torts at the same time were Melville Bigelow, Charles Doe, and Thomas Cooley. See M. Howe, *supra,* note 37 at 83–84, 139.
63. [Holmes], "The Theory of Torts," 7 Am. L. Rev. 652, 660 (1873). Mark DeWolfe Howe attributes this essay to Holmes. M. Howe, *supra,* note 37, at 64.
64. [Holmes], *supra,* note 63, at 659–60.
65. Ibid. at 659.
66. Ibid. at 653.
67. The efforts of Holmes and his contemporaries to develop a general theory of Torts mark one instance in which an American development in nineteenth-century legal scholarship preceded an analogous development in England. The first English treatise to attempt a generalized treatment of Torts, Frederick Pollock's *The Law of Torts,* did not appear until 1887. It was dedicated to Holmes.
68. See [Holmes], *supra,* note 63, at 660.
69. The phrase is Holmes's, *The Common Law* 1 (1881).
70. Ibid. at 89. Holmes acknowledged that fault might not have been a prerequisite "in that period of dry precedent which is so often to be found midway between a creative epoch and a period of solvent philosophical reaction."
71. Wigmore, "Responsibility For Tortious Acts: Its History," 7 Harv. L. Rev. 315, 316 (1894).
72. Deiser, "The Development of Principle in Trespass," 27 Yale L. J. 220, 236 (1917).
73. Isaacs, "Fault and Liability," 31 Harv. L. Rev. 954, 966 (1918).
74. Milsom, *Historical Foundations of the Common Law* 264–65 (1969).
75. 60 Mass. (6 Cush.) 295–96 (1850) [emphasis in original].
76. Milsom, *supra,* note 74, at 336–37.
77. Deiser, *supra,* note 72, at 225, 235. See also Milsom, *supra,* note 74 at 254–56, 269–70, 346–51.
78. See *Percival v. Hickey,* 18 Johns. 257 (N.Y., 1820); *Foot v. Wiswall,* 14 Johns. 304 (N.Y. 1817). See also M. Horwitz, *supra,* note 5, at 85–97.
79. E.g., *Patten v. Halsted,* 1 N.J.L. 277 (1795).
80. E.g., *Lobdell v. New Bedford,* 1 Mass. 153 (1804).

81. See, e.g., 3 N. Dane, *supra,* note 11, at 31–33.
82. See, e.g., *Patten v. Halsted, supra,* note 79. See also M. Horwitz, *supra,* note 5, at 86.
83. 60 Mass. (6 Cush.) 292 (1850).
84. See, e.g., M. Franklin, *Injuries and Remedies: Cases and Materials on Tort Law and Alternatives* 30 (1971); W. Prosser, J. Wade & V. Schwartz, *Cases and Materials on Torts* 9 (6th ed., 1976).
85. *Livingston v. Adams,* 8 Cow. 175 (N.Y., 1828); *Panton v. Holland,* 17 Johns. 92 (N.Y., 1819); *Lehigh Bridge Co. v. Lehigh Coal & Navigation Co.,* 4 Rawle 8 (Pa., 1833). *Livingston v. Adams* and *Lehigh Bridge* were "bursting dam" cases, and *Panton v. Holland* was a case in which a foundation for a house had been dug improperly.
86. *Norway Plains Co. v. Boston & Me. R.R.,* 67 Mass. (1 Gray) 263, 267 (1854). See G. White, *The American Judicial Tradition* 60–61 (1976).
87. See M. Horwitz, *supra,* note 5, at 90 (maintaining that "an exaggerated significance" has been assigned to *Brown v. Kendall*).
88. See 60 Mass. (6 Cush.) 296.
89. M. Horwitz, *supra,* note 5, at 95, uses similar terminology. Professor Horwitz sees mid-nineteenth-century judges as "develop[ing] the idea of duties owed to noncontracting strangers."
90. See [Holmes], *supra,* note 63, at 663.
91. 53 N.H. 442 (1873).
92. 51 N.Y. 476 (1873).
93. L.R., 3 E. & I. App. (H.L.) 330 (1868).
94. 53 N.H. 450–51.
95. Ibid. at 445.
96. Ibid. at 450.
97. Ibid. at 451.
98. Ibid. at 442.
99. *Livingston v. Adams,* 8 Cow. 175 (N.Y., 1828).
100. 51 N.Y. 487 (1873).
101. Ibid. at 484–85.
102. Ibid at 486–87.
103. Ibid. at 491.
104. O. Holmes, *supra,* note 69, at 94–95 (quoting Chief Justice Nelson of New York). Holmes cited *Brown v. Kendall* with approval at 105–106.
105. See 1 F. Hilliard, *The Law of Torts* 115–23 (3rd ed., Boston, 1866).
106. T. Cooley, *A Treatise on the Law of Torts* (1880).
107. Ibid. at 628–58.
108. Ibid. at 659.
109. Ibid.
110. Ibid. at 661–66 (citing cases).
111. 2 J. Ames and J. Smith, *A Selection of Cases on the Law of Torts* (J. Smith, ed., 1893).
112. Ibid. at iii (J. Smith, ed., 1909).
113. 1 J. Wigmore, *Select Cases on the Law of Torts,* Appendix B, at vii, x (1911).

114. Ibid. at xi.
115. Ibid. at x.
116. Ibid. at x, xi.
117. Ibid. at xi.
118. Ibid. at xi–1.
119. Ibid. at vii (emphasis in original).
120. The phrase is Holmes's in "The Theory of Torts," *supra,* note 63, at 662.
121. Ibid. at 660.

Chapter 2

1. D. Meyer, *The Instructed Conscience* 4–10 (1972); L. Veysey, *The Emergence of the American University* 21–56 (1965); Hofstadter, "The Revolution in Higher Education," in A. Schlesinger, Jr. and M. White, eds., *Paths of American Thought* 269, 270–72 (1963).
2. See generally R. Welter, *The Mind of America 1820–1860* (1975); M. Meyers, *The Jacksonian Persuasion* (1957); A. Schlesinger, *The Age of Jackson* (1945).
3. See generally R. Wilson, *In Quest of Community* (1968); A. Kaul, *The American Vision* (1963).
4. See generally E. Pessen, *Jacksonian America* (1969); C. Williamson, *American Suffrage From Property to Democracy* (1960).
5. See generally G. Taylor, *The Transportation Revolution, 1815–1860* (1951). See also T. Haskell, *The Emergence of Professional Social Science* 30–39 (1977). Many of the observations Haskell makes about the emergence of social science disciplines after 1870 parallel my findings about legal education.
6. Henry Adams' account is notable. He said that Harvard, which he attended from 1852 to 1858, "taught little, and that little ill. . . . The entire work of the four years could have been easily put into the work of any four months in after life." *The Education of Henry Adams* 55, 60 (1918 ed.).
7. Ralph Waldo Emerson and Henry David Thoreau were examples. See Wilson, *supra,* note 3 at 9–18.
8. The phrase is Stanley Elkins' in *Slavery: A Problem in American Institutional and Intellectual Life* 175 (1976 ed.). For some examples, see A. Tyler, *Freedom's Ferment: Phases of American Social History from the Colonial Period to the Outbreak of the Civil War* (1944).
9. See R. Chase, *The American Novel and Its Tradition* vii–28 (1957).
10. Thomas Jefferson's conception of the University of Virginia, which opened in 1823, was, of course, a major innovation for its time, but "liberal" and classical in its orientation. See 3 P. Bruce, *History of the University of Virginia* 52–59 (1921). See also R. Storr, *The Beginnings of Graduate Education in America* (1953), for a discussion of developments in higher education in the early nineteenth century.
11. There is some debate about whether the term "revolution" appropriately characterizes developments in higher education after the Civil War. Com-

pare Veysey, *supra*, note 1, at 1–10, with Hofstadter, *supra* note 1, at 269–74, 279–83. My view is that if the term "revolution" has any meaning in intellectual history, it is appropriately used to characterize the educational changes described in this section, for they constituted a fundamental revision in the means of acquiring knowledge in American colleges, universities, and professional schools. Contemporaries used the term "revolution." See, *e.g.,* Veysey, *supra*, note 1, at 1 (quoting Noah Porter, president of Yale from 1871 to 1886).

12. See Veysey, *supra*, note 1, at 121–79.
13. See T. Smith, *Revivalism and Social Reform in Mid-Nineteenth-Century America* (1957).
14. See R. Wilson, *supra*, note 3, at 3–31.
15. D. Meyer, *supra*, note 1, at 137.
16. Ibid. at 138–39.
17. See G. Fredrickson, *The Inner Civil War: Northern Intellectuals and the Crisis of the Union* 199–216 (1965).
18. Ibid. at 79–97.
19. S. Elkins, *supra*, note 8; G. Fredrickson, *supra*, note 17.
20. See Edmund Wilson's reflections on Holmes's Civil War experiences in *Patriotic Gore* 743–96 (1962).
21. On professionalism, see generally B. Bledstein, *The Culture of Professionalism* (1976); R. Wiebe, *The Search for Order 1877–1920* (1967); D. Calhoun, *Professional Lives in America* (1965).
22. Enthusiasm for "science" and "scientific" training was, of course, not unique to the post-Civil War years. Not only had scientific subjects, such as astronomy and physics, been included in antebellum higher education curricula, but influential lawyers such as Joseph Story had aspired to make the subject of law "scientific." There were, however, important differences between the conception of science that emerged throughout higher education after 1870 and earlier conceptions. Antebellum "science" was a version of moral philosophy which assumed a coherent, God-centered universe and derived linear theories of causation consistent with that assumption. Post-Civil War science sought secular explanations for events, stressed complexities in theories of causation, and equated "scientific" training with a specialized process of professional acculturation. See P. Miller, *The Life of the Mind in America* 156–61 (1966); R. Hofstadter and C. Hardy, *The Development and Scope of Higher Education in the United States* (1952).
23. The generalizations advanced here are supported in Haines, "Scientific History as a Teaching Method: The Formative Years," 63 J. Am. Hist. 892 (1977); J. Higham et al., *History* 92–103 (1965); Hofstadter, *supra*, note 1; L. Veysey, supra, note 1.
24. For observations on the scientific method of studying history, see J. Higham, *supra*, note 23, at 92–103.
25. See the discussion of Darwin in T. Haskell, *supra*, note 5, at 243–44.
26. L. Veysey, *supra*, note 1, at 311–24.
27. J. Higham, *supra*, note 23, at 95.

28. Ibid. at 97.
29. Ibid. at 99.
30. Dabney, "Is History a Science?," 10 *The University Magazine* 3 (1894).
31. See J. Auerbach, *Unequal Justice: Lawyers and Social Change in Modern America* 77–89 (1976); R. Wiebe, *supra,* note 21, at 118–22. See also B. Kuklick, *The Rise of American Philosophy* (1977), for an account of the "professionalization" of the discipline of philosophy. W. Johnson, *Schooled Lawyers* (1978), a study of legal education in Wisconsin, supports many of my observations in this section; see especially pp. xii–xiv, 83–119.
32. See generally D. Calhoun, *supra,* note 2.
33. Address to Harvard Law School Association, November 5, 1886, quoted in 2 C. Warren, *History of the Harvard Law School* 374 (2 vols., 1908).
34. C. Langdell, *A Selection of Cases on the Law of Contracts* v–vii (1871).
35. For accounts of the emergence of science throughout higher education, see Veysey, *supra,* note 1, at 121–79; J. Higham, *supra,* note 23, at 92–103.
36. C. Langdell, *supra,* note 34, at vi.
37. S. Williston, *Life and Law* 205 (1940).
38. Ibid. at 204.
39. C. Langdell, *supra,* note 34, at vi.
40. Ibid.
41. Ibid.
42. Ibid. at vii.
43. *Centennial History of the Harvard Law School 1817–1917* 80 (1918).
44. On Story, see *Centennial History, supra,* note 43, at 258–63; G. Dunne, *Justice Joseph Story and the Rise of the Supreme Court* (1970). On Dwight, see J. Goebel, *A History of the School of Law, Columbia University* 33–132 (1955).
45. S. Williston, *supra,* note 37, at 200.
46. See Holmes, "Law in Science and Science in Law," 12 Harv. L. Rev. 443 (1899).
47. [Holmes], Book Review, 5 Am. L. Rev. 539 (1871).
48. 1 M. Howe, ed., *Holmes-Pollock Letters* 17 (1941).
49. [Holmes], Book Review, 14 Am. L. Rev. 233, 234 (1880) [emphasis in original].
50. Gray to Charles W. Eliot, January 8, 1883, quoted in M. Howe, *Justice Oliver Wendell Holmes: The Proving Years* 158 (1963).
51. Ibid.
52. W. Keener, *A Selection of Cases on the Law of Quasi-Contracts* iv (1888).
53. Keener, "The Inductive Method in Legal Education," 17 *Report of the American Bar Association* 473, 488–89 (1894).
54. Ibid. at 489.
55. Ibid.
56. Keener, *supra,* note 52, at iv.
57. Ames, "Discussion of Kale's Paper" (extemporaneous remarks), 30 *Report of the American Bar Association* 1025 (1907).
58. See C. Eliot, *A Late Harvest* 53 (1924).

59. Address, quoted in 2 Warren, *supra,* note 33, at 374.

60. Address, quoted in *Centennial History, supra,* note 43, at 26.

61. C. Langdell, *supra,* note 34, at vi.

62. For an explanation of the conceptualist classification of legal subjects emerging in the 1870s, see Chapter One.

63. *Centennial History of the Harvard Law School, supra,* note 43, at 46.

64. Ibid. at 84.

65. On Eliot, see H. James, *Charles W. Eliot* (1930); H. Hawkins, *Between Harvard and America* (1973).

66. Quoted in *Centennial History, supra,* note 43, at 31.

67. See Stevens, "Two Cheers for 1870: The American Law School," in D. Fleming and B. Bailyn, eds., *Law in American History* 405, 417–19 (1971).

68. See generally P. Wiener, *Evolution and the Founders of Pragmatism* (1949).

69. Keener, *supra,* note 53, at 479.

70. See, e.g., Green, "Proximate and Remote Cause," 4 Am. L. Rev. 201 (1870), reprinted in N. Green, *Essays and Notes on the Law of Tort and Crime* 1 (1933).

71. Holmes, quoted in Keener, *supra,* note 53, at 480.

72. Keener, *supra,* note 53, at 483.

73. Representative selections can be found in *Centennial History, supra,* note 43, at 290–343.

74. Quoted in Keener, *supra,* note 53 at 480.

75. See G. Gilmore, *The Ages of American Law* 52 (1977).

76. Cf. Woodard, "History, Legal History and Legal Education," 53 Va. L. Rev. 89, 102–105 (1967).

77. Keener, *supra,* note 53, at 475.

78. Ibid. at 476.

79. Ibid.

80. Ibid.

81. Ibid. at 477.

82. Ibid.

83. Ibid. at 479–80.

84. Ibid. at 480.

85. Ibid. at 481–82.

86. Ibid. at 482.

87. Ibid.

88. Ibid. at 483.

89. Ibid. at 484.

90. Ibid. at 487.

91. Ibid. at 481 (emphasis in original).

92. Ibid. at 485.

93. Ibid. at 482.

94. J. Wigmore, *A Treatise on the System of Evidence in Trials at Common Law, Including the Statutes and Judicial Decisions of all Jurisdictions of the United States* (1904).

95. S. Williston, *The Law of Contracts* (1920).
96. J. Beale, *A Treatise on the Conflict of Laws* (1916).
97. See, e.g., Llewellyn, "A Realistic Jurisprudence—The Next Step," 30 Colum. L. Rev. 431, 447–48 (1930). See text at notes 278–79, *infra.*
98. E.g., *Centennial History, supra,* note 43; A. Sutherland, *The Law at Harvard, a History of Ideas and Men 1817–1967* 162–225 (1967); 2 C. Warren, *supra,* note 33, at 354–460; S. Williston, *supra,* note 37.
99. S. Williston, *supra,* note 37, at 74.
100. *Centennial History, supra,* note 43, at 178.
101. Ibid. at 233.
102. S. Williston, *supra,* note 37, at 74.
103. For samples, see volumes 1–4 of the Harvard Law Review (1887–1891).
104. *Lumley v. Gye,* 2 El. & Bl. 216, 95 Rev. Rep. 501 (1853).
105. Schofield, "The Principle of Lumley v. Gye, and Its Application," 2 Harv. L. Rev. 19 (1888).
106. Ibid. at 20.
107. *Bowen v. Hall,* 6 Q.B.D. 333 (1881).
108. As quoted in Schofield, *supra,* note 105, at 20.
109. Ibid. at 21.
110. Ibid. at 21–22.
111. Ibid. at 22.
112. Ibid. at 23.
113. Ibid. at 24.
114. Ibid.
115. Ibid. at 26.
116. See Schofield, *supra,* note 105.
117. Ibid. at 22–23.
118. Ibid. at 27.
119. Smith, "Tort and Absolute Liability—Suggested Changes in Classification," 30 Harv. L. Rev. 241, 320 (1917).
120. J. Wigmore, *Select Cases on the Law of Torts* (1911).
121. See N. Dane, *A General Abridgment and Digest of American Law* (1823–1829).
122. See 3 N. Dane, *supra,* note 133, at 31–33.
123. The notion of a universal duty in Torts first appeared in Holmes, "The Theory of Torts," 7 Am. L. Rev. 652, 662 (1873).
124. *Lamson v. American Axe & Tool Co.,* 177 Mass. 144 (1900).
125. Ibid. at 145.
126. Ibid.
127. Ibid.
128. Ibid.
129. F. Hilliard, 2 *The Law of Torts or Private Wrongs,* 467 (3d ed., 1866).
130. T. Shearman and A. Redfield, *A Treatise on the Law of Negligence* 121 (2d ed., 1870).
131. S. Thompson, 2 *The Law of Negligence in Relations Not Resting in Contract* 1147 (1880).
132. Ibid. at 1148.

133. F. Wharton, *A Treatise on the Law of Negligence* 180 (2d ed., 1878).
134. Ibid. at 181.
135. Ibid.
136. Ibid.
137. Ibid.
138. Ibid.
139. Ibid. at 182.
140. Some commentators retained the notion that assumption of risk was a "doctrine of waiver." See, e.g., J. Bishop, *Commentaries on the Non-Contract Law* 311–12 (1889).
141. Warren, *"Volenti Non Fit Injuria* in Acts of Negligence," 8 Harv. L. Rev. 457 (1895).
142. Ibid. at 457.
143. Ibid. at 458.
144. Ibid.
145. Ibid. at 459.
146. Ibid.
147. Warren argued, "The doctrine as established is composed of two parts; first, that plaintiff shall have full knowledge of the nature and extent of the risk; second, that he shall freely and voluntarily incur it" (Ibid. at 464).
148. Ibid. at 466–67.
149. Ibid. at 470.
150. Ibid. at 471.
151. Bohlen, "Voluntary Assumption of Risk," (pts. 1–2), 20 Harv. L. Rev. 14, 91 (1906).
152. Ibid. at 14.
153. Ibid. at 115.
154. Ibid.
155. Ibid.
156. Ibid. at 14.
157. Ibid.
158. Ibid.
159. Melville Bigelow's attitude was representative: "[T]he principles relating to the subject of assum[ption] of risk . . . are now recognized by most if not all of our courts, though in the application of them more or less conflicting dicta may be found, and some conflicting conclusions" (*Elements of the Law of Torts* 367 n. 1 (1896).
160. Act of June 11, 1906, Pub. L. No. 219, ch. 3073, 34 Stat. 232 (1906).
161. Bohlen, *supra,* note 151, at 94 n. 3.
162. M. Franklin, *Injuries and Remedies—Cases and Materials on Tort Law and Alternatives* 202 (1971).
163. *Davies v. Mann,* 10 M. & W. 545, 152 Eng. Rep. 588 (1842).
164. Ibid. at 589.
165. Ibid.
166. S. Thompson, *supra,* note 131, at 1157.
167. F. Wharton, *supra,* note 133, at 291–92.

168. J. Bishop, *supra,* note 140, at 205–208 and nn.
169. G. Chase, *Leading Cases Upon The Law of Torts* 225 (1892).
170. M. Bigelow, *Elements on the Law of Torts* 369 (1896).
171. C. Beach, *A Treatise on the Law of Contributory Negligence* 11 (1885).
172. Ibid. at 10.
173. Ibid. at 11.
174. Ibid. at 461–62.
175. Ibid. at 11.
176. [Wills], "Book Review," 2 L. Q. Rev. 506 (1886). The review was unsigned. Frederick Pollock later identified Wills as the author. See F. Pollock, *The Law of Torts* 473 (12th ed., 1923).
177. [Wills], *supra,* note 176, at 508.
178. Ibid. at 506.
179. Ibid. at 507.
180. Ibid. at 507 (emphasis in original).
181. [Wills], "Book Review," 5 L. Q. Rev. 85, 87 (1889) (emphasis in original).
182. T. Shearman and A. Redfield, *A Treatise on the Law of Negligence* 165 (4th ed., 1888).
183. *Pickett v. Wilmington & W.R.R.,* 117 N.C. 616 (1895).
184. Ibid. at 635.
185. Ibid. at 632.
186. Ibid.
187. T. Shearman and A. Redfield, 1 *A Treatise on the Law of Negligence* 154–55 (5th ed., 1898).
188. 1 S. Thompson, *Commentaries on the Law of Negligence* 229 (1901).
189. Ibid. at 229, 230.
190. Schofield, "Davies v. Mann: Theory of Contributory Negligence," 3 Harv. L. Rev. 263, 271 (1889).
191. Ibid. at 268.
192. Ibid. at 271.
193. Ibid. at 273. At this point Schofield cited Wills's "last . . . clear opportunity" formulation in his review of Beach, *supra,* note 192. Schofield felt that the review was "presumably from the pen of Sir Frederick Pollock" (Ibid. at 273, n. 5).
194. Ibid. at 274, n. 5.
195. Ibid. at 276.
196. Goodrich, "Iowa Applications of the Last Clear Chance Doctrine," 5 Iowa L. Bull. 36, 38 (1919).
197. F. Bohlen, "Contributory Negligence," 21 Harv. L. Rev. 233, 238 (1908).
198. Ibid. at 259.
199. Goodrich, *supra,* note 196, at 38.
200. Note, 26 Harv. L. Rev. 369, 370 (1913).
201. Goodrich, *supra,* note 196, at 38.
202. See, e.g., Schofield, *supra,* note 190, at 274–76; Goodrich, *supra,* note 196.
203. O. Holmes, *The Common Law* 96 (1881).

204. For example, see Holmes's analysis of the "act at peril" doctrine in *The Common Law, supra,* note 203, at 82–107.

205. *Philadelphia & Reading R.R. v. Derby,* 55 U.S. (14 How.) 468, 485–86 (1852). The absolute liability standard did not, of course, guarantee recovery against the employer by an injured third party. Numerous defenses were available, such as the "fellow-servant rule," discussed in text accompanying notes 218–36, *infra.*

206. Dillon, "American Law Concerning Employer's Liability," 24 Am. L. Rev. 175, 176 (1890).

207. Farwell v. Boston & Worcester R.R., 45 Mass. 49 (1842).

208. 41 U.S. (16 Pet.) 1 (1842).

209. 112 U.S. 377 (1884).

210. 149 U.S. 368 (1893).

211. 112 U.S. at 394.

212. F. Wharton, *supra,* note 133, at 211.

213. 2 S. Thompson, *supra,* note 131, at 1026, 1028.

214. C. Beach, *supra,* note 171, at 420–26.

215. 2 S. Thompson, *supra,* note 131, at 1026.

216. Dillon, *supra,* note 206, at 190.

217. C. Beach, *supra,* note 171, at 423.

218. 149 U.S. at 379.

219. Ibid. at 383.

220. Ibid. at 385.

221. Ibid. at 410.

222. Ibid. at 411.

223. Ibid.

224. T. Shearman and A. Redfield, *supra,* note 182, at 392.

225. T. Shearman and A. Redfield, *supra,* note 187, at 419.

226. T. Cooley, *A Treatise on the Law of Torts* 545, 546–47 (Students' Edition: J. Lewis, ed., 1907).

227. Ibid. at 550.

228. Dillon, *supra,* note 206, at 175.

229. A sophisticated law student's guidebook making this assumption and describing techniques of case analysis based on it was E. Wambaugh, *The Study of Cases* (1894).

230. The literature persists in associating scientific methodologies principally with Langdell. See G. Gilmore, *supra,* note 75, at 47–48, 79.

231. See, e.g., Beale, "The Proximate Consequences of an Act," 33 Harv. L. Rev. 633 (1920); Bohlen, "Voluntary Assumption of Risk," *supra,* note 151; Schofield, "Davies v. Mann: Theory of Contributory Negligence," *supra,* note 190; Smith, "Legal Cause in Actions of Tort," 25 Harv. L. Rev. 103, 223, 303 (1911–1912); Wigmore, "Responsibility for Tortious Acts: Its History," 7 Harv. L. Rev. 315, 383, 441 (1894).

232. J. Smith, *supra,* note 231, at 315.

233. H. Terry, "Negligence," 29 Harv. L. Rev. 40, 52 (1915).

234. See generally White, "The Intellectual Origins of Torts in America," 86 Yale L. J. 671, 688–90 (1977).

235. Terry, *supra,* note 233, at 49.
236. Ibid. at 50.
237. Holmes, *supra,* note 203, at 127, 128.
238. Ibid. at 129.
239. See *B. & O. R.R. v. Goodman,* 275 U.S. 66 (1927).
240. *Pokora v. Wabash Ry. Co.,* 292 U.S. 98 (1934).
241. Smith, *supra,* note 231, at 309–10.
242. These questions are central to two works written by Leon Green in the 1920s: *Rationale of Proximate Cause* (1927) and *Judge and Jury* (1930).
243. Llewellyn, *supra,* note 97, at 447–53.
244. See G. Gilmore, *supra,* note 75, at 87.
245. F. Burdick, *The Law of Torts* 536 (1926).

Chapter 3

1. For this reason I have excluded from my sample of reformist thinkers some persons traditionally identified as committed to intraprofessional methodological innovations, such as "behaviorists" in political science, sociology, or psychology. Here I have followed the distinctions implied by Dorothy Ross in "The Development of the Social Sciences in America, 1865–1920" in A. Oleson and J. Voss, ed., *The Organization of Knowledge in Modern America, 1860–1920* (1979). My analysis is also indebted to a body of monographic literature; succeeding footnotes identify the principal sources.
2. See T. Haskell, *The Emergence of Professional Social Science,* 12–47 (1977). While I agree with Professor Haskell that the idea of interdependence came increasingly to be a "guiding assumption" of early twentieth-century reformist thought, I cannot endorse his claim that "interdependence was an objective condition of nineteenth-century society before social thinkers found it and articulated it as such" (p. 16). I use interdependence as a collective perception about social "realities," not as an objective condition of social life. I have profited considerably from exposure to Professor Haskell's views.
3. On the political climate of early twentieth-century America, see A. Link, *Woodrow Wilson and the Progressive Era* (1954). The philosophical dimensions of early twentieth-century reformist thought are treated, from differing vantage points, in D. Noble, *The Progressive Mind, 1890–1917* (1970); M. White, *Social Thought in America: The Revolt Against Formalism* (1949); and E. Purcell, *The Crisis of Democratic Theory* (1973).
4. See generally J. Robinson, *The New History* (1912).
5. See generally A. Bentley, *The Process of Government* (1908).
6. Purcell, *supra,* note 3, at 15–18.
7. E.g., John Dewey; see White, *supra,* note 3, at 146.
8. Pound, "The Need of a Sociological Jurisprudence," 19 Green Bag 607 (1907); Pound, "The Scope and Purpose of Sociological Jurisprudence," 24 Harv. L. Rev. 48 (1911), 25 Harv. L. Rev. 489 (1912).
9. Pound, "Law in Books and Law in Action," 44 Am. L. Rev. 1236 (1910); see also Pound, "Liberty of Contract," 18 Yale L. J., 454 (1909).

10. On the emergence of objectivism and empiricism in early twentieth-century historical scholarship, see J. Higham et al., *History* 104–16 (1965); on analogous developments in the social sciences, see Purcell, *supra,* note 3, at 15–30. D. Hollinger, *Morris R. Cohen and the Scientific Ideal,* 45–61 (1975), summarizes comparable trends in early twentieth-century philosophy.

11. See White, *supra,* note 3; Purcell, *supra,* note 3; Higham, *supra,* note 10; and Hollinger, *supra,* note 10. Each of these authors notes the close connection between early twentieth-century reformist thought and moral relativism. Purcell makes the connection one of his principal themes; see Purcell at 5–11.

12. Standard accounts of the hostility toward universal principles exhibited by early twentieth-century reformist thought can be found in White, *supra,* note 3, at 11–106, and Purcell, *supra,* note 3, at 47–73.

13. Detailed accounts of the attitudes of individual Realists can be found in W. Rumble, *American Legal Realism* (1968) and W. Twining, *Karl Llewellyn and the Realist Movement* (1973). Purcell, *supra,* note 3, at 74–93, and White, "From Realism to Reasoned Elaboration," 59 Va. L. Rev. 279 (1973), discuss the philosophical assumptions of Realist scholars.

14. See, e.g., Pound, "Mechanical Jurisprudence," *supra,* note 10; Pound, "Liberty of Contract," *supra,* note 9; Corbin, "The Law and the Judges," 3 Yale Review 234 (1914). See generally White, "From Sociological Jurisprudence to Realism," 58 Va. L. Rev. 999 (1972).

15. In addition to the sources cited *supra,* note 3, see also S. Fine, *Laissez Faire and the General Welfare State* (1956) and C. Forcey, *The Crossroads of Liberalism* (1967).

16. Pound, "The Need of a Sociological Jurisprudence," *supra,* note 8, at 611.

17. Ibid. at 510.

18. Pound, "The Theory of Judicial Decision," 36 Harv. L. Rev. 641, 802, 940, 955 (1923).

19. Ibid. at 645.

20. This is not to say, of course, that sociological jurisprudence and the later stage of Realism are not distinguishable. I have, in fact, tried to distinguish them in "From Sociological Jurisprudence to Realism," *supra,* note 14. My focus there is on the different views of the sociological jurisprudes and the Realists toward the permanency of moral values.

21. The first use of the term "Realism" as a collective jurisprudential perspective was in Karl Llewellyn's "Some Realism About Realism," 44 Harv. L. Rev. 1222 (1931). See also Llewellyn, "A Realistic Jurisprudence—The Next Step," 30 Colum. L. Rev. 431 (1930) and J. Frank, *Law and the Modern Mind* (1930).

22. *Supra,* note 10.

23. *Supra,* note 21.

24. Pound, *supra,* note 10, at 611.

25. Ibid. at 612.

26. Ibid. at 616.

27. Ibid. at 622.

28. Llewellyn, "A Realistic Jurisprudence," *supra,* note 21, at 450.
29. Ibid. at 464.
30. Green, "The Duty Problem in Negligence Cases: Part I," 28 Colum. L. Rev. 1014, 1016 (1929).
31. On Shaw, see L. Levy, *The Law of the Commonwealth and Chief Justice Shaw* (1957); on Story, see G. Dunne, *Joseph Story and the Rise of the Supreme Court* (1970). See also G. White, *The American Judicial Tradition* 35–63 (1976).
32. E.g. Hessel Yntema, Felix Cohen, and, in their early scholarship, Karl Llewellyn and Jerome Frank. See Purcell, *supra,* note 3, at 89–91.
33. Pound's disassociation began with "The Call for a Realist Jurisprudence," 44 Harv. L. Rev. 697 (1931). This article and the article cited *infra,* note 34, provide evidence *both* for an "incorporationist" theory of the relationship between sociological jurisprudence and Realism and for a theory which distinguishes the two "movements." On balance, Pound and the Realists had a great deal in common, but they chose to focus primarily on their differences.
34. Pound, "Fifty Years of Jurisprudence," 51 Harv. L. Rev. 444, 777, 791 (1938).
35. See Purcell, *supra,* note 3, at 90–94; White, *supra,* note 14, at 280–83.
36. Notably, Jerome Frank and Karl Llewellyn; see Purcell, *supra,* note 3, at 172–74 and White, *supra,* note 14, at 283.
37. References to Green's early years in teaching and law practice are made in Green, "Fifty Years of Tort Law Teaching," 61 NW. U. L. Rev. 499 (1964), and McCormick, "Leon Green and Legal Education," 43 Ill. L. Rev. 5, 6–7 (1948). The most complete account of Green's early career is Robertson, "The Legal Philosophy of Leon Green," 56 Tex. L. Rev. 393, 394–403 (1978).
38. See Green, "Scientific Methods in Law," Bulletin No. 1, Northwestern University School of Law (1929); Green, *supra,* note 30, at 1015–1016 (1929); Green, *The Judicial Process in Tort Cases,* iii–iv (1931); Green, "Unpacking the Court," 90 New Republic 67 (1937).
39. L. Green, *Rationale of Proximate Cause* (1927).
40. Green, "The Duty Problem in Negligence Cases," *supra,* note 30; Green, "The Duty Problem in Negligence Cases: Part II," 29 Colum. L. Rev. 255 (1929).
41. Green, "Relational Interests," 29 Ill. L. Rev. 460, 1041 (1935); "Relational Interests," 30 Ill. L. Rev. 1, 314 (1936).
42. L. Green, *Judge and Jury* (1930).
43. L. Green, *The Judicial Process in Torts Cases, supra,* note 38.
44. Gregory, "Leon Green's Contributions to a Better Understanding of the Law of Torts," 43 Ill. L. Rev. 15 (1948).
45. Ibid. at 19.
46. Ibid. at 5.
47. Green, "The Duty Problem in Negligence Cases," *supra,* note 40.
48. See Green, *supra,* note 42, at 375–417.

49. O. Holmes, *The Common Law* 150–63 (1881).

50. See Green, *supra,* note 42, at 385–91.

51. See Green, "Scientific Methods in Law," *supra,* note 38, at 14–15.

52. Gregory, *supra,* note 44, at 18.

53. E.g. Beale, "The Proximate Consequences of an Act," 33 Harv. L. Rev. 633 (1920).

54. See F. Bohlen, *Studies in the Law of Torts* v–vi (1926); Bohlen, "Old Phrases and New Facts," 83 U. Pa. L. Rev. 305, 308–13 (1935). See also Eldredge, "Francis Herman Bohlen," 91 U. Pa. L. Rev. 387, 388–390 (1943).

55. For a sampling of various efforts to list Realists, see Twining, *supra,* note 13, at 73–83, 408–10.

56. Eldredge, *supra,* note 54, at 391.

57. William Draper Lewis, "Francis Hermann Bohlen," 91 U. Pa. L. Rev. 377, 381 (1943).

58. Ibid. at 380, 381, 382, 384.

59. Eldredge, *supra,* note 54, at 387.

60. Lewis, *supra,* note 57, at 377.

61. Ibid. at 381.

62. Eldredge, *supra,* note 54, at 387, 388.

63. See J. Auerbach, *Unequal Justice* 102–29 (1976).

64. H. Goodrich, *The Story of the American Law Institute* 5–11 (1961).

65. Arnold, "Leon Green—An Appreciation," 43 Ill. L. Rev. 1, 3 (1943).

66. Ibid.

67. Ibid.

68. Bohlen, "Old Phrases and New Facts," *supra,* note 54, at 305.

69. Ibid. at 308.

70. Bohlen, *supra,* note 54, at v.

71. Bohlen, Book Review, 80 U. Pa. L. Rev. 781, 782 (1932).

72. Green, *supra,* note 39, at 65–66, 71; Green, *supra,* note 42, at 292–99.

73. Bohlen, *supra,* note 71, at 783, 782.

74. See Bohlen, "Misrepresentation as Deceit, Negligence or Warranty," 42 Harv. L. Rev. 733 (1929); Green, "Deceit," 16 Va. L. Rev. 749 (1930); Bohlen, "Should Negligent Misrepresentations Be Treated as Negligence or Fraud?" 18 Va. L. Rev. 703 (1932).

75. Polikoff, Book Review, 80 U. Pa. L. Rev. 929 (1932).

76. Green, "The Torts Restatement," 29 Ill. L. Rev. 585 (1935).

77. Ibid. at 585, 592–93, 596.

78. Ibid. at 602.

79. Ibid. at 597.

80. See generally, Green, *supra,* note 39; Green, *supra,* note 30; Green, *supra,* note 40; Green, *supra,* note 42.

81. Bohlen, "The Moral Duty to Aid Others as a Basis of Tort Liability," 56 U. Pa. L. Rev. 217, 316, 336 (1908).

82. Green, "Fifty Years of Tort Law," *supra,* note 37, at 501.

83. E.g. Polikoff, Book Review, *supra,* note 75; Goodhart, 32 Colum. L. Rev. 762 (1932); Gifford, 41 Yale L.J. 1264 (1932).
84. F. Bohlen, *Cases on the Law of Torts* v, vi (1925).
85. See F. Bohlen and F. Harper, *A Short Selection of Cases on the Law of Torts* (1933); F. Bohlen, *Cases on the Law of Torts* (F. Harper, ed., 1941).
86. F. Bohlen and F. Harper, *supra,* note 85, at v.
87. L. Green, *The Judicial Process in Torts Cases, supra,* note 38, at iv, iii, vii.
88. See E. Patterson, *Jurisprudence* 554 (1953); Rumble, *supra,* note 13, at 21–26.
89. See, e.g., F. Bohlen, *Cases on the Law of Torts* iii, 216, 262 (F. Harper, ed., 1941).
90. Vold, Book Review, 25 Corn. L.Q. 151, 154 (1939).
91. E. Thurston and W. Seavey, *Cases on Torts* vii–viii (1942).
92. Vold, Book Review, 10 U. Ch. L. Rev. 359, 361 (1943).
93. H. Shulman and F. James, *Cases and Materials on the Law of Torts,* vii, viii (1942).
94. Ibid. at viii, ix.
95. Halpern, Book Review, 43 Colum. L. Rev. 552, 553 (1943).
96. James, Book Review, 28 Geo. L.J. 1146, 1148 (1940).
97. Shulman, Book Review, 48 Harv. 1445 (1932).
98. Ibid. at 1448.
99. Harper, Book Review, 25 Iowa L. Rev. 182, 183 (1939).
100. 2 J. Ames and J. Smith, *A Selection of Cases on the Law of Torts* 1–96 (2 vols. 1893).
101. Smith, "Legal Cause in Actions of Tort," 25 Harv. L. Rev. 103, 223, 303 (1911–12).
102. Ibid. at 308, 309.
103. Ibid. at 315.
104. Beale, *supra,* note 53, at 636.
105. Ibid. at 658.
106. Green, *supra,* note 39, at 128.
107. Bingham, "Legal Cause," 9 Colum. L. Rev. 16, 136 (1909).
108. Edgerton, 72 U. Pa. L. Rev. 211, 343, 348 (1924).
109. Green, *supra,* note 39, at vi, v.
110. Ibid. at 128.
111. Ibid. at vi.
112. Bauer, Book Review, 77 U. Pa. L. Rev. 147, 148 (1928).
113. Edgerton, Book Review, 29 Colum. L. Rev. 229, 230 (1929).
114. Ibid. at 229.
115. 248 N.Y. 339 (1928).
116. E.g., Cowan, "The Riddle of the Palsgraf Case," 23 Minn. L. Rev. 46 (1938).
117. A collection of scholarly commentary on *Palsgraf* can be found in J. Noonan, *Persons and Masks of the Law,* 191–92 (1976). Some commentators have also questioned the accuracy of the Court of Appeals' ac-

count of the facts of *Palsgraf.* See, e.g., W. Prosser, *Cases and Materials on Torts,* 364 (3rd ed., 1964); Noonan, at 150. An account of Mrs. Palsgraf's accident in the *New York Times,* August 25, 1924 (p. 1) supports the Court of Appeals' rendition of the facts. The *Times* account referred to a "Mrs. Polsgraf."

118. See Prosser, "Palsgraf Revisited," 52 Mich. L. Rev. 1, 4 (1953); Noonan, *supra,* note 119, at 147–49.

119. 248 N.Y. at 345.

120. Ibid. at 345.

121. Ibid. at 349.

122. Ibid. at 350.

123. Ibid. at 352.

124. Ibid. at 343.

125. Professor Robert Keeton has recently disclosed, through publication of a memorandum supplied to him by Warren Seavey, that both the majority and the dissenting opinions in *Palsgraf* may well have been influenced by remarks made by Green in a meeting of the Advisors to the Restatement of Torts sometime in the late 1920s. Seavey, Bohlen, Green, Cardozo, and Robert Deckert, a Philadelphia practitioner, attended the meeting. Green, at that time, had not become disenchanted with the whole idea of a Torts restatement. See Keeton, *"A Palsgraf Anecdote,"* 56 Tex. L. Rev. 513 (1978).

126. Green, "The Palsgraf Case," 30 Colum. L. Rev. 789, 791 (1930).

127. Ibid. at 800, 801.

128. Bohlen, *Cases on the Law of Torts* 144, 239 (1930). Herbert Goodrich, who was a member of the American Law Institute in the 1920s and 1930s and subsequently its Director, described the relationship between Bohlen and Cardozo as follows:

"The Judge and the law professor saw eye to eye on most of the myriad problems in the field of negligence. They liked each other as persons. Francis Bohlen was the only individual who was ever observed to address the Judge as 'Ben'." Goodrich, "Yielding Place to New," in 1 *Benjamin N. Cardozo Memorial Lectures* 319–20 (1972).

129. E.g. [Ehrenzweig], "Loss-Shifting and Quasi-Negligence: A New Interpretation of the *Palsgraf* Case," 8 U. Chi. L. Rev. 729 (1941).

130. E.g. Cowan, *supra,* note 116.

131. E.g. Prosser, *supra,* note 118.

132. E.g. Noonan, *supra,* note 117, at 111–13, 134–51.

133. F. Harper, *The Law of Torts,* 258 (1933).

134. W. Prosser, *Handbook of the Law of Torts,* 319, 320 (1941).

135. Prosser, "Intentional Infliction of Mental Suffering: A New Tort," 37 Mich. L. Rev. 874 (1939).

136. See, e.g., *Chi. B. and Q.R. Co. v. Gelvin,* 238 F. 14 (8th Cir. 1916); *Alexander v. Pacholek,* 222 Mich. 157 (1923).

137. See Rosenthal, "Liability for Injuries Resulting from Fright or Shock,"

Report of the New York State Law Revision Commission, 18 N.Y. Leg. Doc. 65 (E) (1936).

138. Prosser, *supra,* note 134, at 57.

139. Comstock v. Wilson, 257 N.Y. 231 (1931).

140. Great A & P Tea Co. v. Rocy, 160 Md. 189 (1931).

141. Kentucky Traction Co. v. Roman's Guardian, 232 Ky. 285 (1929).

142. St. L. S.W. Ry. Co. v. Alexander, 106 Tex. 518 (1915).

143. Morse v. Chesapeake & Ohio Ry. Co., 117 Ky. 11 (1903).

144. Hall v. Doremus, 175 Atl. 369 New Jersey (1934).

145. Carroll v. N.Y. Pie Baking Co., 213 N.Y.S. 553 (1926).

146. Rosenthal, *supra,* note 137.

147. Goodrich, "Emotional Damage as Legal Damage," 20 Mich. L. Rev. 497 (1922).

148. Green, "Fright Cases," 27 Ill. L. Rev. 761, 873 (1933).

149. Magruder, "Mental and Emotional Disturbance in the Law of Torts," 49 Harv. L. Rev. 1033 (1936).

150. Harper and McNeely, "A Reexamination of the Basis for Liability for Emotional Disturbance," 1938 Wis. L. Rev. 426 (1938).

151. American Law Institute, *Restatement of the Law of Torts,* Section 436 (1934).

152. Prosser, *supra,* note 134, at 211.

153. Ibid. at 212.

154. See, e.g., Holmes, *supra,* note 49, at 144–63; Smith, "Tort and Absolute Liability," 30 Harv. L. Rev. 241, 319, 409 (1917).

155. F. Burdick, *The Law of Torts,* 536 (1926).

156. Ibid. at 542.

157. Harper, *supra,* note 133, at 334.

158. Prosser, *supra,* note 134, at 430.

159. Smith, *supra,* note 154.

160. Prosser, *supra,* note 134, at 431.

161. Ibid. at 468.

162. Cf. Llewellyn to G.B.J. Hughes, August 10, 1954, quoted in Twining, *supra,* note 13, at 476: "[T]he really important contributions of the Realist movement . . . get down under a sound, horse sense technology. . . . In the main, I find the theoretical writing on the subject to have been rather useless." See also Llewellyn's comment to Grant Gilmore in 1960, reported in G. Gilmore, *The Ages of American Law* 138 (1977): "Where you will all go wrong is on thinking that Realism was a theory. It was not. It was merely a methodology."

Chapter 4

1. On Cooley's Michigan Opinions, see Jones, "Thomas M. Cooley and the Michigan Supreme Court," 10 Am. J. Legal Hist. 97 (1966); G. White, *The American Judicial Tradition* 119–21 (1976).

2. For conventional descriptions of the emergence of a perception that judges "made law," see E. Corwin, *The Twilight of the Supreme Court* 113–22, 181–84 (1934); W. Rumble, *American Legal Realism* 48–83 (1968). A comparable description, which focuses more on developments within the legal profession, is in K. Llewellyn, *The Common Law Tradition* 11–15 (1960).

3. *Osborn v. U.S. Bank,* 9 Wheat. 738, 866 (1824).

4. Brewer, "The Nation's Safeguard," *Proceedings of the N.Y. State Bar Assn.* 46 (1893).

5. The careers of Lemuel Shaw, Charles Doe, and Stephen Field are illustrative. See generally L. Levy, *The Law of the Commonwealth and Chief Justice Shaw* (1957); J. Reid, *Chief Justice: the Judicial World of Charles Doe* (1967); and C. Swisher, *Stephen J. Field* (1930). See also White, *supra,* note 1, at 55–63, 91–108, 122–28.

6. Holmes' common law opinions on the Supreme Judicial Court of Massachusetts generally conformed to this pattern. See Llewellyn, *supra,* note 1, at 187–89; Tushnet, "The Logic of Experience: Oliver Wendell Holmes on the Supreme Judicial Court," 63 Va. L. Rev. 975, 976–81 (1977).

7. See, e.g., J. Robinson, *The Mind in the Making* (1921).

8. Holmes in *Southern Pacific Co. v. Jensen,* 244 U.S. 205, 222 (1917) [dissent].

9. B. Cardozo, *The Nature of the Judicial Process* 166–67 (1921).

10. See, e.g., Seavey, "Mr. Justice Cardozo and the Law of Torts," 39 Colum. L. Rev. 20, 21 (1939); Corbin, "Mr. Justice Cardozo and the Law of Contracts," 39 Colum. L. Rev. 56, 57 (1939); G. Gilmore, *The Ages of American Law* 75 (1977).

11. 217 N.Y. 382 (1916).

12. *Torgesen v. Schultz,* 192 N.Y. 156 (1908).

13. Gilmore, *supra,* note 10, at 135.

14. 217 N.Y. at 391.

15. 231 N.Y. 229 (1921).

16. *Supra,* note 9, at 141.

17. 231 N.Y. at 234.

18. Ibid.

19. Ibid. at 233.

20. *Supra,* note 9, at 110.

21. 231 N.Y. at 235–36.

22. Ibid. at 235.

23. Ibid. at 233.

24. Ibid. at 235.

25. Ibid. at 236.

26. 217 N.Y. at 390.

27. Ibid.

28. Ibid. at 389–90.

29. Two New York cases extending the *MacPherson* principle during Cardozo's lifetime are *Smith v. Peerless Glass Co.,* 259 N.Y. 292 (1932), and *Genesee*

County Patrons Fire Relief Ass'n v. Sonneborn Sons, 263 N.Y. 463 (1934). For subsequent developments, see James, "Scope of Duty in Negligence Cases," 47 N.W. U. L. Rev. 778 (1953).

30. 247 N.Y. 340 (1928).
31. *McCarty v. Natural Carbonic Gas Co.,* 189 N.Y. 40 (1907).
32. *Muller v. McKesson,* 73 N.Y. 195 (1878).
33. *Clifford v. Dam,* 81 N.Y. 53 (1880); *McGuire v. Spence,* 91 N.Y. 302 (1883).
34. 247 N.Y. at 347.
35. Ibid. at 350.
36. Ibid. at 348 (in original).
37. Ibid. at 350.
38. See M. Horwitz, The *Transformation of American Law, 1780–1860* 74–78 (1977).
39. E.g., *Boomer v. Atlantic Cement Co.,* 26 N.Y. 2d 219 (1970); *Jost v. Dairyland Power Cooperative,* 45 Wis. 2d. 164 (1969).
40. Compare Cardozo's essay, "The Moral Element in Matthew Arnold," written in 1889, with his "Faith and a Doubting World," an address delivered to the New York County Lawyers' Association in 1931. Both essays stress "the place and potency of . . . moralities" (p. 105); the latter "deplore[s] . . . the stock distinctions between morals and law" (p. 106). The essays are reprinted in M. Hall, ed., *Selected Writings of Benjamin Nathan Cardozo* (1947).
41. See Cardozo's discussion of "The March of Civilization," in B. Cardozo, *The Paradoxes of Legal Science* 57–58 (1928).
42. See discussion in Chapter 3.
43. See Edgerton, "Negligence, Inadvertence and Indifference," 39 Harv. L. Rev. 849 (1926); Seavey, "Negligence—Subjective or Objective," 41 Harv. L. Rev. 1 (1927).
44. Compare Labatt, "Negligence in Relation to Privity of Contract," 16 L. Q. Rev. 168 (1900) and Smith, "Liability for Negligent Language," 14 Harv. L. Rev. 184 (1900) with Bohlen, "Should Negligent Misrepresentations Be Treated as Negligence or Fraud," 18 Va. L. Rev. 703 (1932).
45. See Williston, "Liability for Honest Misrepresentation," 24 Harv. L. Rev. 415 (1911); Bohlen, "Misrepresentation as Deceit, Negligence or Warranty," 42 Harv. L. Rev. 733 (1929); Green, "Deceit," 16 Va. L. Rev. 749 (1930); Weisiger, "The Bases of Liability for Misrepresentation," 24 Ill. L. Rev. 866 (1930).
46. 233 N.Y. 236 (1922).
47. Ibid. at 239.
48. Ibid. at 242.
49. *Lawrence v. Fox,* 20 N.Y. 268 (1859); *Seaver v. Ransom,* 224 N.Y. 233 (1918).
50. Bohlen, "The Basis of Affirmative Obligations in the Law of Tort," 53 Am. L. Reg. 209 (1905).
51. 233 N.Y. at 242.

52. 255 N.Y. 170 (1931).
53. *Jaillet v. Cashman*, 235 N.Y. 511 (1923); *International Products Co. v. Erie R.R.*, 244 N.Y. 331 (1927); *Courteen Seed Co. v. Hong Kong and S.B. Corp.*, 245 N.Y. 377 (1927); *Doyle v. Chatham & Phoenix Nat. Bank*, 253 N.Y. 369 (1930).
54. 225 N.Y. at 179.
55. Ibid. at 188.
56. Ibid. at 183.
57. Ibid. at 190.
58. Ibid. at 192–93.
59. *Beatty v. Guggenheim*, 225 N.Y. 380 (1919).
60. *Meinhard v. Salmon*, 249 N.Y. 458 (1928).
61. *Junius Construction Corp. v. Cohen*, 257 N.Y. 393 (1931).
62. See Cardozo's comments in *The Paradoxes of Legal Science, supra*, note 41, at 74–77. See also discussion in Chapter Three, pp.
63. See discussion in *The Paradoxes of Legal Science, supra*, note 41, at 72–77. In the course of that discussion Cardozo said that the determination of negligence "[I]nvolved at every turn . . . the equilibration of social interests"; that judgments about negligent conduct "yield quickly to the pressure of new facts with new social implications"; and that in "the law of torts . . . there are so many questions, elementary in the sense of being primary and basic, that remain unsettled even now."
64. See Cardozo, ["Jurisprudence"], in Hall, ed., *supra*, note 40, at 7. Cardozo's remarks were originally delivered to the New York State Bar Association; see 55 *New York State Bar Assn. Report* 263 (1932).

Chapter 5

1. Cf. R. Pound, *The Formative Era of American Law* 82 (1938).
2. Pound, "The Call for a Realist Jurisprudence, 44 Harv. L. Rev. 697 (1931); Cardozo, ["Jurisprudence"], 55 *New York State Bar Assn. Report* 263 (1932).
3. See, e.g., Lucey, "Natural Law and American Legal Realism," 30 Geo. L. J. 493 (1942).
4. L. Fuller, *The Law In Quest of Itself* (1940).
5. E.g., Llewellyn, "On Reading and Using the Newer Jurisprudence," 40 Colum. L. Rev. 581 (1940); J. Frank, *Law and the Modern Mind* xvii (1949 ed.).
6. B. Cardozo, *The Paradoxes of Legal Science* 4–5, 58 (1928).
7. Fuller, "Reason and Fiat in Case Law," 59 Harv. L. Rev. 376 (1946).
8. These themes are prevalent in H. Hart and A. Sacks, *The Legal Process* (tent. ed., 1958).
9. Moore and Hope, "An Institutional Approach to the Law of Commercial Banking," 38 Yale L. J. 703 (1929); Hamilton, "The Problem of Anti-Trust Reform," 32 Colum. L. Rev. 173 (1932); Frank, "Realism in Jurisprudence," 7 Am. L. School Rev. 1063 (1934).

10. E.g., Sturges and Clark, "Legal Theory and Real Property Mortgages," 37 Yale L. J. 691 (1928), which Grant Gilmore has called "of no conceivable interest to Sturges or anyone else" (G. Gilmore, *The Ages of American Law* 81 [1977]).

11. E. Levi, *Legal Reasoning* (1949).

12. H. Hart and A. Sacks, *supra,* note 8.

13. Bickel and Wellington, "Legislative Purpose and the Judicial Process," 71 Harv. L. Rev. 1 (1957).

14. Hart, "The Time Chart of the Justices," 73 Harv. L. Rev. 84 (1959).

15. Bickel, "The Passive Virtues," 75 Harv. L. Rev. 40 (1961).

16. K. Llewellyn, *The Common Law Tradition* 19–50 (1960).

17. Wechsler, "Toward Neutral Principles of Constitutional Law," 73 Harv. L. Rev. 1 (1959).

18. Id. at 23–24.

19. Hart and Sacks, *supra,* note 8, at 1–10.

20. Cf. L. Fuller, *The Morality of Law* (1964).

21. E.g., L. Hartz, *The Liberal Tradition in America* (1955).

22. E.g., R. Dahl, *Who Governs?* (1961).

23. D. Potter, *People of Plenty* (1954); E. Erikson, *Childhood and Society* (1950); R. Lewis, *The American Adam* (1955).

24. See Chapter Three.

25. C. Gregory, *Legislative Loss Distribution in Negligence Actions* (1936); [Ehrenzweig], "Loss-Shifting and Quasi-Negligence," 8 U. Chi. L. Rev. 729 (1941); James, "Accident Liability Reconsidered: The Impact of Liability Insurance," 57 Yale L. J. 549 (1948).

26. The first such legislation, originating in England, was the Employers' Liability Act, 43 and 44 Vict. 42 (1880).

27. *Bain v. Atkins,* 181 Mass. 240, 241 (1902).

28. E.g., Corbin, "Liability of Water Companies for Losses by Fire," 19 Yale L. J. 425 (1910); Douglas, "Vicarious Liability and the Administration of Risk," 38 Yale L. J. 584 (1929); Feezer, "Capacity to Bear Loss as a Factor in the Decision in Certain Types of Torts Cases," 78 U. Pa. L. Rev. 805 (1930); Laube, "The Social Vice of Accident Indemnity," 80 U. Pa. L. Rev. 189 (1931).

29. E.g., *Sanders v. Frankfort Ins. Co.,* 72 N.H. 485 (1904); *Stenbom v. Brown-Corliss Engine Co.,* 137 Wis. 564 (1909); *Patterson v. Adam,* 119 Minn. 308 (1912).

30. *Merchants Mutual Automobile Liability Insurance Co. v. Smart,* 267 U.S. 126 (1925).

31. Note, "Direct Rights of Action Against Public Liability Insurers," 11 Tulane L. Rev. 443 (1937); *Oertel v. Williams,* 214 Wis. 68 (1934).

32. Feezer, *supra,* note 28, at 808–809.

33. E.g., Gregory, *supra,* note 25; Feezer, *supra,* note 28.

34. Green, "Tort Law Public Law in Disguise," 38 Tex. L. Rev. 1, 257, 269 (1959–60).

35. Ibid. at 2, 1.

36. Ibid. at 266.
37. Ibid.
38. Ibid. at 268.
39. Ibid.
40. See Pound, "The Economic Interpretation and the Law of Torts," 53 Harv. L. Rev. 365, 366–67 (1940); Keeton, "Creative Continuity in the Law of Torts," 75 Harv. L. Rev. 463, 469–72 (1962).
41. Keeton, *supra,* note 40.
42. See Chapter Two.
43. See Chapter Three.
44. Pound, *supra,* note 2.
45. The casebooks were L. Green (Northwestern), *The Judicial Process in Torts Cases* (1931); H. Shulman and F. James (Yale), *Cases and Materials on the Law of Torts* (1942); and C. Gregory and H. Kalven (Chicago), *Cases and Materials on Torts* (1959). The fourth casebook, W. Prosser (Berkeley) and Y. Smith (Columbia), *Cases and Materials on Torts* (1951) was "doctrinal" in its emphasis.
46. See W. Roalfe, *John Henry Wigmore* 34–39 (1977); F. Ellsworth, *Law on the Midway* 63–110 (1977).
47. Green, "Protection of Trade Relations Under Tort Law," 47 Va. L. Rev. 559 (1961); James, "Tort Law in Midstream," 8 Buffalo L. Rev. 315 (1959).
48. Wade, "William L. Prosser: Some Impressions and Recollections," 60 Calif. L. Rev. 1255 (1972).
49. See Malone, "More in Sorrow Than in Anger," 60 Calif. L. Rev. 1252 (1972).
50. W. Prosser, *Law of Torts* 174 (1971).
51. W. Prosser, *Law of Torts* 18 (1941).
52. In 1932, at the very beginning of his academic career, Prosser reviewed Green's *Judge and Jury*. After claiming that "neither Dean Green nor any other realist" had provided "a method by which we can decide, in any given case, which 'interests' to consider, and to which 'factors' to give the greater weight," Prosser predicted that judges would generally "steer [their] course[s] . . . by the magnetic needle of stare decisis" (Prosser, Book Review, 16 Minn. L. Rev. 222, 223 [1932]). By 1941, however, Prosser's perspective had integrated Green's approach, as the subsequent discussion in the text indicates. By 1953 Prosser said, in an article on the *Palsgraf* case, that Green had been "for a quarter century a voice crying in the wilderness; and as one of the original scoffers at his doctrine, I make him belated obeisance" (Prosser, "Palsgraf Revisited," 52 Mich. L. Rev. 1, 32 [1953]).
53. Ibid. at 17.
54. Ibid. at 17, 15.
55. Prosser, *supra,* note 50, at 14–23.
56. Prosser, *supra,* note 51, at 17.
57. Ibid. at 17–18.

58. References are to the 1971 edition: see Prosser, *supra,* note 50, at 427–29.
59. Ibid. at 429.
60. Prosser, *supra,* note 51, at 411.
61. Prosser, *supra,* note 50, at 429–30.
62. Ibid. at 431.
63. "All courts": Alabama, Arizona, Indiana, Maine, New Jersey (Id. at 429, n. 22); "a substantial number": Ohio, New York, Oklahoma, Rhode Island, Alabama (Ibid. at 430, n. 30); "a considerable majority": North Carolina, Kentucky, Kansas, Vermont. (Ibid. at 430, n. 31).
64. Ibid. at 433.
65. Prosser, "Palsgraf Revisited," *supra,* note 52, at 32.
66. Ibid.
67. Ibid. at 56.
68. Prosser, "Intentional Infliction of Mental Suffering: A New Tort," 37 Mich. L. Rev. 874 (1939).
69. Restatement of Torts § 46 (1948 Supp.); see cases cited in W. Prosser, *Law of Torts* 42–45 (1955).
70. Prosser, "Libel Per Quod," 79 Harv. L. Rev. 733 (1966).
71. Prosser, "Injurious Falsehood: A Basis of Liability," 59 Colum. L. Rev. 425 (1959).
72. Prosser, "False Imprisonment: Consciousness of Confinement," 55 Colum. L. Rev. 847 (1955).
73. Prosser, "Privacy," 48 Calif. L. Rev. 383 (1960).
74. Malone, Book Review, 43 Calif. L. Rev. 740 (1955).
75. Wilson, Book Review, 27 Corn. L. Q. 159, 160 (1941).
76. Vold, Book Review, 11 Ford. L. Rev. 239, 240 (1942).
77. See, e.g., Harris, "Idealism Emergent in Jurisprudence," 10 Tul. L. Rev. 169 (1936); Mechem, "The Jurisprudence of Despair," 21 Iowa L. Rev. 669 (1936).
78. Eldredge, Book Review, 90 U. Pa. L. Rev. 505, 506 (1942).
79. Prosser, Book Review, 4 La. L. Rev. 156 (1941).
80. See, e.g., Goodrich, "Iowa Applications of the Last Clear Chance Doctrine," 5 Iowa L. Bull. 36 (1919); Note, 26 Harv. L. Rev. 369 (1913).
81. 35 Stat. 65 (1908).
82. 38 Stat. 1164 (1915).
83. 41 Stat. 988 (1920).
84. See Prosser, "Comparative Negligence," in *Selected Topics on the Law of Torts* 22–23 (1954).
85. Turk, "Comparative Negligence on the March," 28 Chi.-Kent L. Rev. 189, 304, 336 (1950).
86. See V. Schwartz, *Comparative Negligence* 2–3 (thirteen states adopting legislation between 1971 and 1973).
87. *Hoffman v. Jones,* 280 So. 2d 431 (Fla. 1973) *Li v. Yellow Cab Co. of California,* 13 Cal. 3d 804 (1975).
88. Keeton, *supra,* note 40, at 475, 478.
89. Gregory, *supra,* note 25, at 4.

90. E.g., Gregory, *supra,* note 25, at 154–72; Prosser, *supra,* note 84, at 68–69.
91. Prosser, *supra,* note 84, at 30.
92. Prosser, *Law of Torts* 445 (1964).
93. Prosser, *supra,* note 84, at 17–67.
94. Gregory, *supra,* note 25, at 49.
95. C. Beach, *A Treatise on the Law of Contributory Negligence* 12 (1892).
96. Hart and Sacks, *supra,* note 8, at 6–9.
97. Keeton, *supra,* note 40, at 486–93.
98. Cf. Hart & Sacks, *supra,* note 8.
99. Prosser, *supra,* note 51, at 468.
100. Ibid. at 688–89.
101. Ibid. at 689.
102. Prosser, *supra,* note 69, at 506.
103. Ibid. at 510–11.
104. Prosser, *supra,* note 51, at 692.
105. E.g. James, "General Products—Should Manufacturers Be Liable Without Negligence?" 24 Tenn. L. Rev. 923 (1957).
106. Green, "Should the Manufacturer of General Products Be Liable Without Negligence?" ibid. 928.
107. Plant, "Strict Liability of Manufacturers for Injuries Caused By Defects In Products—An Opposing View," ibid. at 938.
108. Noel, "Manufacturers of Products—The Drift Toward Strict Liability," ibid. at 963.
109. James, "Products Liability," 34 Texas L. Rev. 44 (1955).
110. 69 Yale L. J. 1099 (1960).
111. Ibid. at 1110.
112. Ibid. at 1112.
113. Ibid. at 1113–14.
114. Ibid. at 1112.
115. Ibid. at 1122.
116. See, e.g., Prosser, *supra,* note 51, at 689–92; Prosser, *supra,* note 69, at at 506–10.
117. Prosser, *supra,* note 110, at 1122.
118. Ibid. at 1123.
119. Ibid. at 1134.
120. Ibid. at 1140.
121. Prosser, "The Fall of the Citadel," 50 Minn. L. Rev. 791 (1966).
122. Ibid. at 793–94.
123. 32 N.J. 358 (1960).
124. 12 N.Y. 2d. 432 (1963).
125. 59 Cal. 2d. 57 (1963).
126. Restatement (Second) Torts § 402A (1965).
127. See James, "The Scope of Duty in Negligence Cases," 47 N.W. L. Rev. 778 (1953).
128. Jaffe, "Res Ipsa Loquitur Vindicated," 1 Buffalo L. Rev. 1 (1951).
129. See *Henningsen v. Bloomfield Motors, supra,* note 123; *Lartique v. R. J.*

Reynolds Tobacco Co., 317 F.2d 19 (5th Cir. 1963); *Seely v. White Motor Co.,* 403 P.2d 145 (Cal. 1965).

130. Prosser, *supra,* note 110, at 1120, 1121–22.
131. Prosser, *supra,* note 121, at 800.
132. Prosser, *supra,* note 50, at 547.
133. Ibid. at 554.
134. Prosser, *supra,* note 51, at 1050.
135. Warren and Brandeis, "The Right to Privacy," 4 Harv. L. Rev. 193 (1890).
136. Prosser, *supra,* note 69, at 639.
137. *Sidis v. F-R Pub. Corp.,* 113 F.2d 806 (2d Cir. 1940).
138. Prosser, *supra,* note 51, at 1050–62.
139. Cf. Bloustein, "Privacy as an Aspect of Human Dignity," 39 N.Y.U. L. Rev. 962 (1964).
140. See, e.g., *Roberson v. Rochester Folding Box Co.,* 171 N.Y. 538 (1902); *Pavesich v. New England Life Insurance Co.,* 122 Ga. 190 (1904).
141. *Melvin v. Reid,* 112 Cal. App. 285 (1931).
142. Prosser, *supra,* note 51, at 1054.
143. Prosser, *supra,* note 69, at 638.
144. *Gill v. Curtis Pub. Co.,* 38 Cal. 2d 273 (1952).
145. *Goldberg v. Ideal Pub. Co.,* 210 N.Y.S. 2d 928 (1960).
146. Prosser, *supra,* note 69, at 639.
147. Prosser, *supra,* note 92, at 839.
148. Prosser, *supra* note 50, at 816.
149. Prosser, *supra* note 69, at 637.
150. Prosser, "Privacy," 48 Calif. L. Rev. 383, 389, 422 (1960).
151. Prosser, *supra,* note 50, at 816.
152. Prosser, *supra,* note 150, at 422.
153. *Time Inc. v. Hill,* 385 U.S. 374 (1967).
154. *Gertz. v. Robert Welch, Inc.,* 418 U.S. 323 (1974).
155. *Hill, supra,* note 153, at 383, n. 7; *Gertz, supra,* note 154; *Cox Broadcasting v. Cohn,* 420 U.S. 469 (1975).
156. See generally F. Harper and F. James, *The Law of Torts* (3 vols., 1956); W. Blum and H. Kalven, *Public Law Perspectives on a Private Law Problem* (1965).
157. Prosser, *supra,* note 92, at xi.
158. Prosser, *supra,* note 50, at 16–23.

Chapter 6

1. Traynor, "La Rude Vita, La Dolce Giustizia; Or Hard Cases Can Make Good Law," 29 U. Chi. L. Rev. 223, 234 (1962).
2. 38 Cal. 2d 330 (1952).
3. Ibid. at 335.
4. Ibid. at 336.
5. Ibid. at 338.

6. Ibid.
7. Ibid.
8. Traynor, "Law and Social Change in a Democratic Society," 1956 U. Ill. L.F. 230, 233.
9. Kalven, "Torts: The Quest for Appropriate Standards," 53 Calif. L. Rev. 189, 190 (1965).
10. Jaffe, "Res Ipsa Loquitur Vindicated," 1 Buffalo L. Rev. 1, 13 (1951).
11. Kalven, *supra,* note 9, at 189.
12. Traynor also received a Ph.D. in philosophy at the time he received his law degree from Berkeley in 1927.
13. O. Holmes, *The Common Law* 123–29 (1881).
14. *Toschi v. Christian,* 24 Cal.2d 354, 364–65 (1944).
15. 29 Cal.2d 866 (1947).
16. Ibid. at 871.
17. Ibid. at 872.
18. Ibid.
19. 22 Cal.2d 72 (1943).
20. Ibid. at 74.
21. Ibid. at 75.
22. Ibid. at 76.
23. Ibid. at 77 (Shenk, J.).
24. 29 Cal.2d 581 (1947).
25. Ibid. at 586.
26. See generally G. White, *The American Judicial Tradition* 200–368 (1976).
27. Traynor, "Badlands in an Appellate Judge's Realm of Reason," 7 Utah L. Rev. 157, 167 (1960).
28. Traynor, *supra,* note 1, at 234.
29. *Startup v. Pacific Elec. Ry. Co., supra,* note 15; see Traynor, *supra,* note 27, at 169.
30. Traynor, "Better Days in Court for a New Day's Problems," 17 Vand. L. Rev. 109, 115 (1963).
31. *In re Estate of Mason,* 62 Cal.2d 213 (1965); see Traynor, "Statutes Revolving in Common-Law Orbits," 17 Cath. U. L. Rev. 401, 417 (1968).
32. Traynor, "Reasoning in a Circle of Law," 56 Va. L. Rev. 739, 740 (1970).
33. Ibid. at 749, 750, 751.
34. Traynor, *"Mapp v. Ohio* at Large in the Fifty States," 1962 Duke L.J. 319.
35. *State Rubbish Collectors Ass'n. v. Siliznoff, supra* note 2.
36. See W. Prosser, *Law of Torts* 357–98 (1971).
37. 19 Cal.2d 647 (1942).
38. Ibid. at 658.
39. Ibid. at 659.
40. See *Restatement (Second), Torts* § 343A(1) (Tent. Draft No. 5, 1960).
41. *Escola v. Coca Cola Bottling Co.,* 24 Cal.2d 453, 461 (1944) (concurrence).
42. *Devens v. Goldberg,* 33 Cal.2d 173, 181 (1948) (dissent).
43. Ibid. at 183.

44. 48 Cal.2d 778 (1957).
45. Ibid. at 782, 783.
46. Section 1714: "Everyone is responsible . . . for an injury occasioned to another by his want of ordinary care or skill in the management of his property or person" (Ibid. at 785).
47. Ibid. at 786, 787.
48. Ibid. at 792.
49. *Rowland v. Christian,* 69 Cal.2d 108 (1968).
50. Ibid. at 119.
51. 43 Cal.2d 60 (1954).
52. Ibid. at 63.
53. Ibid. at 66.
54. E.g., *McEvoy v. American Pool Corp.,* 32 Cal.2d 295 (1948); *Benton v. Sloss,* 38 Cal.2d 399 (1952).
55. 43 Cal.2d 69.
56. 44 Cal.2d 772 (1955).
57. Ibid. at 776–77.
58. Ibid. at 776.
59. Ibid. at 777.
60. *Supra,* note 41.
61. W. Prosser, *The Law of Torts* 689 (1941).
62. *Supra,* note 41, at 462.
63. *Supra,* note 61, at 689.
64. *Supra,* note 41, at 462.
65. *Supra,* note 61, at 689.
66. *Supra,* note 41, at 462–63.
67. *Supra,* note 61, at 689.
68. *Supra,* note 41, at 464.
69. *Supra,* note 61, at 690–91.
70. *Supra,* note 41, at 465–66.
71. *Supra,* note 63, at 690, 692; see *Ketterer v. Armour & Co.,* 200 F. 322, 323 (D.C.N.Y. 1912).
72. *Supra,* note 41, at 465–66.
73. *Supra,* note 61, at 692.
74. *Supra,* note 41, at 468.
75. *Supra,* note 61, at 689.
76. Perkins, "Unwholesome Food as a Source of Liability," 5 Iowa L. Bull. 6, 86 (1919).
77. Jeanblanc, "Manufacturers' Liability to Persons Other Than Their Immediate Vendees," 24 Va. L. Rev. 134 (1937).
78. Feezer, "Manufacturer's Liability for Injuries Caused by His Products," 37 Mich. L. Rev. 1 (1938).
79. Patterson, "The Apportionment of Business Risks Through Legal Devices," 24 Colum. L. Rev. 335 (1924).
80. Bogert and Fink, "Business Practices Regarding Warranties in the Sale of Goods," 25 Ill. L. Rev. 400 (1930).

81. *Supra,* note 61, at 693.
82. *Supra,* note 41, at 463.
83. 33 Cal.2d 514 (1949).
84. Ibid. at 523, 530 (concurrence).
85. Ibid.
86. Id. at 532.
87. Id. at 533.
88. 50 Cal.2d 217 (1958).
89. Id. at 235, 237–38 (concurrence and dissent).
90. Id. at 235–36.
91. Id. at 236–37.
92. 59 Cal.2d 57 (1963).
93. Prosser had been an advocate of strict liability since the 1940s, when in "Res Ipsa Loquitur in California," 37 Calif. L. Rev. 183 (1949), he cited *Escola* and spoke of *res ipsa* as "a step along the road to liability without fault" (Id. at 224).
94. Id. at 63.
95. Id. at 61.
96. For an interesting effort to expand an analysis of power and powerlessness to other areas of tort law, see M. Shapo, *The Duty to Act* (1977).
97. 59 Cal.2d at 63.
98. 61 Cal.2d 256 (1964).
99. Ibid. at 262.
100. Ibid. at 263.
101. 63 Cal.2d 9 (1965).
102. Ibid. at 13–14.
103. Ibid. at 14–15.
104. Ibid. at 19.
105. Ibid. at 20 (Peters, J.).
106. Ibid. at 16.
107. Ibid. at 19.
108. Ibid.
109. These hypotheticals are based on *Santor v. A & M Karagheusian, Inc.,* 44 N.J. 52 (1965).
110. *Supra,* note 101, at 18.
111. *H.R. Moch Co. v. Rensselaer Water Co.,* 247 N.Y. 160 (1928).
112. *Supra,* note 101, at 19.
113. Traynor, "Statutes Revolving in Common Law Orbits," *supra,* note 31, at 402n.

Chapter 7

1. See Savoy, "Towards a New Politics of Legal Education," 79 Yale L.J. 444 (1970); Kennedy, "How the Law School Fails: A Polemic," 1 Yale Rev. L. & Social Action 71 (1970); Stone, "Legal Education on the Couch," 85 Harv. L. Rev. 392 (1971).

2. M. Shapo, *Tort and Compensation Law* xv (1976).

3. P. Keeton and R. Keeton, *Cases and Materials on the Law of Torts* xvi (1977).

4. G. Gregory, H. Kalven, and R. Epstein, *Cases and Materials on Torts* xxii (1977) [hereafter cited as Epstein].

5. See discussion in Chapter Three.

6. W. Seavey, P. Keeton, and R. Keeton, *Cases and Materials on the Law of Torts* ix (1964).

7. P. Keeton and R. Keeton, *Cases and Materials on the Law of Torts* xvii (1971).

8. Keeton and Keeton, *supra,* note 3, at xxiv.

9. Ibid. at 759.

10. Ibid. at 761.

11. Ibid. at 775.

12. Posner, "Strict Liability—A Comment," 2 J. Leg. Studies 205 (1973).

13. Posner, "A Theory of Negligence," 1 J. Leg. Studies 29, 33 (1972).

14. Posner, *supra,* note 12, at 221.

15. Posner, *supra,* note 13, at 74–75.

16. Calabresi and Hirschoff, "Toward a Test for Strict Liability in Torts," 81 Yale L.J. 1055, 1060–64 (1972). Calabresi's views were expressed in somewhat different form in *The Costs of Accidents* (1970). I have taken his 1972 article to represent a refinement of the positions he advocated in 1970.

17. Posner, *supra,* note 12, at 214.

18. Calabresi, *supra,* note 16, at 1057, 1058.

19. Fletcher, "Fairness and Utility in Tort Theory," 85 Harv. L. Rev. 537, 550 (1972).

20. Ibid. at 542.

21. Ibid.

22. Ibid. at 553.

23. Ibid. at 573.

24. Ibid. at 538, 560.

25. Ibid. at 572.

26. Two differences are that a search for the "cheapest cost-avoider" might produce someone who creates no risk at all (someone disturbed by jet planes who can wear earplugs), and that one's ability to avoid risks does not correlate with the gravity of these risks. Calabresi is concerned with risk-avoidance, Fletcher with weighing the comparable gravity of risks.

27. Ibid. at 564.

28. See Chapter One.

29. Epstein, "A Theory of Strict Liability," 2 J. Leg. Studies 151, 165n (1973).

30. Epstein, "International Harms," 4 J. Leg. Studies 391, 442 (1975).

31. Epstein, *supra,* note 29, at 151.

32. Ibid. at 203–204.

33. Ibid. at 165n.

34. Epstein, *supra,* note 30, at 441.

35. Epstein, *supra,* note 29, at 160–86.
36. Epstein, "Defenses and Subsequent Pleas in a System of Strict Liability," 3 J. Leg. Studies 165, 169 (1974).
37. Epstein, *supra,* note 30, at 416–18.
38. Epstein, *supra,* note 36, at 169–70.
39. Ibid. at 207–11.
40. Epstein, *supra,* note 29, at 203–204.
41. Epstein, *supra,* note 30, at 442.
42. Cf. Ames, "Law and Morals," 22 Harv. L. Rev. 97, 99 (1908).
43. Epstein, *supra,* note 30, at 423–40.
44. Posner, *supra,* note 12, at 214.
45. This example is based on *Pike v. Frank G. Hough Co.,* 2 Cal.3d 465 (1970).
46. Cf. *Michaels v. Gannett Co.,* 199 N.Y.S.2d 778 (1960). A strict liability standard in defamation was found constitutionally impermissible in *Gertz v. Robert Welch, Inc.,* 418 U.S. 323 (1974).
47. For judicial changes of contributory negligence and charitable immunity doctrines see, respectively, *Li v. Yellow Cab Company of California,* 13 Cal.3d 804 (1975); *Muskopf v. Corning Hospital District,* 55 Cal.2d 211 (1961).
48. The two areas in which legislative activity has been most pronounced are products liability and medical malpractice. Since 1978 eleven states have passed products liability laws, and since 1975 forty-three states have passed legislation affecting tort law in medical malpractice cases. See 394 Products Liability Reports 3–4 (1978); Comment, "An Analysis of State Legislative Responses to the Medical Malpractice Crisis," 1975 Duke L.J. 1417. The constitutionality of malpractice legislation has been challenged: see Redish, "Legislative Response to the Medical Malpractice Insurance Crisis: Constitutional Implications," 55 Tex. L. Rev. 759 (1977).
49. See, e.g., J. O'Connell, *Ending Insult to Injury* (1975).
50. Most strikingly in *Gertz v. Robert Welch, Inc.,* supra, note 46.
51. See, e.g. *Cronin v. J.B.E. Olson Corp.,* 8 Cal.3d 121 (1972), rejecting Section 402A's requirement that a product's "defect" make it "unreasonably dangerous" to consumers.
52. See, e.g., R. Berger, *Government By Judiciary* (1977).

Index

Absolute liability, 17. *See also* "act at peril" standard of liability; strict liability
Academics as lawmakers, 6–7, 240–43
"Act at peril" standard of liability, 13–15, 128, 224, 225, 231, 236, 240
Adams, Henry, 6
Addison, Charles G., 12
Admonitory function of tort law, xvi, 155, 164, 181, 231, 237–39
American Law Institute (A.L.I.), 97, 98, 101, 104, 124; origins, 80, 83. *See also* Restatement of Torts
Ames, James Barr: casebook on Torts, 18, 34, 39, 84, 154, 216; at Harvard Law School, 29, 30, 31, 155
Andrews, William S., 98–101
Antiuniversalism in twentieth-century reformist thought, 65, 68
Arnold, Thurman W., 80
Assumption of risk: development of, 41–45; use by commentators, 60–62, 83–87, 107, 124, 173, 217, 227; use in courts, 166, 184
Atomism, in tort law, 4, 5, 57, 232, 233

Baltimore & Ohio R.R. v. Baugh, 52–54
Beach, Charles F., 46, 52, 53
Beale, Joseph H., 32, 34, 56, 78, 80, 84, 154, 216; theory of causation 93, 94
Bingham, John A., 94
Blackstone, William: classification system of law, 3, 4; conception of Torts, 14
Bogert, George G., 200

Bohlen, Francis H.: and assumption of risk doctrine, 44–45; *Cases on Torts,* 84–85, 88; friendship with Cardozo, 128, 132; and last clear chance doctrine, 48–49, 84, 86–87; personality, 78–79, 156; relationship to legal science, 83–86; relationship with Leon Green, 78–87, 146, 150–51; Reporter for the Restatement of Torts, 79–83, 93, 100
Bowen v. Hall, 35
Brandeis, Louis D., 173
Brewer, David J., 53, 116
Brown v. Collins, 16–17
Brown v. Kendall, 14–16
Burdick, Francis M., 61, 108

Calabresi, Guido, 221–23, 225, 229–30
Cardozo, Benjamin Nathan: conception of judging, 116, 119–24, 130–38, 181, 189, 208; contrast with Traynor, 188–89, 193, 196–97, 208; *Glanzer* case, 132; *MacFarlane* case, 127–29; *MacPherson* case, 125–27; and misrepresentation, 131–36; and moral dimensions of law, 129–36; *Nature of Judicial Process,* 120–24; and negligence theory, 99–102, 107–108, 112, 124–29, 197; *Palsgraf* case, 124–27; relationship to Realism, 138–40; theory of causation, 97–101, 124, 126–27, 193, 196–97; *Ultramares* case, 132–33
Case method, xiii, xiv, 27–29, 31–33, 37, 72, 154, 214. *See also* scientific method

279